JOHN SLOAN

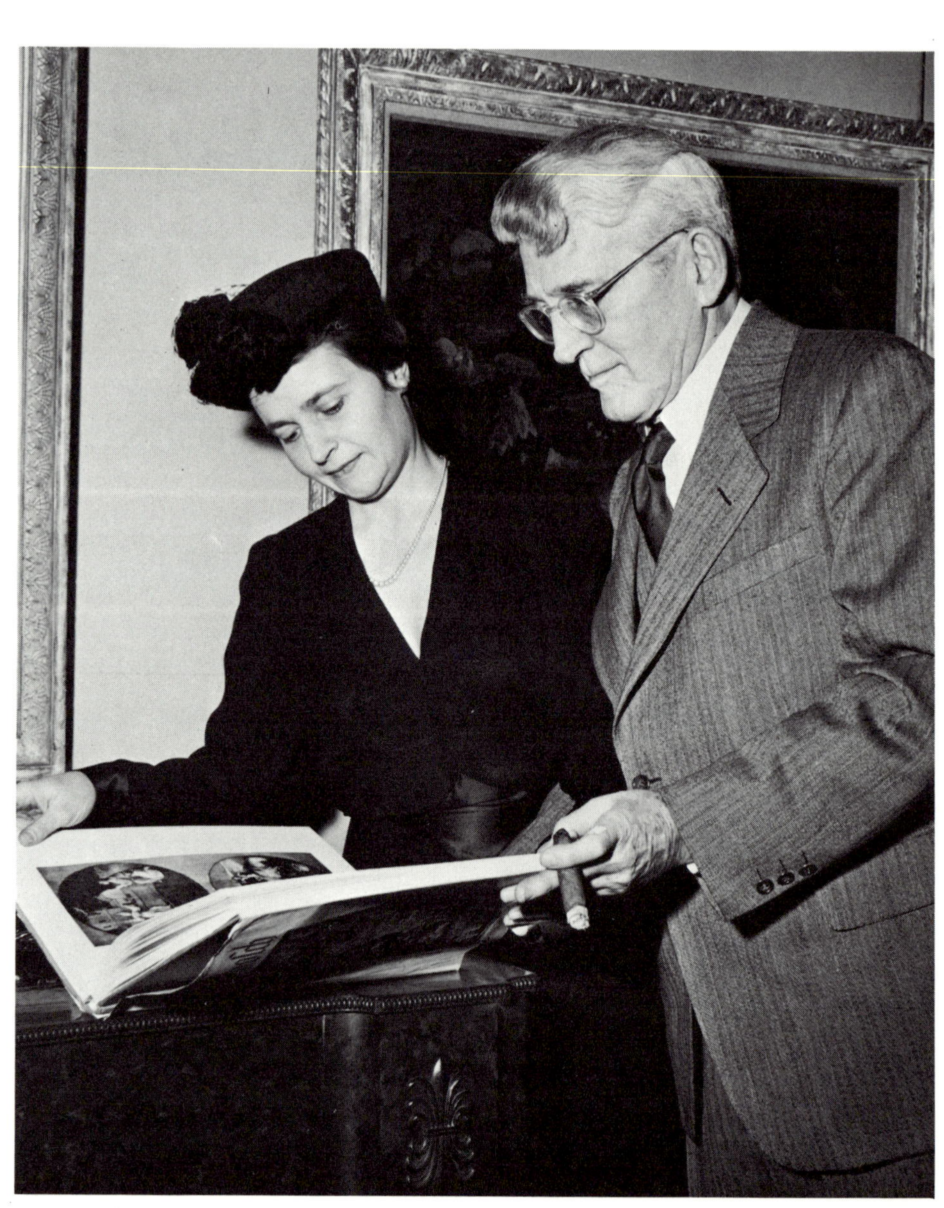

JOHN SLOAN

BRUCE ST. JOHN

PRAEGER PUBLISHERS

NEW YORK • WASHINGTON • LONDON

FRONTISPIECE. Photograph of John and Helen Farr Sloan. 1947.
John Sloan Collection, Delaware Art Museum, Wilmington.
Photo Acme Newspictures, New York.

PRAEGER PUBLISHERS
111 Fourth Avenue, New York, N.Y. 10003, U.S.A.
5, Cromwell Place, London S.W.7, England

Published in the United States of America in 1971
by Praeger Publishers, Inc.

© 1971 by Praeger Publishers, Inc.

Library of Congress Catalog Card Number: 74–117478

Printed in the United States of America

Credits

The excerpt from Peter Morse's *John Sloan's Prints: A catalogue raisonné of the etchings, lithographs, and posters* (New Haven: Yale University Press, 1950); the excerpts from *Gist of Art* (New York: American Artists Group, 1939); the excerpts from *John Sloan's New York Scene* (New York: Harper & Row, 1965); and the excerpts from the unpublished notes of John and Helen Farr Sloan are reprinted by permission of Helen Farr Sloan.

To my daughter Donna, an expert on
life with her father and a help and encouragement to him as well

CONTENTS

LIST OF ILLUSTRATIONS

PREFACE

For several years I have considered writing a book about John Sloan, his life and times—a period in American history that has always held a special interest for me. The first major step in my involvement with Sloan's art was the research and preparation for the 50th-anniversary celebration of the Exhibition of Independent Artists (1910), which was recreated at the Delaware Art Museum, Wilmington, in 1960. At that time, the artist's widow made Sloan's diaries available to me, and shortly thereafter she arrived at her decision to establish what is now known as the John Sloan Collection. The Delaware Art Museum is fortunate in being the home of that collection, which includes personal papers, correspondence, the artist's own library, art books relating to Sloan's times, and paintings by Sloan and many of his associates. The museum also maintains a master catalog of Sloan's paintings, drawings, and graphic work.

Several projects have evolved from the cataloguing of this important research collection The first was a major exhibition in 1961, "The Life and Times of John Sloan," shown both at the Delaware Art Center, as it was then called, and the Pennsylvania Academy of the Fine Arts in Philadelphia. Immediately following that exhibition, I organized a Sloan show for the Traveling Exhibition Service of the Smithsonian Institution. In 1965, I edited Sloan's early diaries, publishing them under the title *John Sloan's New York Scene 1906–1913.*

The present volume is not intended as a critical analysis of Sloan's art. It is rather a survey of his entire œuvre from one major stylistic period to another, its purpose being to motivate further study and investigation. Sloan's place in the mainstream of American art history has been well established, yet it is too soon—only 19 years after his death—to expect a definitive judgment on the aesthetic quality of his art.

The illustrations have been carefully selected to show the most representative examples of Sloan's style in all periods and in all media. Special effort has also been made to illustrate, particularly in the color plates, work that is less familiar.

Much careful checking of published facts about Sloan's life and work has been done here at the Delaware Art Museum since the establishment of the Sloan Study Collection. It has been done not only by the artist's widow but also by several graduate students working with original materials in the preparation of their theses. I have tried to take advantage of their efforts in the preparation of this text in order to correct mistakes and misinterpretations that now exist in print concerning Sloan.

I want to acknowledge the encouragement and support of Helen Farr Sloan, not only in the preparation of this book, but also in the years of preliminary research. Her notes, those of her late husband, correspondence, diaries have— along with the volumes listed in the Selected Bibliography—been the main sources for the facts provided here. We owe her a debt of gratitude for her sense of responsibility in her custodianship of Sloan's documents and her continuing awareness of their importance, for Sloan left behind not only the wealth of his own work but also writings that are a key to his times.

This is also an opportunity for me to express special thanks to Antoinette Kraushaar, of the Kraushaar Galleries, New York, for her interest and support in so many ways and over a period of many years. She has been very generous in giving valuable time to long discussions about Sloan and his friends, as well as placing her files at my disposal.

I must also mention with gratitude the cooperation of the many museums and private collectors whose works are reproduced in this book.

February, 1971

BRUCE ST. JOHN
Director
Delaware Art Museum
Wilmington, Delaware

PROLOGUE

A central component of the American art heritage is a strong realist tradition from the colonial limners and the Peale family to William Sidney Mount, Eastman Johnson, and Thomas Eakins. This was the tradition to which John Sloan belonged.

His early work was done in an international style carried to this country largely by means of graphic work. Sloan had visual contact with original works of art at the Pennsylvania Academy in Philadelphia. His Art Nouveau poster style was influenced by Pre-Raphaelitism (through Walter Crane) and Japanese prints; Rembrandt too was a favorite, whose work he studied during his early years in New York. The Armory Show gave him another opportunity to see the work of the Impressionists and Post-Impressionists. Sloan studied their art carefully, and after 1916 he moved from Renoir back in time to study Rubens and then Titian. He also studied the early Italian and Flemish masters; indeed, some of the best of his late work shows the result of his contemplative study of Bellini.

The long span of Sloan's life saw many changes in both social and art history. Just before the turn of the century the American Impressionists joined in an exciting and important exhibition of The Ten; Sloan himself was vitally involved in the revolutionary 1908 exhibition that shook the art world and won for its participants the label of "revolutionary black gang." Though not personally involved, he was aware of Alfred Stieglitz's movement to introduce modern European art to America.

After the Armory Show and during the 1930's and 1940's American art was eclipsed by that of Paris; much of it was social realism, and Sloan's painting was not part of that tradition. He continued to be a realist but was more concerned with painting problems and depicting the human figure than with social problems.

Sloan died before the full impact of Abstract Expressionism was felt in the 1950's, yet it is interesting to note that some of his students—Alexander Calder, David Smith, Adolph Gottlieb, and Barnett Newman among them—have become major figures in contemporary art.

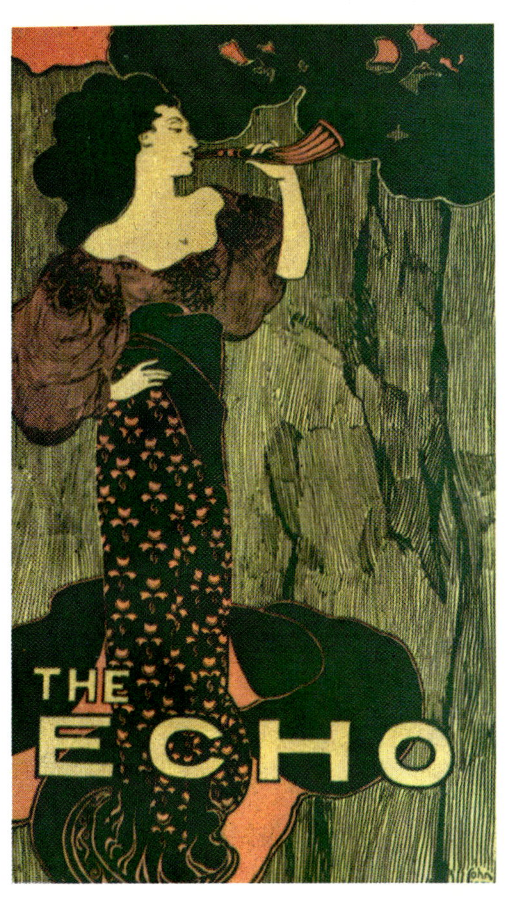

PLATE I. Cover for *The Echo*. 1894–95. Poster drawing, 9 7/8″ x 5 3/5″. John Sloan Collection, Delaware Art Museum, Wilmington.

PLATE II. *East Entrance, City Hall, Philadelphia*. 1901. Oil on canvas, 27¼″ x 36″. The Columbus Gallery of Fine Arts, Columbus, Ohio: F. Howald Fund Purchase.

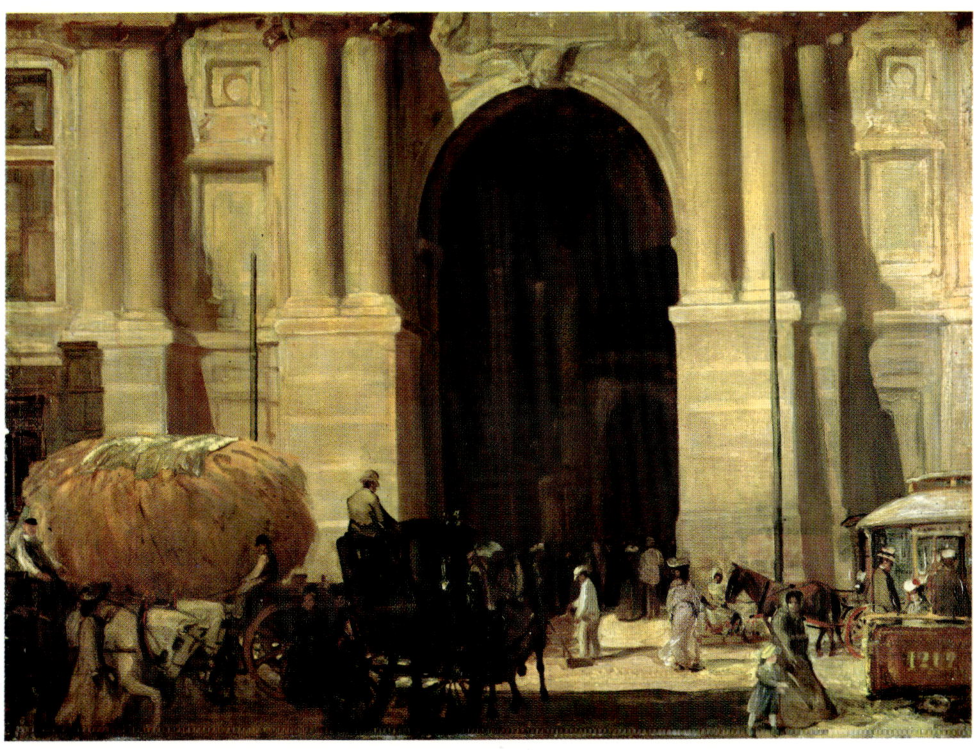

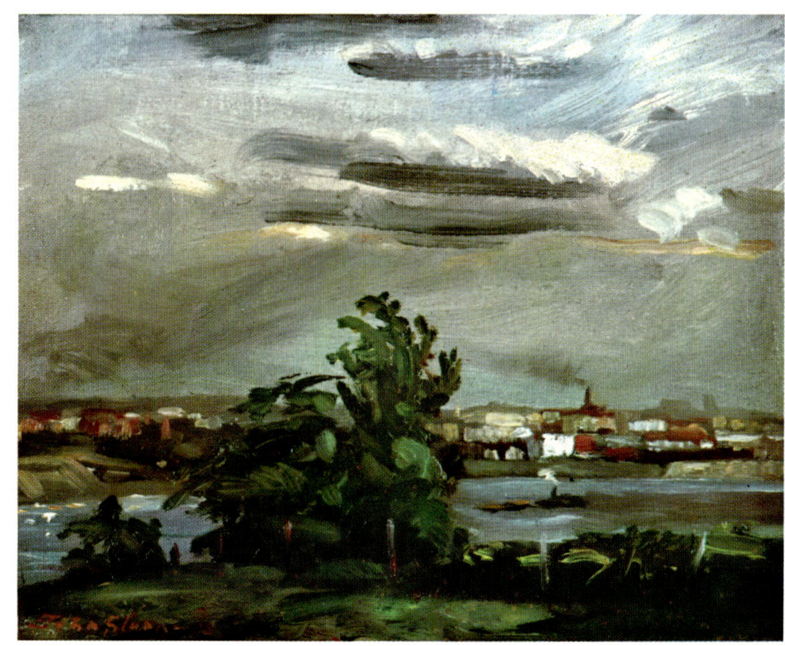

PLATE III. *Coytesville on the Palisades.* 1908. Oil on canvas, 8¾″ x 11″. Wilmington Society of the Fine Arts, Delaware Art Museum, Wilmington.

PLATE IV. *Six O'Clock Winter.* 1912. Oil on canvas, 26″ x 32″. The Phillips Collection, Washington, D.C.

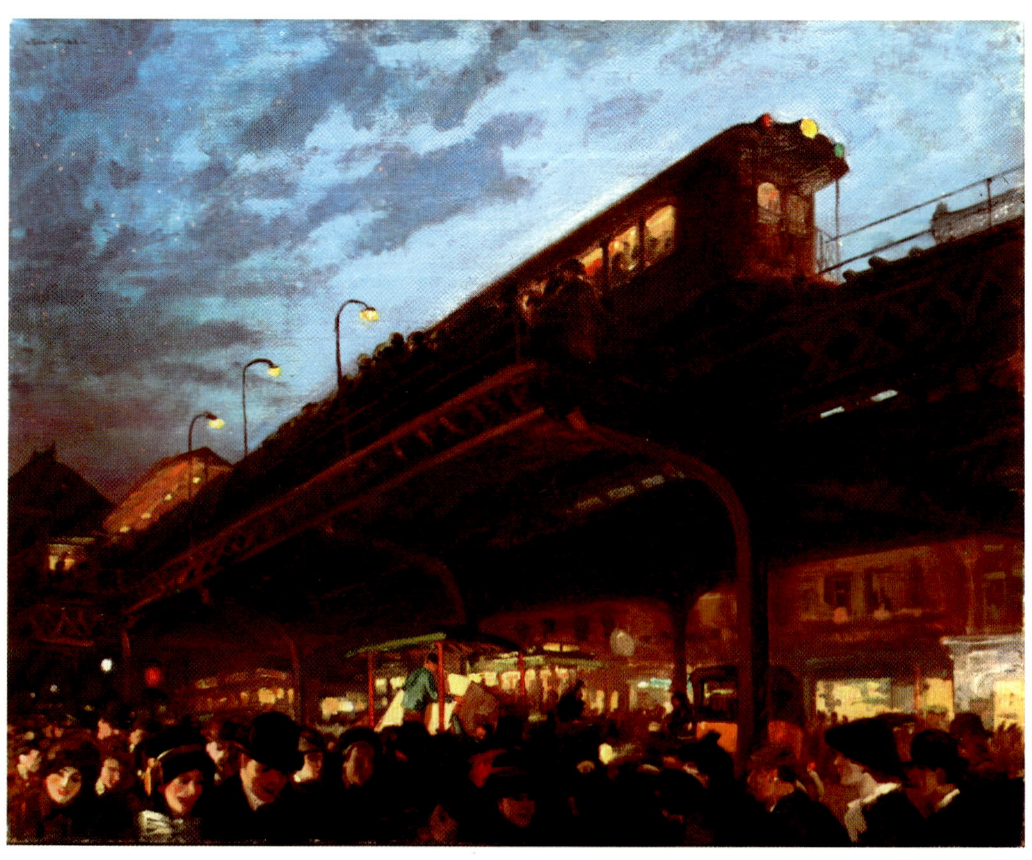

CHAPTER ONE   1871–91

John Sloan was born on August 2, 1871, at Lock Haven, a small lumber town in central Pennsylvania. His father, James Dixon Sloan, was descended from a long line of Scottish Presbyterians, cabinetmakers by trade. Sloan's father was to have followed in the family business, but growing competition from furniture factories in the Civil War period doomed his venture to failure. Manually talented and intelligent, James Sloan was nevertheless a poor business man. Nothing he worked at turned out successfully, and so, after several failures at jobs, he moved his family to Philadelphia in 1876.

Because of his father's lineage, John Sloan thought of himself as descended from Celtic or Irish ancestors, frequently referring to his "Irish" background, which in reality seems to have been more Scottish. He was christened John French Sloan after his paternal grandfather; in later years, after he began to paint in earnest, he dropped his middle name, considering it a "romantic encumbrance."

His mother, Henrietta Ireland Sloan, was an English teacher in Lock Haven when she met and married James Dixon Sloan. Her family, primarily of English lineage, claimed kinship with the famous scientist Joseph Priestley through his cousin Samuel Priestley, Sloan's great-grandfather. The latter had settled in Smyrna, Delaware, in 1816. Before that he had been trained in the family paper business in Leeds, England; and while living for a short time in Belfast, Northern Ireland, had married into the Ireland family, who were also in the paper business. Sloan's great-uncle, Alexander Priestley, was to have a very strong influence on his literary and artistic development. His aunt, Emma Ireland, who had attended school in Switzerland, married William H. Ward, the son of Marcus Ward, whose company in Belfast published greeting cards and books and also made fine stationery. Alfred Ireland, Sloan's uncle, was the firm's American representative. Emma and William Ward lived in London and ran the English branch of the business. William Ward was a highly intelligent man and knew Walter Crane, who designed greeting cards and illustrated books for Marcus Ward & Company. He discovered Kate Greenaway and encouraged his father to use her designs.

Kate Greenaway was greatly influenced by the Pre-Raphaelites, and one of her major accomplishments as an illustrator of children's books was her unification of text and illustrations in a decorative style. Crane, one of England's best-known illustrators in the late nineteenth century, was also influenced by the Pre-Raphaelites in his allegorical paintings and became a leader in the Arts and Crafts Movement, following William Morris.

Sloan's mother, a strong woman, influenced Sloan mainly in the development of his character, and his love and respect for her are clearly reflected and immortalized in his great etching, *Mother,* done in 1906. He was also indebted to his mother's uncle, the inventor Alexander Priestley, in whose library he spent time looking at elephant folios of prints by Hogarth and Rowlandson, books illustrated by George Cruikshank and Gustave Doré, and *Punch* and *Harper's Monthly,* with illustrations by George du Maurier, John Leech, and Edwin Austin Abbey. Indeed, throughout his youth Sloan read prodigiously; his mother had taught him to read before he entered school. He had little interest in sports and spent most of his spare time in the library. By the time he was twelve, he had read all of Dickens and Shakespeare. He also kept a notebook with magazine clippings that included reproductions of works by Dürer and Botticelli. One of the strongest influences in the early years was Walter Crane, whose concept of design was important when Sloan first started to draw. There were many books published by Marcus Ward and illustrated by Crane in the Sloan library.

Sloan's early literary education and its relation to English art, which itself has a strong literary tradition, bear examination. His first venture into illustration, for instance, was at the age of twelve, when he illustrated his own copy of Robert Louis Stevenson's *Treasure Island* (*Ill. 1*). The existence of these illustrations is an example of the influence the English literary tradition had on Sloan even at that early age. To be sure, they did not reveal an extraordinary native talent, but they did indicate the direction of his future stylistic development.

Sloan's father, who had an important influence on his life, encouraged his children in arts and crafts. Well read (he was said to reread Dickens and Pepys every year) and skillful with tools, he was also familiar with printmaking, drawing, and even painting on china. In fact, it was with his father's set of oil paints that Sloan painted his self-portrait of 1890 (*Ill. 3*). In 1876, James Sloan took his son to see the great Centennial Exposition in Philadelphia. This international exhibition, which was held from May 10 to November 10, 1876, was the celebration of the 100th anniversary of America's independence and was the largest world's fair held up to that time. Virtually a new city was built on the banks of the Schuylkill River, with seven main exhibition buildings, some built by foreign and state governments.

The aftermath of the depression of 1873 adversely affected the fortunes of the Sloan family. James Sloan put up his home as collateral for a note to provide his brother Nelson with money to save the family business. The note was not paid off and the Sloans lost their home. When it became obvious that he could no longer make a decent living in Lock Haven, the elder Sloan moved his family to Philadelphia (1876). For several months prior to moving into a house at 1921 Camac Street, the family stayed with Grandmother Ireland in Germantown. For one year, Sloan attended a small private school, but thereafter he was enrolled in public schools.

Around 1885, John Sloan entered Philadelphia's Central High School, where he was the classmate of Albert Barnes and William Glackens. Barnes was later to become wealthy and famous as the inventor of Argyrol and as an important collector of modern art, while Glackens was to become closely associated with Sloan in the formation of The Eight. At this time, however, the three knew each other only slightly. Mrs. Sloan kept her son out of school for one semester because of his nearsightedness, and he did not continue in their class.

After two years at Central, his father told Sloan that he would have to leave school to help support the family. This reversal was due to the failure, in 1886, of a small stationery store operated by James Sloan. Thereupon the young Sloan got a job as assistant cashier with Porter and Coates. The firm was a leading dealer in books and prints in Philadelphia. Thus in 1887, at the age of sixteen, Sloan began his long working life. Fortunately, he had considerable time to examine and even read the many fine books there. It was here too that he first saw original etchings by Dürer and Rembrandt, and engravings after Rubens. (He had seen original Hogarth prints earlier in his uncle Alexander Priestley's library.) He became more familiar with the illustrative work of John Leech and read avidly the writings of Balzac, Flaubert, and De Maupassant. At this time Sloan began to make pen-and-ink drawings from originals by Dürer and Rembrandt, which he sold for five dollars each.

In 1888 Sloan decided to learn the art of etching. At that time there was no placc in Philadelphia where a young artist could learn the technique, so he taught himself, using the third edition of the English art critic Philip Gilbert Hamerton's *Etcher's Handbook*, published in London in 1881. In 1889 he bought *Practical Notes On Etching* by R. S. Chattock, which had been published in 1883. His earliest effort (1888) was a *Head of Rembrandt* in drypoint. *Dedham Castle* (*Ill. 2*), also done in 1888, was another early print, of which Sloan wrote:

> This pale little plate, the earliest of my efforts at etching, is so timidly bitten that it looks like a drypoint. The exciting action of the acid evidently frightened me so that it is hard for me to believe that the lines ever saw acid. Done at the age of seventeen. Made from a print, or copy, or watercolor that hung over the mantlepiece.[1]

A. Edward Newton, who was later to be known as an important bibliophile, was an assistant in the print department at Porter and Coates at the time Sloan worked there. He decided to set up his own business and asked Sloan to come with him in 1890. There Sloan designed greeting cards, matchboxes, and calendars, and continued to do etchings. He did a series of heads of English authors (*Ill. 4*), a series from drawings of Westminster Abbey, and a series of the homes of American poets for calendars.

Newton offered to take Sloan to Europe to study the masters but retracted the offer when he learned how young Sloan was. Sloan himself did not wish to go to Europe, and purposely never did. Even after he began to paint seriously, he was convinced that he had to remain in America so that what he produced would be purely "American." Still, he had great respect for European painters, particularly Manet and Rembrandt. He did, however, join a freehand drawing class at the Spring Garden Institute, which he attended through the fall and winter of 1890–91. While there, he produced pen-and-ink drawings (*Ill. 5*) and several watercolor studies (*Ill. 6*). Watercolor never became important in Sloan's work, and only a few such studies are extant. In October, 1889, Sloan had bought John Collier's *Manual of Oil Painting*, published in London by Cassell in 1886. It was from this manual that he taught himself to paint; a self-portrait of 1890 (*Ill. 3*) provides an existing link to the book.

The pay at Newton's was too low to satisfy Sloan's needs, and he left in the fall of 1891 to establish himself as a free-lance commercial artist. He provided advertisements for such companies as the Bradley Coal Company and designed greeting cards, calendars, and lettering for baptismal certificates and commencement diplomas. He also submitted three drawings to the humor magazine *Judge,* and they were accepted. The titles are recorded as *A Guilt*

Frame, Charge of the Light Brigade, and *Getting a Head of Him.* It is possible that they were paid for but not published. This modest financial success enabled Sloan to afford a tiny studio at 703 Walnut Street, which gave him a measure of independence, though he continued to live at home until he was about thirty.

(See Illustrations 1–6)

CHAPTER TWO   1892–1903

In February of 1892 Sloan took a full-time job with the art department of the *Philadelphia Inquirer*. In those days the newspaper employed artists to make on-the-spot drawings of events and to create cartoons and advertisements. Quick drawing was essential, and it soon became apparent that this was not Sloan's forte. Instead, he was kept busy in the art department doing poster-style drawings for the feature pages and Sunday supplements.

During this period Sloan shared a studio at 705 Walnut Street (*Ill. 8*) with Joe E. Laub, a fellow artist on the *Inquirer* staff. A happier period in Sloan's life began now as he made friends with other members of the staff, many of whom were to remain friends for the rest of his life. He re-established his acquaintance with William Glackens; on Sunday afternoons in summer, Glackens, Laub, and Sloan biked and sketched in the beautiful countryside around Philadelphia.

Reminiscing about his early years, Sloan said: "I might have been a doctor, lawyer, or preacher"—referring to the fact that a university career had been planned for him.[2] When circumstances interfered and he was forced to leave school to help support his family, his first job was a step toward an art career. While working for Porter and Coates, he discovered he could sell his drawings and greeting cards. Pressure to earn money to help his family provided an impetus to put his drawing ability to use. A letter of introduction (which Sloan never used) from his uncle, William H. Ward, to C. W. Beck, manager of the Philadelphia Engraving Company, bears witness to Sloan's determination to succeed and to his independence. He drew a great deal and was thoroughly familiar with Ruskin's *Elements of Drawing* before he studied at the Pennsylvania Academy of the Fine Arts. In 1889 he had begun to teach himself to paint, but until Henri encouraged him to do so seriously, he had not considered a career as a painter. During the period from 1892 until 1895, his working hours at the *Inquirer* were morning and afternoon. After 1895, when he began working for the *Press* in the afternoon and evening, he had his mornings free and began to paint more. Encouragement came not only from Henri but also as a result of being included in major exhibitions at the Pennsylvania Academy, the Carnegie Institute, and the Art Institute of Chicago— all in 1900. As has already been pointed out, Sloan did not have the quick sketching facility of other newspaper artists and always had to work hard at his drawing and painting. Years later he said: "I accomplished more than some of the others in our group because I had less talent than they did and so I had to work harder." [3]

In the fall of 1892 Sloan enrolled in a night class under Thomas Anshutz at the Pennsylvania Academy of the Fine Arts. Anshutz was a fine teacher who carried on the tradition of American realism as embodied in the works of Thomas Eakins. The system of teaching at the Academy was to begin drawing from casts, "to work from the antique," and from there to graduate to the life class. Sloan had already had some drawing instruction at the Spring Garden Institute and, bored with drawing from casts, began to make sketches of other members of the class. This displeased Anshutz, and there was a brief clash between the two. In spite of this, Sloan had great respect for Anshutz as a teacher. Early in 1893 Anshutz went to Europe, and many of his students were not satisfied with his replacement. Sloan, along with Edward Wyatt Davis, Glackens, and several others, formed the Charcoal Club in March, 1893.[4] In addition to their dislike of the replacement, all were bored with drawing from casts and were probably interested in lower fees, since economic conditions were not good at the time. They were also most interested in using life models. Most of the members of the Club were illustrators and were accustomed to drawing from memory and from their observation of life, which accounts for their boredom with academic procedures. During the lifetime of the Club, semi-weekly meetings were held during which Sloan criticized compositions done as homework. Henri occasionally gave informal criticisms of classwork. It was here that many of the members had their first experience in drawing from a nude model. By fall, the Club had served its purpose and went out of existence (*Ill. 7*). Sloan returned briefly to classes at the Academy.

Another significant event in Sloan's life occurred simultaneously. At a party in Charles Grafly's studio, Sloan met Robert Henri (*Ill. 16*), who helped to change the course of his life. Almost at once they discovered their mutual interest in Walt Whitman's *Leaves of Grass*. Their friendship grew during the following year, and in September of 1893 Joe Laub and Sloan rented Henri's old studio at 806 Walnut Street. Henri was away for a time; when he returned all three shared the studio and it became a meeting ground for the influential group of young artists later dubbed The Eight. The term Ashcan School was not applied to The Eight or their associates during the early years of the twentieth century. Strictly speaking, the correct term for Henri and others who followed the tradition of Eakins and Anshutz is realist. Those artists who found their subject matter in New York City streets, alleys, and docks were called the New York Realists. Their concern was with life in its everyday aspect as opposed to the photographic realism and romantic subject matter preferred by the Academy.

The first appearance in print of the term Ashcan School seems to have been in *Art in America,* in an article written in 1934 by Holger Cahill and Alfred H. Barr, Jr. It has since become a popular term to describe the work of the New York Realists. Unfortunately, the term suggests a group dealing with very narrow subject matter, whereas it was originally intended to indicate its basic interest in all kinds of themes that had previously been considered unworthy of an artist's attention. Cahill and Barr were attempting to categorize a segment of the American scene and to differentiate between the regional realists (Curry and Benton), the social realists (Shahn and Evergood), and the New York Realists (Henri and his followers).

Meanwhile, Sloan's poster style was maturing. One of his first poster-style drawings was published in the *Inquirer* in 1892. It clearly showed the influence of Walter Crane, the Pre-Raphaelite School, and his own independent study of Japanese prints. His fully developed poster style evolved after his brief encounter, in the summer of 1893, with Beisen Kubota, a Japanese newspaper artist who had been visiting the Chicago World's Fair (also called the Columbian Exposition). Sloan carefully examined his sketchbook of brush-and-ink drawings. This contact increased the influence of Japanese brushwork in Sloan's poster style (*Ill. 10*). Later on, Sloan said of their meeting that he "began drawing in a flat, sort of Japanese, black-and-white style. I was given recognition as one of the 'poster movement.' That was before I had ever seen the work of Beardsley, McCarter, Bradley, Steinlen, and Toulouse-Lautrec."[5] The combined influence of Crane and Japanese drawing proved to be successful. In 1894 an article on Sloan's work was published in the Chicago *Inland Printer,* a technical magazine concerned with developing quality printing. His work was also published in the *Chicago Chap Book,* affording him his first national recognition as an artist. Although he worked primarily for the *Philadelphia Inquirer,* Sloan also contributed work to *Gil Blas* and *The Echo* (*Plate I*) and was art editor of *Moods,* a literary and art magazine published in Philadelphia in 1895, to which Henri and Glackens also contributed.

In December of 1895, Sloan moved from the *Inquirer* to the *Philadelphia Press,* where he was given more interesting assignments and a higher salary. He was assigned primarily to feature stories and Sunday supplements; in addition to continuing his poster-style illustrations, he did much of his newspaper work in pen-and-ink drawings.

Perhaps one reason for Henri's influence on Sloan's career was their common respect for the ideas expressed by George Moore in his book, *Modern Painting* (1893), along with their admiration for Thomas Eakins, who shared with Sloan a strong aversion to leaving his native region. Moore too had expounded a "stay-home" theory. Both Eakins and Moore emphasized the importance of life in art. These were the ideas that Henri promoted to his circle of young newspaper artists in Philadelphia. It is most likely that many discussions during Henri's Tuesday evenings emphasized the ideas with which they were to explode the current mode of academic realism: to find their subject matter in the real world around them, to paint life as they saw it— squalid or gay, beautiful or ugly, but always real.

Around 1897, under Henri's influence, Sloan was encouraged to expand his primary interest in illustration and the graphic arts and to begin painting seriously. A number of his portraits of this period, done in a rather dark palette, show Henri's influence and that of Manet, Goya, Velázquez, and Hals, whom Henri introduced to Sloan through reproductions (these were the painters most admired by Henri). One such portrait was of William Glackens, done about 1895–96. Sloan painted approximately ten portraits during this period.

In 1896, at the invitation of Henry J. Thouron, Sloan executed two murals called *Music* and *Opera* for the Pennsylvania Academy of the Fine Arts. Thouron was a well-known painter who had studied at the Pennsylvania Academy and later in Paris. He returned to the United States and taught at the Academy, where he gained an excellent reputation as a teacher of composition. Sloan was proud of Thouron's sponsorship, especially as he had never studied with him, and felt that the commission was an honor. From then until 1903, Sloan painted approximately fifteen more portraits, which form an interesting body of work from this little-known early period. *The Model (Ill. 12)* is a good example of his style at that time.

Late in 1897 or early 1898, Sloan began to paint scenes of Philadelphia, all of which showed the influence of Henri in their choice of colors. In the summer of 1898, he was lured briefly to New York to work on the *New York*

Herald for Frank Crane, who had been art department manager for the *Philadelphia Press*. Crane had offered him a weekly salary of $50; this, together with the fact that some of the *Press* artists had moved on to New York, made Sloan decide to go. He did not, however, find the city to his liking—a strange reaction, considering his later love for New York—because he had left many of his good friends behind and was not pleased with working conditions. By fall, Sloan returned to the *Philadelphia Press* at a weekly salary of $45. He was now the most important member of the art department staff and was turning out a great deal of work.

Sloan continued to paint portraits and scenes of Philadelphia. In November, 1899, Henri sent Sloan a set of Daumier lithographs from Paris, which added another stylistic dimension to Sloan's work. His style in painting, drawing, and etching became increasingly confident and clearly showed his study of Leech, Charles Keene, Gavarni, Daumier, and Steinlen. His painting, while touched with the quality of illustration, was creative and imaginative and showed a serious consideration of the work of Manet, Goya, Velázquez, and Hals.

In 1900 the Pennsylvania Academy of the Fine Arts included Sloan's work in its annual exhibition for the first time (it continued to do so each year through 1907). In the same year the painting *Independence Square* was exhibited in the Carnegie Institute's Fifth Annual Exhibition; his work was also included in an exhibition at the Art Institute of Chicago. This surely indicated a measure of success in his painting, since he had only begun to paint steadily about four years earlier.

In 1902 Sloan began his first major work in etching: fifty-three illustrations for a deluxe edition of the novels of Charles Paul de Kock. To prepare for the job, Sloan read extensively about French history and costumes and studied maps of Paris. The quality of the illustrations indicates the creative powers of his imagination, for, in spite of the fact that he had never visited France, they captured the flavor of that country exactly (*Ill. 15*).

In April, 1901, Henri invited Sloan to participate in a group exhibition at the Allan Gallery in New York. The other participating artists included Glackens and Alfred H. Maurer. This was Sloan's first exposure to the New York public. He also showed works in the first annual exhibition of the Newspaper Artists Association, which was held in Philadelphia and New York in 1901. He served as secretary-treasurer of the Philadelphia exhibitions held in 1901, 1902, and 1903. Sloan frequently acted in this kind of administrative capacity for group exhibitions and in organizations throughout his life.

On August 5, 1901, John Sloan and Anna Marie (Dolly) Wall were married in Philadelphia. Dolly, an auditor in Lit's Department Store, had been introduced to Sloan through the Edward Davises in 1898. The marriage, which suffered through bad times, was destined to last for forty-two years. To quote from the introduction by Helen Farr Sloan in *John Sloan's New York Scene 1906–1913*:

> There were to be long years of financial worry and illness borne with deep loyalty to each other.
>
> Dolly was really Irish and her parents were Roman Catholics from the old country. She had the milk-white skin, blue eyes, soft voice and the tenderness and temper of her racial stock. She and her two sisters lost their father and mother when they were very little and were raised by an older half-brother and his English Quaker wife. This "aunt" was a second mother to Dolly, but the brother was high-tempered. His daughters told me, years after Sloan died, that their father had never been able to understand Dolly. She had a tendency to drink and started to drink when she was fifteen years old, which led to bitter misunderstanding with her family. By the time Sloan met her, Dolly was estranged from the Church. Very fortunately, she had come under the care of an excellent physician, Dr. Collier Bower, who recognized that she had a neurosis "too deep-seated to be cured," he told Sloan, and advised him to think of Dolly as his "game leg." [6]

Bower also advised Sloan to keep a diary, left open carelessly, which Dolly could easily read to be assured of her husband's love.

In November, 1903, Sloan left the art department of the *Philadelphia Press*. The newspaper had dropped its Sunday supplement and subscribed to a syndicated one, so there was no longer sufficient art work for him to do. He began making weekly word-charade puzzles for the *Press* on a free-lance basis at $20 to $30 per puzzle (*Ill. 14*). This relationship with the *Press* continued until 1910 and provided his main source of regular income during those years.

Again at Henri's invitation, Sloan was included in an exhibition of non-academic painters at New York's National Arts Club in January, 1904. This time the group included Henri, George Luks, Glackens, Arthur B. Davies, and Maurice Prendergast. Charles FitzGerald, a well-known art critic at the time, reviewed the exhibition favorably, saying that it was the most significant in recent years.

By the time Sloan had left the *Press,* his fellow artist-reporters—Glackens, Luks, and Everett Shinn—had already moved to New York. Their jobs as quick-sketch artist-reporters came to an end when the half-tone process was introduced and when the use of photographs became possible in newspaper reproduction. Because they were his closest friends, and because many other artists who belonged to the Walnut Street group had also migrated to New York, Dolly and John Sloan moved there in April, 1904.

At first they rented a studio in the Sherwood Building at the corner of 57th Street and Sixth Avenue, where the Henris were living. By August they had settled in their own apartment at 165 West 23d Street. And so the Philadelphia period of Sloan's life came to an end. For the rest of his life he was to be identified with the cities of New York and Santa Fe, which he painted with great affection.

(See Illustrations 7–17, Plates I and II)

CHAPTER THREE   1904–13

Now began a period of activity and vitality (*Ill. 18*) that is described in Sloan's own words in the diaries he kept between 1906 and 1913. The discussions that took place after 1904 at Mouquin's (the café immortalized in Glackens's painting *Chez Mouquin*) on the corner of 28th Street and Sixth Avenue were the source of many ideas for exhibitions and meetings that culminated eventually in the revolutionary Armory Show of 1913.

In those early discussions the specific characteristics of the Armory Show were not decided. Certainly it was not the original intention of the group to include foreign work. Their primary concern was with their own contemporary American artists. The Eight briefly considered inviting some foreign artists but decided against it. Henri encouraged his companions to be concerned about the then limited exhibition facilities for artists in New York.

Many informal meetings were held at the artists' studios during the early years to discuss various exhibition ideas. Jerome Myers and Walter Pach, although not members of the original Eight, were close friends and associates and lent their ideas and support to some of the meetings. After the first exhibition of The Eight in 1908, the next important group show for Henri and his followers was the Exhibition of Independent Artists, held in 1910. The final step in the progression of major events leading up to the Armory Show was the formation of the Association of American Painters and Sculptors. All the members of The Eight except Shinn were invited to join, along with many other prominent New York artists who had been involved in the 1910 exhibition. This group had come into existence primarily to organize and exhibit a larger version of the 1910 show; Arthur B. Davies was elected its first President in 1912.

In 1905–6 Sloan produced a series of ten etchings on city life: *Fifth Avenue Critics (Ill. 19); Fun, One Cent; Connoisseurs of Prints; Man Monkey; Show Case; Woman's Page; Turning Out the Light; Man, Wife, and Child; Roofs, Summer Night;* and *The Little Bride.* Henri was so enthusiastic about Sloan's new endeavors that he offered him financial help, which might permit him to give up commercial work for a time (by now Sloan was doing magazine illustrations for *Collier's* and *Century,* but they provided a rather uncertain and not very lucrative source of income). In spite of his urgent need for money, Sloan did not accept the offer, taking instead a small loan of $100, which he soon paid back.

In 1906 the American Watercolor Society invited Sloan to show his group of etchings, but returned four it considered "too vulgar" for public exhibition. The incident is described in the May 2 entry in Sloan's diary:

> In the afternoon four etchings of the set which had been invited by Mr. Mielatz of the committee on etchings at the Water Color Society Exhibition were returned to me. Great surprise as he had even furnished the frames. In the evening I attended the "stag" Private View, saw Mielatz and asked for an explanation. He said other members of the committee had thought these four were rather "too vulgar" for a public exhibition. I asked to be introduced to some of these sensitive souls but he would not comply. I was madder than I can describe. Asked to have the remaining six taken down but this is against the rules . . .[7]

In contrast to this unpleasantness, three of Sloan's paintings and several of the etchings were exhibited at the Modern Gallery, where they received much favorable comment, especially from Charles FitzGerald in the *New York Evening Sun.* In April, 1906, a set of the ten city-life etchings was sold to Henry W. Ranger and another to W. H. Kent of the Metropolitan Museum of Art. At their request, Sloan also donated a set of fifty-seven etchings to the Lenox Library Collection.

One of Sloan's major contributions to American art was as a teacher, beginning in 1906 when he substituted for Henri for one month at the New York School of Art (George Bellows, Edward Hopper, and Walter Pach were all students of Henri at the time). In July of the following year he accepted a position as instructor at the Pittsburgh Art Students League. He commuted weekly to this class (in life, portrait, and composition) from October until December, when the school was no longer able to pay his salary.

On April 4, 1907, a significant meeting took place at Henri's studio, attended by Sloan, Luks, Arthur B. Davies, Glackens, and Ernest Lawson, the core members of The Eight. On that date Sloan wrote in his diary: "After dinner

PLATE V. *Dolly Reading*. 1914. Oil on canvas, 20″ x 24″.
Private collection.

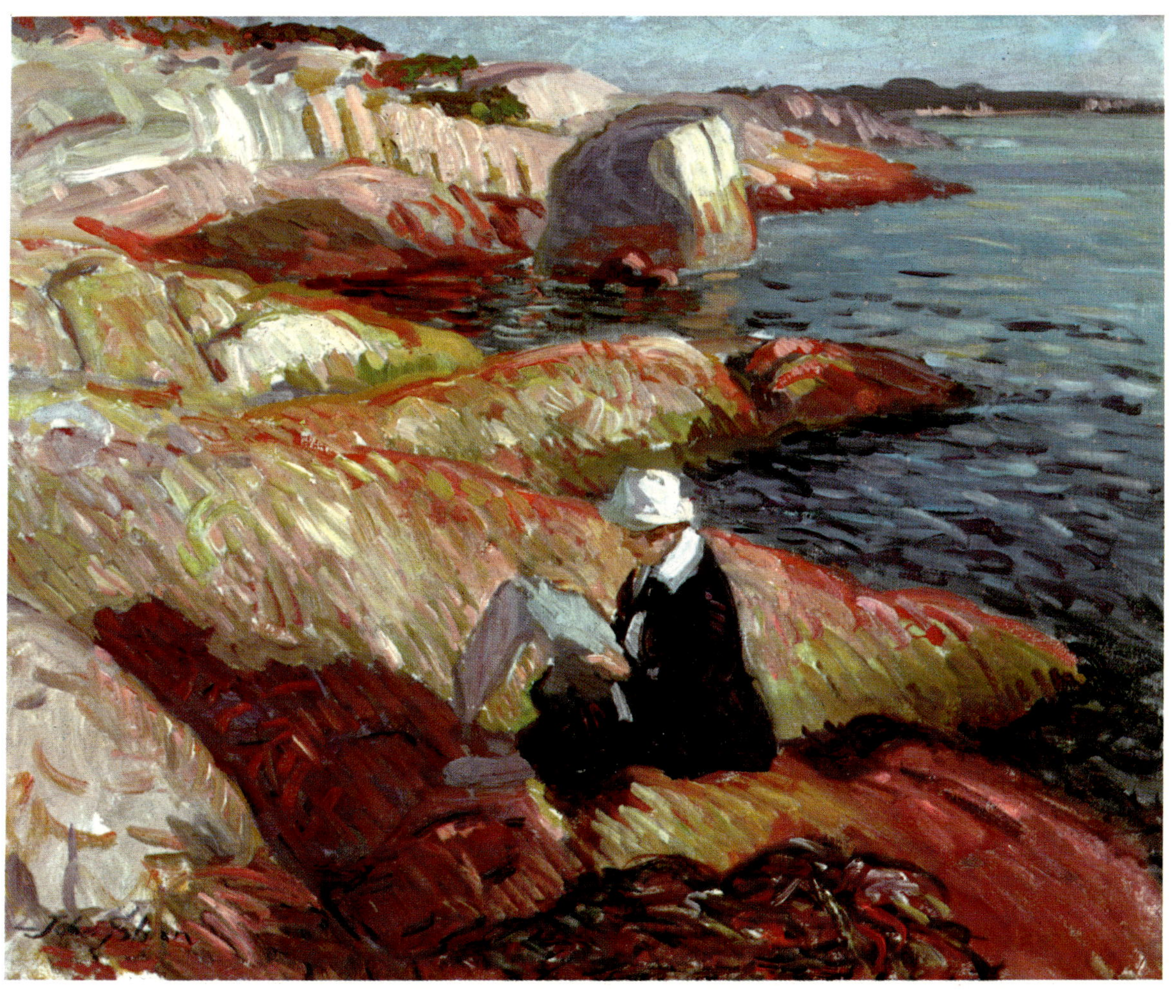

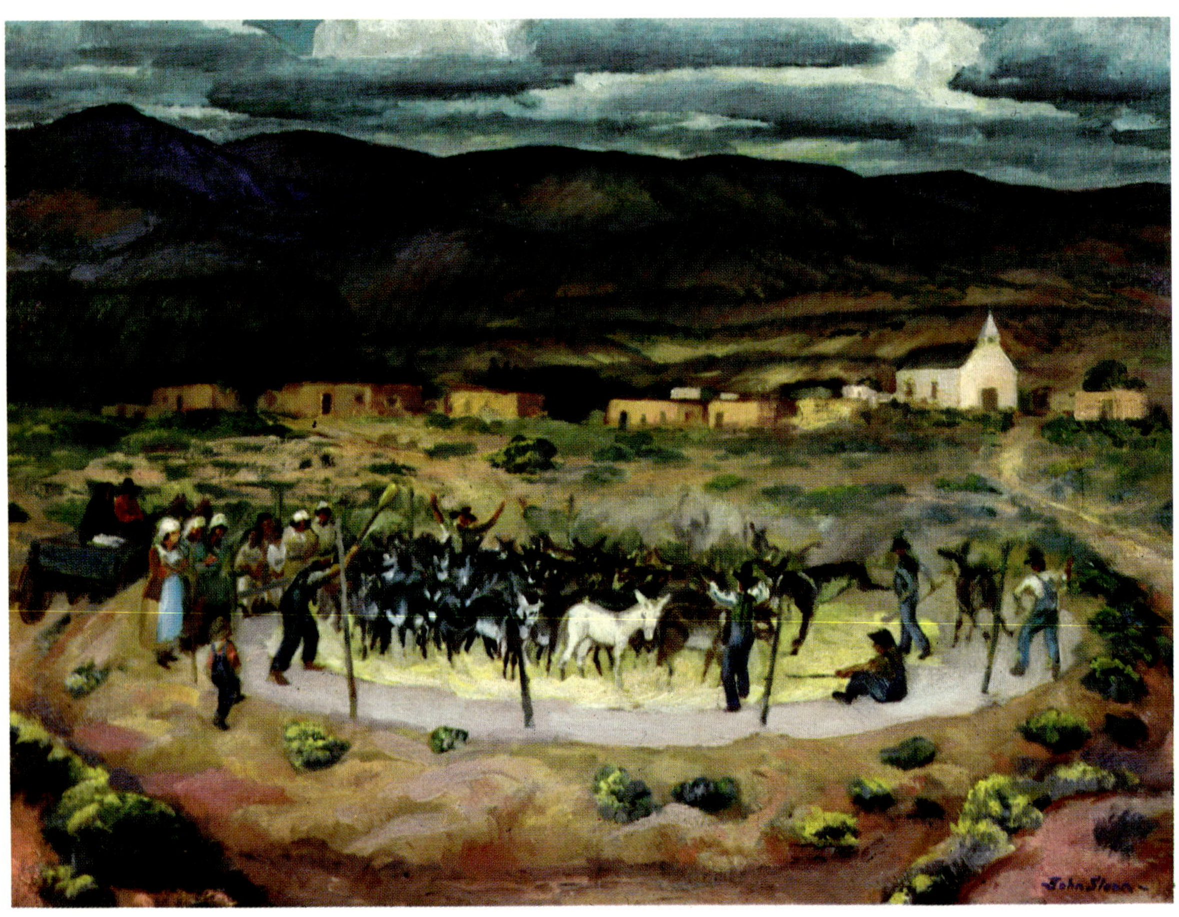

PLATE VI. *Burros Threshing.* 1922. Oil on canvas, 32″ x 24″.
Collection of Mr. Titus C. Geesey, Wilmington.

I went to a meeting at Henri's to talk over a possible exhibition of the 'crowd's' work next year. . . . The spirit to push the thing through seems strong."[8] The April 9 entry relates how Davies had seen William Macbeth, who offered two rooms in his gallery for the exhibition; the arrangements with Macbeth were for him to receive 25% of any possible sales, while the group (which had by now taken in Everett Shinn and Maurice Prendergast as well) would guarantee $500 (later reduced to $400) for the use of the rooms. On February 3, 1908, the first exhibition of The Eight opened at the William Macbeth Gallery in New York. Sloan's diary entry reads:

> Exhibition at Macbeth's opens. . . . Davies called, said that he thought the show looked quite well but a little crowded in some places—which is true enough but don't seem to me to matter in a group arrangement—hang "taste" anyway! . . . They report a great crowd at the gallery, and young du Bois [Guy Pène du Bois], the artist and critic of *The American,* came in most enthusiastic over the show. He wants photos for article but I have very few of pictures which are there.[9]

Sloan exhibited the following pictures: *The Cot* (Bowdoin College Museum of Art, Brunswick, Maine), *Dust Storm, Fifth Avenue* (*Ill. 22*), *Easter Eve* (Collection of Miss Ruth Martin, New York), *Election Night* (Rochester Memorial Art Gallery, University of Rochester, New York), *Hairdresser's Window* (*Ill. 23*), *Movies, Five Cents* (private collection), *Nursemaids, Madison Square* (Sheldon Memorial Art Gallery, University of Nebraska, Lincoln), and *Sixth Avenue and Thirtieth Street* (*Ill. 24*). It is hard now to believe that paintings such as these could arouse such fury in the press at the time that the group's members were labeled the "apostles of ugliness."

Thus the now-famous exhibition of "The Eight" was launched. The tendency to remember only the epithets hurled at the artists is great, yet the press was kinder than those epithets would indicate. Certainly some harsh things were said; it is possible that some of the criticism directed at Sloan related to the incident concerning his "vulgar" etchings. Nevertheless, the exhibition as a whole was a great success. Paintings by Henri, Luks, Davies, Shinn, and Lawson were sold for a total in excess of $4,000. Although Sloan did not sell any works, he was gratified by the success of his friends.

In May, 1908, Sloan began to experiment with the medium of lithography. Arthur G. Dove, who was planning to be in Europe for at least a year, offered to lend Sloan his lithographic press in the interim. The offer was accepted with enthusiasm, and the press was moved into Sloan's apartment the next day. Lithographs did not become a major part of Sloan's œuvre, since he could not afford to have them printed. The ten lithographs he completed form an interesting segment of his printmaking career (*Ills. 30 and 31*). Six were done in 1908, one in 1919, one in 1921, and two in 1923.

In June, 1909, Henri told Sloan of a new color system invented by Hardesty G. Maratta. Maratta was a painter, probably not too successful, who wrote and lectured on color theory and who also manufactured and sold paints. Within a few days Sloan began working with this new set of paints, manufactured in "regular intervals" of "full" colors and neutrals. Sloan's diary entry for June 13 is accompanied in the published version by a quotation from his later notes:

> *The palette is an instrument that can be orchestrated to build form. If we stumble around in colors we are like a musician who would have to tune every note on the piano each time he sits down to play or compose. I liked the Maratta colors because they provided the painter with a battery of pigments that were accurately mixed. We had twelve "full colors" around the color wheel (a triangle is more accurate for purpose of mixing because there are only three primary colors, red, yellow and blue); twelve semi-neutral colors, and twelve neutrals very low down in the scale of intensity. With these twelve major notes, we could plan color chords, similar in some ways to those of music. For instance, a 3–4–5 chord might go from yellow to blue-green to red. I painted hundreds of landscapes, portraits and other subjects—and no two of them have the same color scheme. Before starting to paint, I would decide on a point of view about the color, whether it was to come out of a tonality (chiaroscuro) or perhaps I would emphasize some dominant colors with neutrals for foils. If the limited palette I had chosen to work with proved inadequate to get the kind of plastic realization I wanted, I could always open the palette up, using some of the colors that had been held in reserve. If you use all the strong colors and most powerful contrasts of light and dark right at the beginning, you have nothing extra to fall back on when you need to invent a more powerful or more subtle way of creating form.[10]*

Sloan felt that this was a more perfect "set of tools" than the old palette, with its raw mineral colors and earth hues, irregular and unrelated. Later notes and comments by Sloan and Helen Farr Sloan indicate that he used the Maratta paints until he began spending his summers in Santa Fe. Wartime restrictions made it increasingly difficult for Maratta to get the fine pigments he used at first, and so Sloan began to make up his own bi-colors and hues (he had always added certain colors, such as viridian, alizarin, cobalt, cobalt violet, and ultramarine to the Maratta pigments). Sloan worked with set palettes until 1928, by which time he had started to employ underpainting and glazing.

On July 22, 1909, the Sloans went out to dinner in New York and met John

Butler Yeats, father of the Irish poet William Butler Yeats. For many years, until his death in 1922, he remained a close friend and confidant, as well as a firm believer in Sloan's ability as a painter. Yeats himself was a competent artist and draftsman, and there exist some excellent drawings of both John and Dolly Sloan done by him during their years of close association. It was through Yeats that Sloan was introduced to John Quinn, an art collector. Quinn, too, became a good friend and bought some of Sloan's etchings, even though he was not much interested in American art.

One of the more serious problems confronting the New York art world in those years was the shortage of exhibition space and the limited opportunity for young artists to show their work. Sloan and his friends were much concerned with this and, after the exhibition of The Eight, had many discussions that led gradually to a determination to remedy the situation. Early in these talks Henri, Sloan, Davies, and Jerome Myers offered various plans for revolting against the National Academy and its support of academic realism. Sloan's diary entry of February 24, 1910, reads:

> Sent *Pigeons* [*Ill. 35*] and *Three A.M.* to the National Academy Jury. The last one won't have a chance I'm sure. It is the Tenderloin picture I painted last year. One girl in her shift cooking, the other gossiping over a cup of tea. Quite too much for them." [11]

On March 9, he wrote:

> Back *rejected!* From the N.A.D. jury came the *City Pigeons* and *Three A.M.* The latter I sent them as much as a joke like slipping a pair of men's drawers into an old maid's laundry, so that its refusal I expected surely. The first, *Pigeons,* I thought had a chance to pass but I evidently underrated it. It looks as though they had cut me off from the exhibition game: must find some way to show the things.[12]

On April 1, 1910, some 2,000 persons swarmed to the opening of the first open no-jury no-award exhibition of American artists at 29-31 West 35th Street in New York City. The idea for this revolutionary exhibition had been nurtured and discussed for some time by Henri, Sloan, Myers, Davies, Pach, Shinn, Glackens, and others.

Early in January, 1910, the news that the National Academy had found a site on which to build new galleries had sent Jerome Myers to Sloan, full of ideas for the exhibition that had been discussed previously. In a talk with Sloan later the same day, Henri had suggested that a society of artists be started under the name "Independent American Artists." He had further suggested that patrons be secured who would put up money in advance with the privilege of choosing paintings from the exhibit, and that twenty artists be asked to contribute $100 each.

A meeting was called on January 10, 1910, to discuss the idea of both the exhibition and the society, with Myers, Von Gottschalk, Shinn, Henri, Pach, Sloan, and Luks attending. Henri's later comment on this meeting was that there seemed to be little "do-something" spirit. By the end of January, Sloan was impatient to proceed with all arrangements: *I am going to go at this thing* with Ullman. [Ullman had offered to take over raising money for the backing of the show, but Henri had objected to his doing so.] I *believe* we *can do it* and it will be worth while trying anyhow. . . ." [13]

Sloan suggested the name "Association of American Artists" for the exhibition and gave Ullman $75 in cash and a $25 check to be used for rent and preliminary expenses in starting a fund for an exhibition of the new group. He wrote later to Ullman cancelling the plan because the others had become more active in organizing the exhibition.

As early as February, 1910, Myers had spoken of an international exhibition. Davies too seemed to feel that the plans for the exhibit should have been expanded to the international scale, but he was not to have his wish until 1913.

On March 11, 1910, Henri, Walt Kuhn, and Sloan met to discuss the exhibit. By the middle of the month Guy Pène du Bois, along with Clara Tice and P. Scott Stafford, two of Henri's pupils, had joined in the scheme and furnished extra backing money. By March 22, sufficient money had been collected so that the exhibition was assured.

The entrance fees had been decided on and pictures started coming in about March 25. The fee for one picture was $10; for two, $18; for three, $25; and $30 for four. Glenn Coleman and Stafford were enlisted to work on the wall hangings that would provide a suitable background for the pictures. At first the walls were hung with cheesecloth, but it was decided that it was too white and translucent. Henri and Sloan finally bought a large amount of fine gray Linon de Paris, with which the galleries were rehung. The Hanging Committee included Henri, Glackens, du Bois, and Kuhn.

On March 29, Kuhn and Sloan worked on the catalog until three in the morning, and the printer's proofs were finally checked two days later. Writers from the newspapers previewed the show on April 1, and everything was in readiness for the opening that evening. Although the galleries were artificially lit, each painting had an individual light. All three floors of the building were used, with the third floor set aside for drawings and etchings. The total number of entries was 260 paintings, 219 drawings, and 20 pieces of sculpture. One hundred and three artists exhibited, many of whom were Henri's pupils.

That the opening was a success can hardly be questioned, with some 2,000 persons in attendance (figures on total attendance for the show are not available). On that memorable opening night, however, only three items were sold. They were drawings by Henri, a sketch by Edith Haworth, and a picture by Clara Tice. As with any exhibition, newspaper comment was varied and conflicting, some favorable, some vitriolic.

The exhibition was taken down on April 28, 1910. It was never entirely forgotten, for even today we can see some of the results of the ideas planted during the organization of the Armory Show of 1913 and finally, in 1917, in the formation of the Society of Independent Artists.

Henri was always active in trying to promote and arrange exhibitions to help young artists, whether or not they were his own students. He approached the widow of the composer Edward MacDowell with an idea for a series of shows at the MacDowell Club on West 55th Street. Against the opposition of some club members, who felt that such a suggestion favored painting over the other arts, exhibitions were inaugurated there in 1911. Sloan, as usual, was active in helping to organize the exhibits. The shows went on for several years and provided still another exhibition ground for artists that was not controlled by the Academy or the jury system.

As early as 1909, Sloan had been contributing cartoons to *The Call,* a weekly (later bi-weekly) Socialist magazine. In his diaries he often mentioned, with some vehemence, the evils perpetrated against the working classes by the power structure. His appeal, however, was for reform rather than actual revolt against the government; the idea of change was linked in his mind to the orderly democratic process of the vote. Therefore, it was with a certain naiveté that Sloan sometimes contributed drawings and cartoons to *The Call* and later to *The Masses (Ills. 44–46)* with the conviction that they would not be used for political purposes.

Sloan's comments in his diaries clarify his feelings on the relationship of his art to politics. On April 15, 1909, he wrote:

In the afternoon, Barrell [Charles Wisner Barrell] called and he and I took a walk. As we walked we talked on Socialism. He is, of course, a thorough advocate of the cause—and I can't help feeling that the movement is right in the main. I am rather more interested in the human beings themselves than in the schemes for betterment. In fact, I rather wonder if they will be so interesting when they are all comfortable and happy.[14]

On May 5, 1909, he relates:

> Vlag came again today and brought Herman Bloch who is art writer for the Socialist daily newspaper *The Call*. I was glad to meet him. Told him that I had no intention of working for any Socialist object in my etchings and paintings though I do think that it is the proper party to cast votes for at this time in America. Bloch is soft spoken and not as alert and practical as Vlag. Bloch speaks of a man being religiously interested in his work. This may mean well but does not sound "healthy" to me.[15]

Many of Sloan's artist friends—Glackens, Luks, Shinn, Bellows, and Stuart Davis among them—also contributed to *The Masses* in the years from 1912 until 1916. Sloan became acting art editor of the magazine in December, 1912. During that period he produced some of his finest black-and-white drawings. In his later notes, Sloan points out that for two years the illustrations he provided for *The Masses* were one of his greatest interests in life.

After the outbreak of World War I in August, 1914, Sloan, disillusioned with the failure of the Socialist party to prevent war, ceased sending cartoons to the magazine, believing that instead of being a vehicle for social satire it had become a mere mouthpiece for doctrinaire propaganda. (One of Sloan's major quarrels with Max Eastman and Art Young of *The Masses* was that they obscured the purely humanitarian purpose of his drawings by changing the captions to give them political significance.) Sloan was asked especially to attend a meeting on April 6, 1916, to defend his humanistic viewpoint against the propagandistic and doctrinaire; when the meeting left him unreconciled, he resigned from the magazine the next day. His early support of the Socialist party was clearly the result of an enthusiasm for righting social wrongs. In later years he refused to join the Artists' Congress or the Artists' Union because he did not believe in their ideas. In 1933 he refused an invitation from Moscow to exhibit in the American Section of the International Bureau of Revolutionary Artists.

Not long after the closing of the Exhibition of Independent Artists in 1910, the Association of American Painters and Sculptors was formed. Some of the prime organizers of that group were those who had been most influential in the formation of the earlier group. The Association became the sponsoring group for the Armory Show. For many reasons, Sloan—who was invited by Walt Kuhn to join the show in February, 1912—was not active in its organization. He was extremely busy with his work on *The Masses,* with his own painting, and teaching private pupils; he did not attend more than one or two preliminary meetings but did work hard on the hanging committee. He was represented in the show by two paintings and five etchings. The paintings were *Sunday, Girls Drying Their Hair* (*Ill. 43;* Addison Gallery of American Art) and *McSorley's Ale House* (*Ill. 40;* Detroit Institute of Arts). The etchings were *Girl and Beggar, Mother, Night Windows, Anshutz on Anatomy,* and *The Picture Buyer* (*Ill. 37*).

Davies, Kuhn, and the lawyer-collector John Quinn advocated an exhibition that would include many foreign works. Sloan's later notes indicate that there was considerable dissent among the members of the Association about the organization of the Armory Show. Some of this was in the form of opposition to the importation of foreign work, but a more fundamental cause of friction was the lack of democratic discussion about methods of financing the show. Davies and Kuhn made a trip to Europe and there met Walter Pach, who was very influential in the selection of the foreign section of the exhibit. Henri, Sloan, and several other artists resigned from the Association after the show because they were unable to obtain the treasurer's financial report.

In an interview with Carl Zigrosser [16] in 1947, Sloan remarked that the Armory Show had undoubtedly had a strong and subtle effect on his work. He felt that it had led him to a greater interest in color, plasticity, and the geometry of form. He was certainly not opposed to the modernist principles underlying the show: "While I did make only one excursion into the abstract field [Sloan was referring to the aquatint *Mosaic*] . . . the impact of the ultra modern work has greatly influenced my thinking." [17] Although Sloan in fact recognized the importance of the new trend toward abstraction, he never felt at ease with this style and always felt the need to express himself in terms of realism (*Plate IV*).

(*See Illustrations 18–46, Plates III and IV*)

CHAPTER FOUR   1914–18

From 1909 on, Sloan had been going through a process he called "opening up the palette." This meant modifying his palette and using a greater variety of color themes. The Armory Show gave him the opportunity to see numerous works by Cézanne, Matisse, Van Gogh, and Renoir and to realize the importance of color in their work.

In the summer of 1914, the Sloans shared a cottage with friends in Gloucester, Massachusetts. In that new environment he painted as many as ten to twelve landscapes and portraits each week (*Plate V*). Sloan felt that the landscape genre enabled the artist to free himself of stale color habits and that the variety of forms in nature yielded opportunities for new color combinations and plastic rhythms. The Sloans spent every succeeding summer through 1918 in Gloucester, the site of some of his most beautiful landscape paintings. During this transitional period in his career, Sloan continued to paint cityscapes, including *Backyards, Greenwich Village (Ill. 47)* in 1914 and *Sun and Wind on the Roof* in 1915, although they were now done in a much lighter palette than the early city pictures.

Gradually, however, as the city changed, Sloan lost some of his interest in urban life as a theme with pictorial possibilities. With the coming of Prohibition, restaurants changed their character, and such old haunts as Petitpas' and Mouquin's were no longer as colorful. The old neighborhoods of New York that had fascinated Sloan in the early years were also changing; large buildings were rising and business began to encroach on such picturesque areas as the Tenderloin, which had been a rich source of inspiration for paintings. One of his major city pictures was *Grand Central Station (Ills. 62 and 63)*, in which he successfully solved the pictorial problem of depicting crowds of people while retaining a sense of order and design.

The Armory Show caused Sloan to change some of his ideas about painting. Sloan said in his later notes that he had learned the value of developing the habit of painting, of not waiting for an idea or inspiration to come before beginning to paint. After the Armory Show, he grew increasingly concerned with the plastic problems involved in painting and far less with thematic ones. Sloan said in his notes that after 1912 he was much more apt to use the medium of etching for "city subjects" because he did not always visualize such pictures in terms of color. One of his most popular etchings, *Fifth Avenue Critics* (*Ill. 19*), was done in 1905. Thirty-five years later he made a second version of the subject in oil, which he entitled *Fifth Avenue Critics, 1905* (*Ill. 88*). This is the only example in Sloan's œuvre of a painting based on an earlier work. Sloan himself commented on the evolution of his style in the catalog for a 1946 exhibition of his work at Dartmouth College:

> My etching of 1905 from which this painting is derived has always been an outstanding best seller among the prints. This picture was painted in 1940 and is far more concerned with color plasticity than paintings contemporary with the etching. Limousines and taxis have taken the place of the vehicles of that day but the humans are the same.[18]

An interesting comparison with this late painting is provided by *Gray and Brass* (*Ill. 26*), a work of 1907, painted with a low-key palette and with a greater concern for fluent brushwork.

Sloan's stature as an artist grew steadily after World War I. In 1915 he met Gertrude Vanderbilt Whitney, a meeting that ultimately resulted in his first one-man exhibition at Mrs. Whitney's studio from January 26 through February 6, 1916. Mrs. Whitney was one of the earliest patrons of American art. (A few years later, Sloan did a fine portrait of Juliana Force, the first director of the Whitney Museum and also a staunch supporter of American art and artists [*Ill. 56*]). Later that year, from February 10 through April 10, Sloan had a one-man show at the Hudson Guild in New York, sponsored by the People's Art Guild. It was also at this time that Sloan's long-time association with the Kraushaar Galleries began (*Ill. 70*). His first one-man show there was held from March 19 through April 7, 1917. John F. Kraushaar was one of the first art dealers to promote the work of the New York realists. Sloan's association with the Kraushaar family, which extended to John Kraushaar's son Charles and his daughter Antoinette, was a personal as well as a business relationship, which continued until Sloan's death in 1951.

Sloan began teaching at the Art Students League of New York in 1916 and continued to be affiliated with that school until 1938, except for the period from 1932 to 1935. In that period he taught at Alexander Archipenko's art school in New York for two months and, after George Luks's death in 1934, was elected head of Luks's school, also in New York. In addition to those formal associations, Sloan had private pupils in New York and Gloucester from as early as 1912. Thus, teaching gradually replaced illustration as his main source of income.

The year 1917 witnessed the organization and inaugural exhibition of the Society of Independent Artists. Walter Pach, who had spent many years abroad and was familiar with French artists' organizations, was its prime organizer. Marcel Duchamp and Francis Picabia were his assistants; they were living in the United States during World War I. They helped Pach to fashion the new American Society along the lines of the French organization that had been in existence from the time of the Salon des Refusés in 1863.

Glackens was elected first President of the Society—an appropriate choice, as he had been chairman of the American section of the Armory Show. Sloan served on the hanging committee for its first exhibition, held in April at the Grand Central Palace. Historically, the forerunners of this open, jury-free, no-prize exhibition were the group exhibitions inspired by Henri and his followers, principally the Exhibition of Independent Artists in 1910.

Sloan was elected President of the Society of Independent Artists in 1918, a post he held until the Society discontinued its exhibitions in 1944. The Society accomplished enormously important work of a kind that appealed to Sloan, who, like many artists of his generation, was actively concerned for the well-being of his fellow artists. It enabled unknown artists to exhibit their work to the public without first having to submit it to a jury. Moreover, its refusal to confer prizes or awards of any kind eliminated a possible cause of jealous rivalries and ill will among artists. Many artists who were later to become famous had their first opportunity to show their works in the Society's annual exhibitions.

The founders included not only American realists in the tradition of Eakins and Homer, but also artists of stature from Europe. Duchamp and Picabia, somewhat revolutionary in their ideas, represented the avant-garde. For many years, the photographer Alfred Stieglitz and the artists who exhibited at his 291 Gallery formed the core of the American avant-garde.

As President of the Society, Sloan worked tirelessly to keep the organization vital and active. Only World War II and the physical difficulties of organizing large exhibitions under wartime restrictions caused the eventual termination of this worthy enterprise.

In 1917, Sloan was forty-six years old. He had sold few paintings but had exhibited in Paris in 1910, in an international exhibition in Rome in 1911, and had received the bronze medal for etchings at the Pan-Pacific International Exposition in San Francisco in 1915.

(See Illustrations 47–54, Plate V)

CHAPTER FIVE   1919–27

In 1919, John and Dolly made their first trip to Santa Fe, New Mexico, which Henri had visited a few years earlier, strongly recommending its climate and the wide variety of subject matter it afforded the artist. In 1920, the Sloans returned to Santa Fe and bought a house there. Sloan used a studio formerly occupied by Henri, and provided by the Museum of New Mexico. After 1920, Sloan built his own studio in the garden of his home. Each year thereafter, with the exception of 1933 and 1951, the Sloans spent three or four months in Santa Fe, where he often gave private lessons to pupils. The clear, dry atmosphere of the desert, the cloud formations, the mountain ranges, and the foliage around Santa Fe—all so different from the New England scenery— provided a new source of excitement for him (*Plate VI*). Although he still painted many landscapes on the spot, as he had in Gloucester, Sloan now began to paint more often from drawings, working on the canvases in his studio after starting them out of doors. From 1914 on in Gloucester, and from 1919 on in Santa Fe, Sloan painted more in the summers, when he was free from his regular teaching duties at the Art Students League.

Hotel Dance, Santa Fe (*Ill. 57*) was painted on Sloan's first trip in 1919. The artist's comment on the painting, years later, was:

> Our contemporary life soon becomes history. This festive gathering at the old De Vargas hotel, in the large, high-ceilinged dining room draped with flags covering the windows, is an echo of the past. The old hotel went up in flames years ago. The dances have also gone up in price and social pretense.[19]

The painting shows the same interest in the panorama of human life as do the early New York scenes.

Besides being captivated by the New Mexico landscape, Sloan grew intensely interested in Indian art and culture, an interest reflected in many paintings of that period. Among them were *Eagles of Tesuque (Ill. 58)*, *The Eagle Dance, Koshare,* and *Koshare in the Dust*. In *Gist of Art*, Sloan remarked of *Eagles of Tesuque:*

> Within nine miles of a Europeanized city, for three hundred years the little Pueblo of Tesuque has made a noble fight against combined poverty and civilization. The population is small and on the day when we saw this ceremony a mere handful appeared as spectators.[20]

In the case of Indian ceremonies, his paintings were always done from memory, because the Indians were sensitive about the sketching and photographing of their dances and tribal rites. He observed the rituals and costumes with great care and always sought to render them as faithfully as possible.

Sloan was one of the earliest champions of Indian painting and crafts. His interest in American Indians and his respect for their work continued to grow during his years in Santa Fe. Strong religious opposition to the Indian ceremonials arose in the mid-1920's, when an effort was made to suppress them. Sloan and other artists sympathetic to the Indian cause united successfully to promote tribal art and to protect the Indians' religious culture. Their efforts culminated in the great Exposition of Indian Tribal Arts in 1931–32— the first national exhibition of works by the American Indian to treat them as art rather than ethnology.[21] As President of the Society of Independent Artists, he encouraged the showing of works by Indian artists in the Society's exhibitions. The show took place at the Grand Central Art Galleries in New York. Later it traveled through the United States under the auspices of the College Art Association. The exhibition was largely paid for and sponsored by Amelia Elizabeth White. Sloan and Dolly worked together to organize it. Sloan was its president. For several years, Miss White paid Dolly a salary to manage the Exposition and the Gallery of American Indian Art in New York. The salary helped the Sloans through the Depression Years.

Sloan's early years in Santa Fe also introduced him to the old Spanish culture of the Southwest. He was fascinated by the dignity and gaiety of the descendants of the *conquistadores* and enjoyed painting them, as in the fine *Two Sisters (Ill. 59)*, painted in 1925. Of this painting, Sloan commented later: "A case of double exposure or dual personality or second sight. . . . A double attempt at a portrait of a single Santa Fe girl—Alejandra Rael, Aleck for short, since married. A handsome Spanish-American type. Composed right well—the picture, I mean." [22]

In 1919, after a hiatus of many years, Sloan returned briefly to lithography.

He accepted an invitation from Pratt Institute in Brooklyn to give a demonstration of the medium for students. His seventh lithograph, *Saturday Afternoon on the Roof (Ill. 55)*, also called *Man on the Roof,* was done at that demonstration. In 1921, he produced *Snake Dance,* and in 1923 two others—*Sunday, Girls Drying Their Hair on the Roof* and *Shine, Washington Square.*

Sloan's main source of income now was teaching, both privately and at the Art Students League. Sales of his work were never sufficient alone to earn him a living until the 1940's. His first sale to a major museum occurred in 1921; the painting, acquired by the Metropolitan Museum of Art, was a 1906 work, *Dust Storm, Fifth Avenue (Ill. 22).* John Butler Yeats, who had great faith in Sloan's paintings and called them "poems of the city" *(Plate VII),* had tried to interest his friend John Quinn in Sloan's work. Quinn visited Sloan on June 12, 1910, and was offered *Dust Storm* for $350. He said during the visit he would buy one of Sloan's paintings; he never did, but before leaving he did order a complete set of the De Kock etchings. In 1926, Gertrude Vanderbilt Whitney bought a set of Sloan's etchings and donated them to the Metropolitan.

For many years, Mr. and Mrs. George Otis Hamlin had been close friends of John and Dolly Sloan. In 1923, to pay medical bills, twenty of Sloan's paintings were sold to the Hamlins for $5,000. The price was publicized at that time as $20,000 in order to protect Sloan's prices at the Kraushaar Gallery. Sloan later persuaded the Hamlins to will the entire collection to Bowdoin College in Maine.

Sloan continued to teach and exhibit frequently during this period. In 1920, five of his paintings were included in the overseas show of American paintings at the International Exhibition in Venice. The move to Santa Fe and Sloan's exposure to the Indian and Spanish cultures of the American Southwest had an important and lasting effect on his life and work.

(See Illustrations 55–73, Plates VI and VII)

CHAPTER SIX   1928–43

Early in 1928 Sloan adopted a new painting technique, monochrome under-painting in oil and glazing with transparent and semi-opaque oil colors. That summer he substituted tempera underpainting for oil and began to use some linework superimposed over glazes. Some years later, in *Gist of Art,* Sloan said of linework: "I like to use linework to give added significance to the surfaces in the light and to increase the sensation of light and shade." [23] Of *Nude on Navajo Blanket (Plate VIII)*, painted in the new technique in 1929, he commented:

> A very complete panel in which little use is made of the linear technique except in turning from the light. This is a decided variation from our general principle which calls for the lines as color-textural definition of the lightened surface. More visual than some, perhaps. The increase in volume of the far side of the figure is very successful because quite unnoticeable. [24]

Of a later painting, the portrait of Amelia Elizabeth White done in 1934–35 (*Ill. 81*), Sloan wrote:

> My sitter asserts her liking for this picture which to my mind rates her high in ability to look on a picture as a created work. These examples of the linear super-glazing texture are difficult to photograph. I see no reason why a painter should not pride himself on producing pictures which are exclusively themselves. [25]

Sloan's subject matter continued to include city scenes—though fewer than before—landscapes, and portraits (*Plate IX*). Increasingly, his interest was in the single figure and nude studies. Sales of his work continued to be insignifi-cant as a source of income. In 1928 a projected sale of $40,000 worth of paintings failed to materialize, a serious financial setback for Sloan, who had borrowed $7,500 to lend to a friend on the basis of the contract. The friend did not repay the loan, and Sloan had to spend the Depression years retiring his debt.

In this period, Sloan's works were increasingly exposed to the public through exhibitions, but it was his early paintings and etchings that were most readily accepted. The critics always showed more interest in, and respect for, Sloan's early work. It sometimes annoyed him that the later work in Gloucester and Santa Fe was not taken seriously. The public exposure did, however, account in part for some sales. In 1928, his *Lafayette Hotel* (*Ill. 73*) was purchased and given to the Metropolitan Museum of Art, and *The Cow* sold to Duncan Phillips. In 1933, the Corcoran Gallery of Art in Washington, D.C., purchased *Yeats at Petitpas'* (*Ill. 36*).

Sloan exhibited five paintings in the Museum of Modern Art's show in 1929, entitled "Nineteen Living Americans." Almost every year throughout the 1930's he had one-man shows: In 1931 there was a show at the McClees Gallery in Philadelphia; in 1933 a large exhibition of etchings at the Corcoran Gallery of Art; and in 1934 one at the Montross Gallery in New York. The Whitney Museum of American Art held a large exhibition in March, 1936, of one hundred of Sloan's etchings. The following December the Jerome Stavola Art Gallery in Hartford, Connecticut, honored him with a major one-man exhibit. These were all followed by a major retrospective at the Addison Gallery of American Art in Andover, Massachusetts, in 1938. In 1939, on the occasion of the publication of *Gist of Art,* the Wanamaker Department Stores in New York and Philadelphia had exhibitions of Sloan's work. In 1942 a one-man show was organized and traveled from Chicago to Denver, Santa Fe, Albuquerque, and Fort Worth.

The fact that exhibition opportunities were so much more available to artists in New York was in no small part due to the efforts of Sloan, Henri, and their associates. The Society of Independent Artists promoted exhibition opportunities not only for its own members but for all artists. Indeed, a study of the catalogs of the Society's exhibitions reveals in many instances the first appearance on the art scene of painters whose names now rank at the top of the contemporary American art world.

The directors of the Society of Independent Artists gave Sloan a testimonial dinner in 1941 in honor of the twenty-fifth anniversary of the Society's founding and in recognition of his twenty-fourth year as President. Sloan remained President of the Society until after the last exhibition in 1944 when, because of dwindling finances, lack of exhibition space, and insufficient interest and support, it became dormant. (The Society could be revived at any time. Its records are on deposit at the Delaware Art Museum; Stuart Klonis of the Art Students League and Helen Farr Sloan are still officers of its last Board.)

Adelaide Garvin, in her column "Art and Artists" in *The Critic,* August–September, 1958, wrote that Sloan, even at the age of eighty, could have been called the angriest of young men. She was referring to the critical attitude Sloan held toward contemporary abstract painting. In a lecture at Bucknell University in 1946, he had remarked that he felt it was going from "the abstract, to the abstruse, to the absurd." Nevertheless, Sloan had been fascinated by the new work shown in the Armory Show, saying that he felt the modern movement was a medicine that would help cure the disease of copying the appearance of things. He never questioned the validity of the Abstract Expressionist movement, but he did fear the lengths to which a complete rejection of objective reality could go. In *Gist of Art* (1939), Sloan articulated some of his reservations about modern art: "The stumbling block in modern art is that the artist becomes more interested in craftsmanship than anything else. Cubism is not art in itself. It is the grammar and composition of art. The ultra-modern movement has made us conscious of the skeleton of tradition." [26] He cautioned young artists:

> Avoid imitative painting, the copying of light shapes and shadow shapes. But this does not mean being alienated too far from representation. Work which is purely non-representational loses some of the texture of life. Students cannot have too much training in cubism but there has to be an interest in life before the work takes on a healthy creative vigor.[27]

In 1930 the College Art Association organized a series of six radio broadcasts. Sloan spoke on the first of these, his topic being "The Assimilation of Modern Art." During these years Sloan was interviewed frequently and was sought after as a speaker and writer on art. In 1931 he received the Carroll H. Beck Gold Medal for his portrait of *Vagis the Sculptor* (*Ill. 77*). During the next year he was made an honorary member and President of the Art Students League. The etching *Sunbathers on the Roof* (*Ill. 89*) was made for the American College Society of Print Collectors in 1941. In the following year his etching *Fifth Avenue 1909* won first prize in the Artists for Victory Exhibition.

Sloan's willingness to fight for a cause in which he believed came to the fore in 1932, when he resigned as President of the League after it refused to appoint George Grosz as an instructor. Sloan felt that Grosz had a great deal to contribute to the League as a teacher, even though the two men held quite different aesthetic ideas. "The reason I wanted an artist like George Grosz on the teaching staff of the Art Students League," Sloan wrote later, "was because he had had that thorough training in academic drawing. It sticks out all over his work, and yet he can draw like a wise child." [28]

The controversy inaugurated a period of estrangement from the League. In the fall of 1932, Sloan joined the staff of Alexander Archipenko's art school in New York, where he taught painting and drawing for two months. George Luks, his friend and associate from Philadelphia days, died in 1933. Sloan was elected head of the George Luks School in the next year by the students and executors and taught there until May, 1935. Sloan returned to the Art Students League for a while in 1933 and resumed his regular teaching schedule there in 1935. He continued to teach there through 1938.

In 1937 Sloan began his second major etching commission, a series of sixteen scenes illustrating W. Somerset Maugham's novel *Of Human Bondage* (*Ill. 86*). One of his most charming and humorous etchings, *A Thirst for Art*, was done in 1939 (*Ill. 87*). Art show openings in the 1930's were not especially enjoyable for Sloan, whose mocking statement about these functions shows a crowd attracted to one of them mainly by the refreshments offered rather than by any interest in art.

Although Sloan and other Americans had exhibited in Europe, very little was known there about American art. In June, 1941, Sir John Rothenstein wrote in an article ("Painting in America") for *Horizon, A Review of Literature and Art:*

Of the older men, none seemed to me to equal John Sloan (b. 1871), who is essentially the painter of the low life of Victorian downtown New York. Sloan is a vigorous, scintillating realist, who prefers low, silvery tones, a master of atmosphere and gesture. So close is his affinity with Sickert that I asked whether he knew him. "I've followed Sickert's development for many years," he said, "feeling that we saw many things rather alike, but we've never met. You see," to my surprise he added, "I've never been abroad."

(*See Illustrations 74–89, Plates VIII and IX*)

CHAPTER SEVEN   1944–51

Dolly Sloan died on May 4, 1943. Nine months later, on February 5, 1944, Sloan married Helen Farr. They had met in the fall of 1927, when Helen, then sixteen years old, entered Sloan's class at the Art Students League. From the first day, she took notes in his classes. As time went on she became a close friend and, in 1939, *Gist of Art,* subtitled *Principles and Practise expounded in the Classroom and Studio, recorded with the assistance of Helen Farr,* was published. In Chapter One, Sloan aptly describes the book as a "record of the thoughts and impulses that have been behind my work and teaching." [29]

After their marriage, Helen Sloan continued to take notes of interviews and to sort, file, and annotate her husband's many letters and documents, recognizing the historical importance of such papers and their value as social history. There were times when the typing of notes and the keeping of diaries irritated Sloan because he was busy painting and was more interested in the present than the past. Nevertheless, he resumed his diaries in 1944, reread a few pages of his early diaries, and delivered comments on his early work, which his wife faithfully recorded. Those recollections of his early years are an important contribution to American art history.

By 1918 or 1919, Sloan had grown less interested in the work of Hals, Manet, and Velázquez and more so in that of Carpaccio, Signorelli, Mantegna (whose *Dead Christ* he never tired of looking at in reproductions), and other Italian painters. He was fascinated by their draftsmanship.

In his teaching at the Art Students League Sloan referred many times to the early Italian painters. He once said, "There are many kinds of good painting, but one thing is true of them all: it is the power of drawing which makes a painter great. Carpaccio, Bellini, Veronese, Breughel, Rembrandt, Delacroix, and all the others were great painters because they were draughtsmen." [30] In his discussions on drawing and geometric forms, he remarked: "The Italians were constantly concerned with theories of beauty based on geometrical plans. When a man is a great master this interest in mathematics serves to discipline his thought rather than to devitalize it." [31] In discussing color in painting he said: "The early Italians and Flemish used it in this way to reinforce the pattern of the design." [32] Sloan's interest in the early Italians prompted him to look at other masters. During the period immediately after the Armory Show he began to study the work of Renoir and subsequently that of Rubens and Titian.

Although he was always initially inspired by subject matter, he gradually grew more interested in painterly problems, particularly after the Armory Show. His late work, though somewhat uneven (from 1922 on Sloan's work was interrupted by six major operations), was sometimes more powerful and creative than that of his younger days; *Monument in the Plaza* (*Plate X*), a 1949 work, is an example. Comparison of the early *Yolande in the Large Hat* (*Ill. 34*) with the late portrait *Yolande van R.* (*Ill. 93*), done in 1946, affords an interesting view of his stylistic development. The first portrait is in his early style; its low-key palette fuses the influences of Hals, Manet, and Velázquez. The brushwork is freer and more dashing and the modeling is more classical. In the later portrait we see the results of the more colorful palette of his later style and the increased concern with a different kind of plastic design. The draftsmanship, chiaroscuro, and use of color are inspired now by his study of Renoir, Rubens, and Titian. *Monument in the Plaza* is influenced by his study of Bellini.

Sloan participated in major exhibitions throughout these years. He was represented by twenty-two paintings and some etchings and lithographs in the Philadelphia Museum of Art's large "Artists of the *Philadelphia Press*" exhibition in 1945. In 1946, Dartmouth College (of which his cousin, John Sloan Dickey, was President) organized a large exhibition of his work to commemorate his seventy-fifth birthday; Sloan himself wrote the foreword to the catalog. The Kraushaar Galleries gave him a retrospective show in 1948. The last major exhibition in his lifetime was a two-man show with his old friend Randall Davey, which was put on at the New Mexico Alliance for the Arts in Santa Fe. Finally, though he did not live to see it, Sloan worked with Lloyd Goodrich of the Whitney Museum in planning a major retrospective, which ran there from January 10 to March 2, 1952. The show was then put on display at the Corcoran Gallery of Art in Washington (March 15 to April 20) and at the Toledo Museum of Art (May 4 to June 8).

Honors continued to come to Sloan near the end of his life: In 1950 he was elected to the American Academy of Arts and Sciences in recognition of his work as an artist and received the Gold Medal for Painting from the American Academy of Arts and Letters. Sloan had never been in favor of jury shows or prizes and awards for artists. In his opinion, such acclaim usually went to the worst art, and he firmly believed prizes were harmful, especially to the young artist. In his acceptance of the Gold Medal he chose to believe it was for his independence rather than for his art and took further comfort from the thought that he was much too old for it to have any harmful effects on his career.

In 1951, Sloan's doctor advised him not to go to Santa Fe for the summer. He vacationed instead in Hanover, New Hampshire, at the invitation of his namesake, the President of Dartmouth. There, he foresook the colors of the Southwest for the green New England landscape, as in *Mink Brook* (*Ill. 100*).

The summer was an active and pleasant one. Sloan busied himself with painting for many hours a day and visited with friends. Late in August it was discovered that Sloan had cancer. Now in his eighty-first year, he entered the hospital at Hanover to prepare for another operation. Calm and un-worried, he passed the time looking at art books and talking about painting. In spite of his youthful outlook and zest for living, however, Sloan died of post-operative medical complications on September 7, 1951.

(See Illustrations 90–100, Plate X)

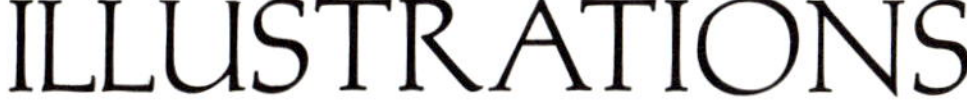
ILLUSTRATIONS

The cannon-shot was followed, after a considerable interval, by a volley of small arms.

Another pause, and then, not a quarter of a mile in front of me, I beheld the Union Jack flutter in the air above a wood.

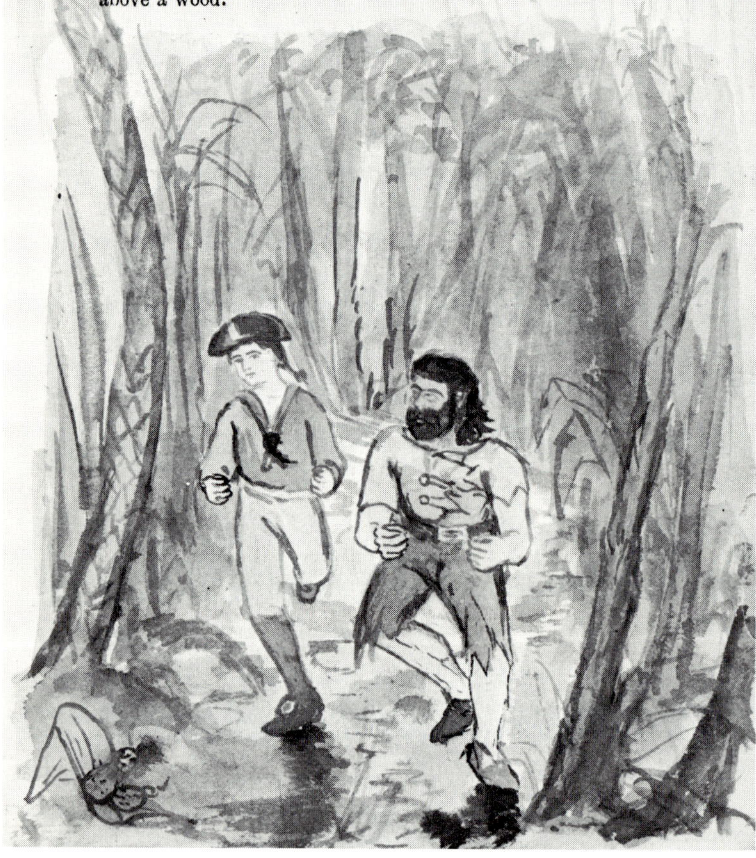

1. Illustration for *Treasure Island*. 1884. Wash drawing, 7⅜″ x 4¾″. John Sloan Collection, Delaware Art Museum, Wilmington. *Photo Lubitsh & Bungarz, Wilmington.*

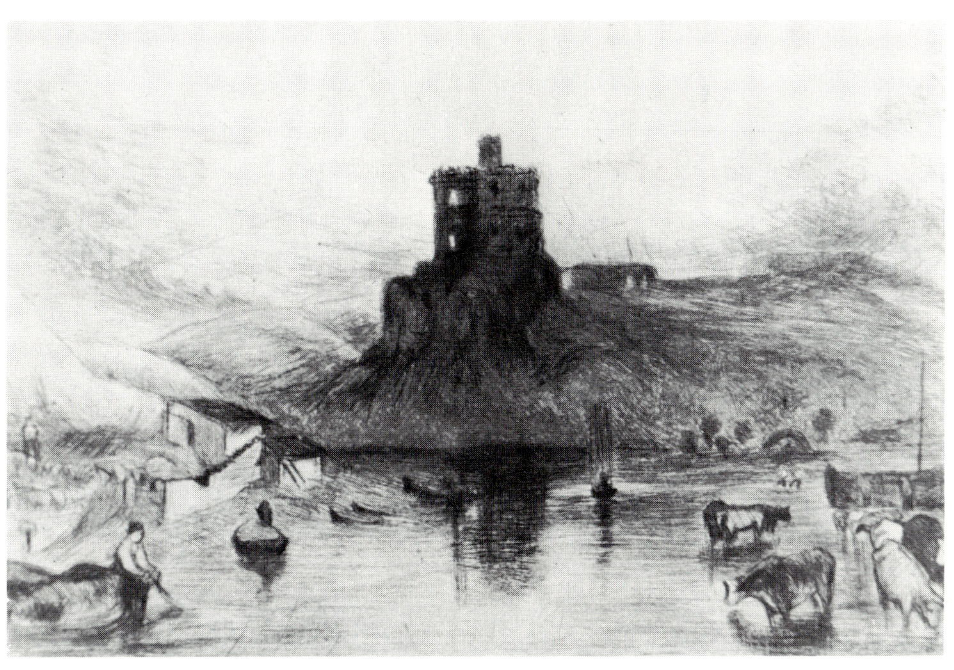

2. *Dedham Castle.* 1888. Etching, 3¼″ x 5″.
Wilmington Society of the Fine Arts, Delaware Art Museum, Wilmington.

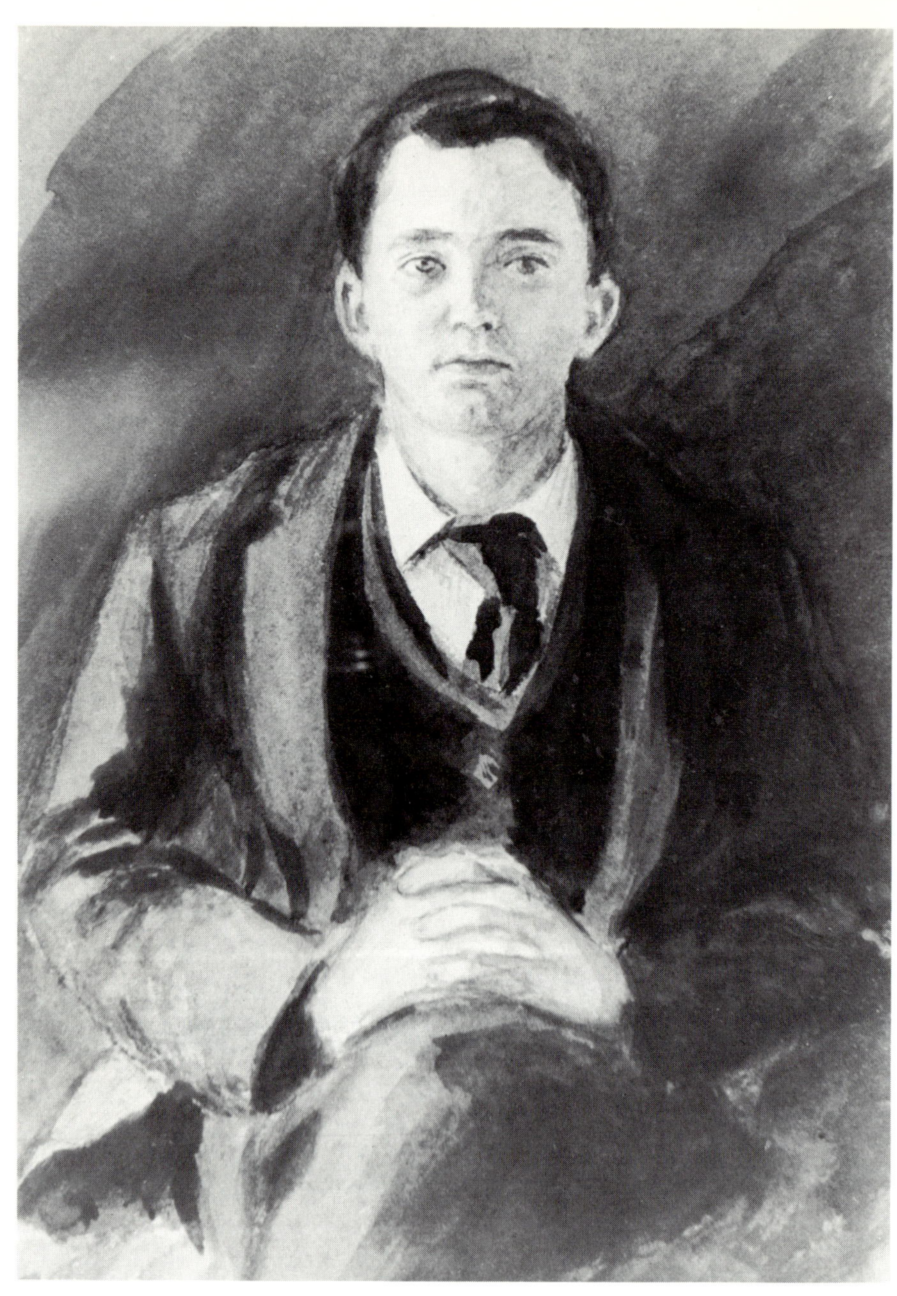

3. *Self-Portrait*. 1890. Oil on canvas, 14″ x 12″.
John Sloan Collection, Delaware Art Museum, Wilmington.

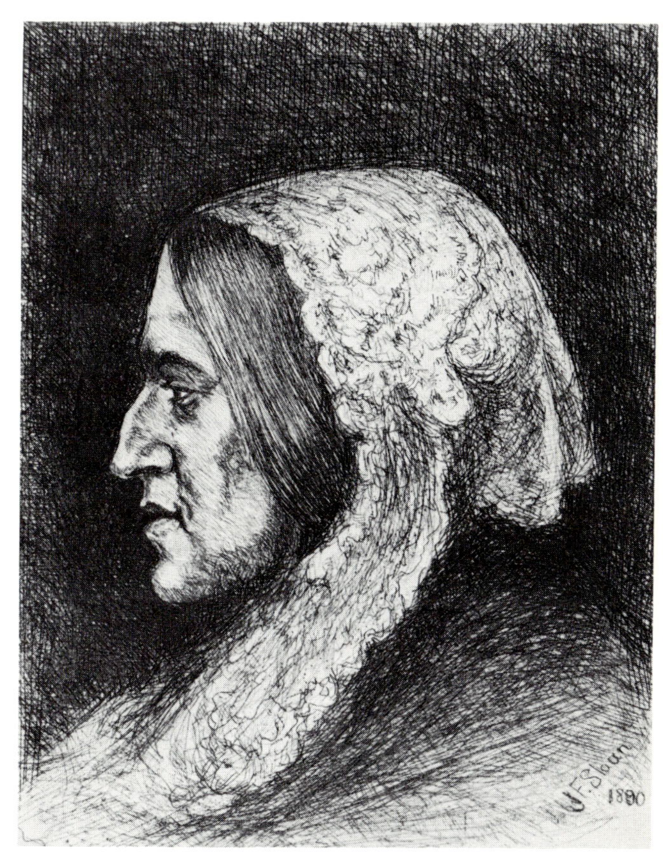

4. *George Eliot.* 1890. Etching, 4½″ x 3½″.
Wilmington Society of the Fine Arts, Delaware Art Museum,
Wilmington.
Photo Lubitsh & Bungarz, Wilmington.

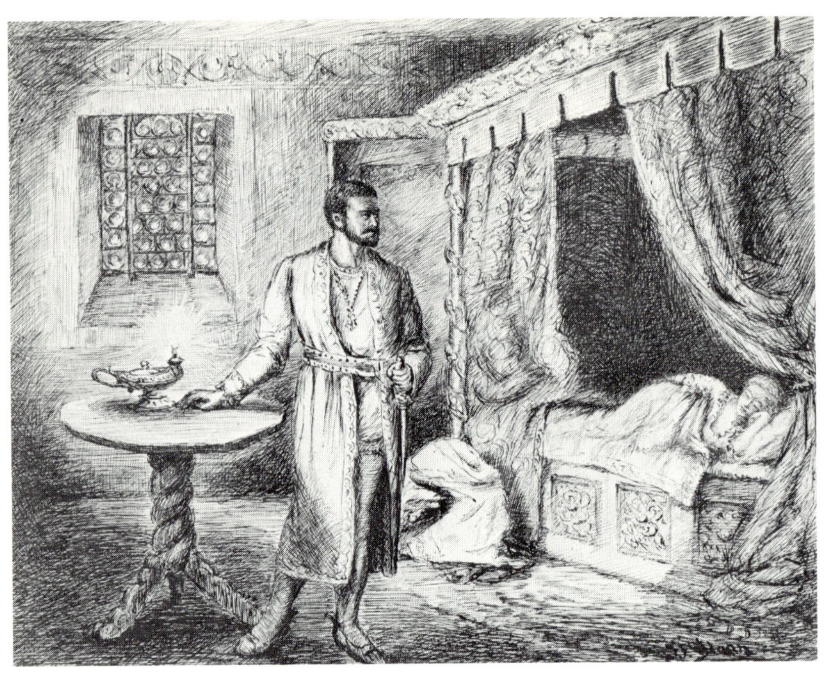

Above

5. Untitled drawing. 1891. Pen and ink, 9½″ x 12″.
John Sloan Collection, Delaware Art Museum, Wilmington.
Photo Lubitsh & Bungarz, Wilmington.

6. *Landscape. c.* 1890–92. Watercolor, 7¼″ x 10¼″.
John Sloan Collection, Delaware Art Museum, Wilmington.

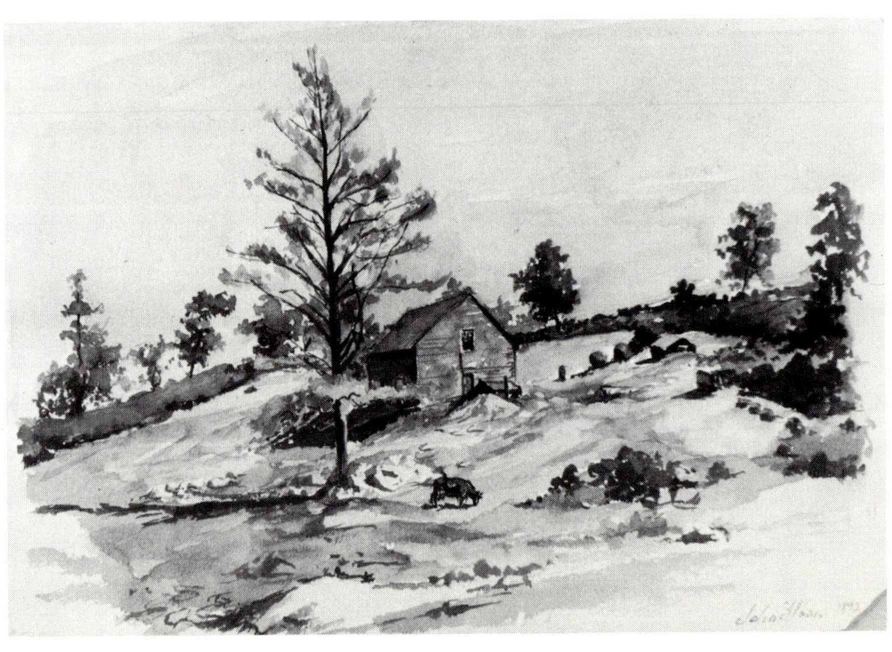

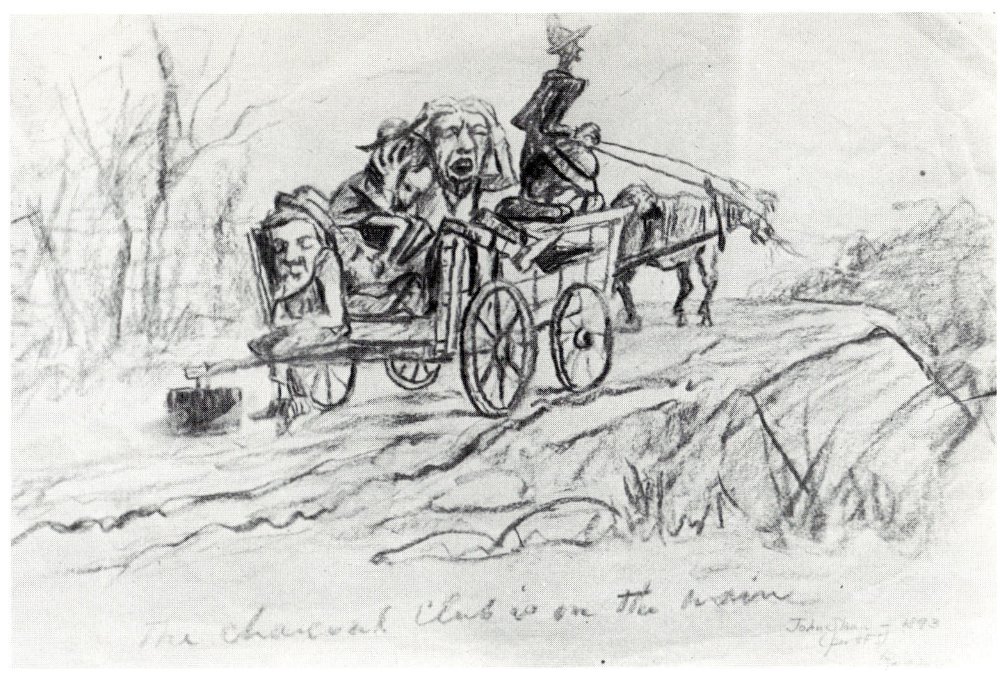

Above

7. *The Charcoal Club Is on the Wain.* 1893. Charcoal drawing, 9½″ x 14⅞″.
Wilmington Society of the Fine Arts, Delaware Art Museum, Wilmington.

8. Photograph of John Sloan in the studio at 705 Walnut Street. 1893.
John Sloan Collection, Delaware Art Museum, Wilmington.

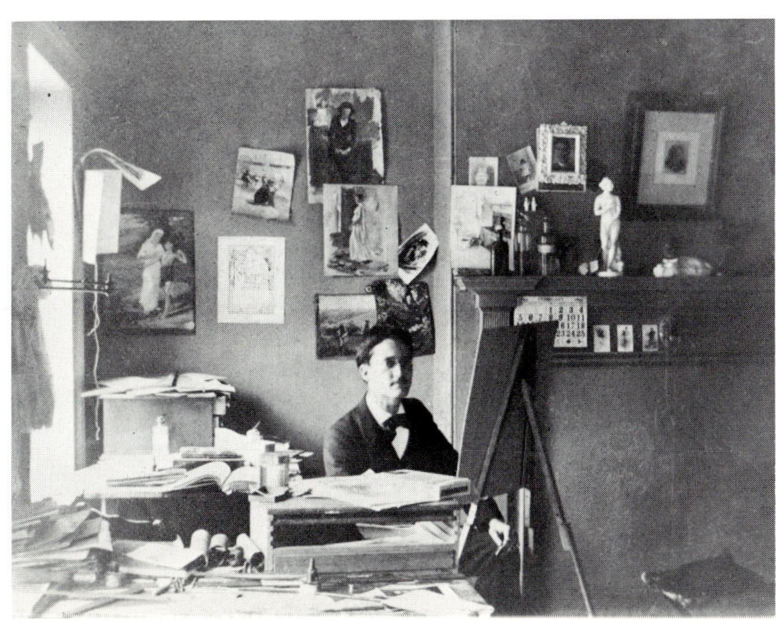

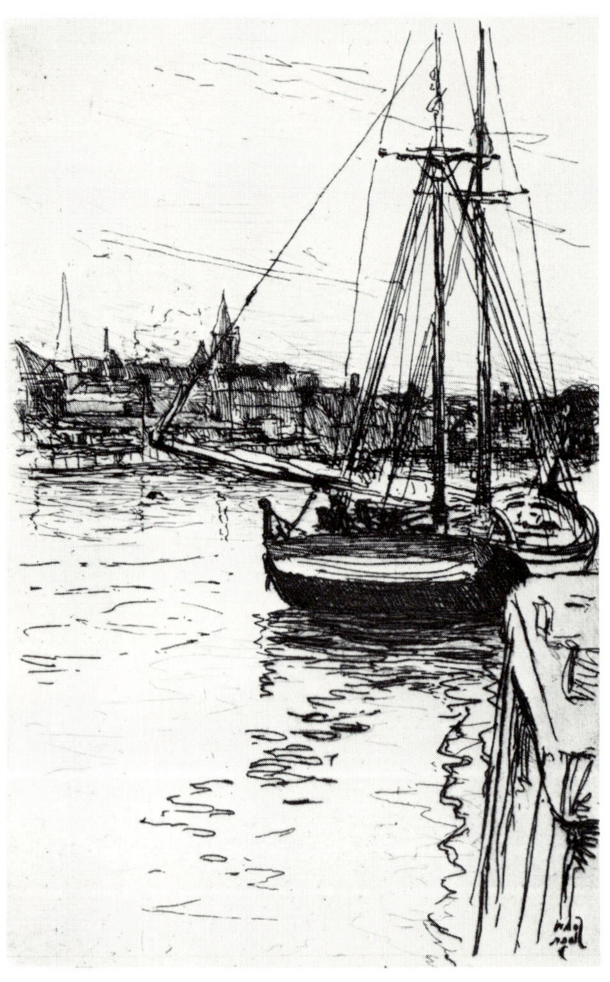

9. *Schuylkill River*. 1894. Etching, 8¼″ x 5¼″. Wilmington Society of the Fine Arts, Delaware Art Museum, Wilmington.

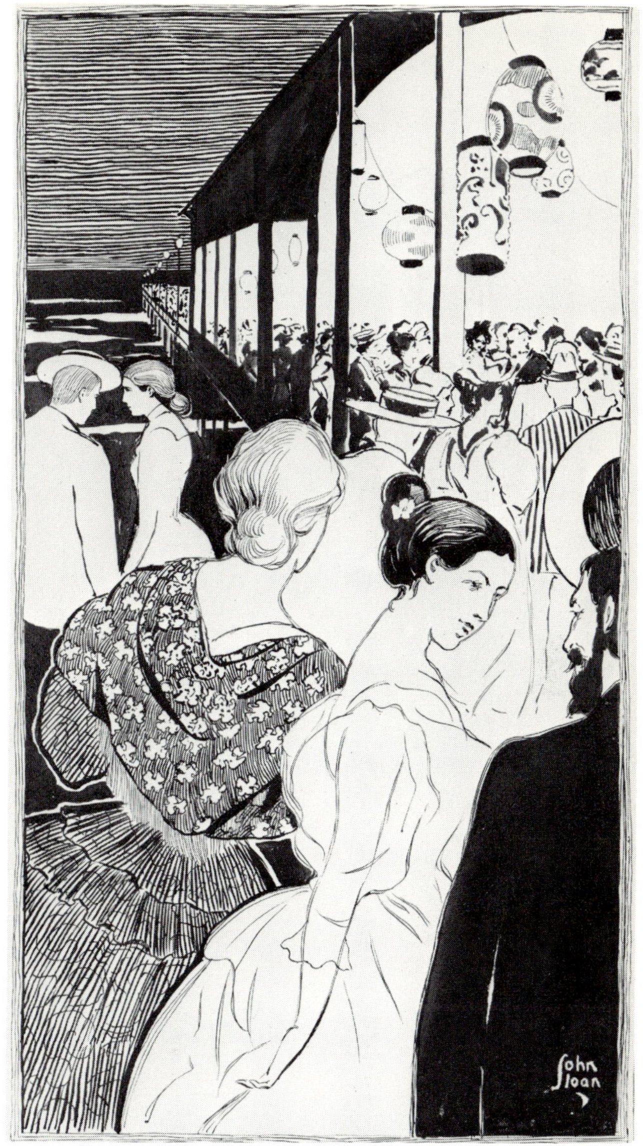

10. *Night on the Boardwalk*. 1894. Pen and ink, 12½″
x 6¾″. John Sloan Collection, Delaware Art Museum,
Wilmington.

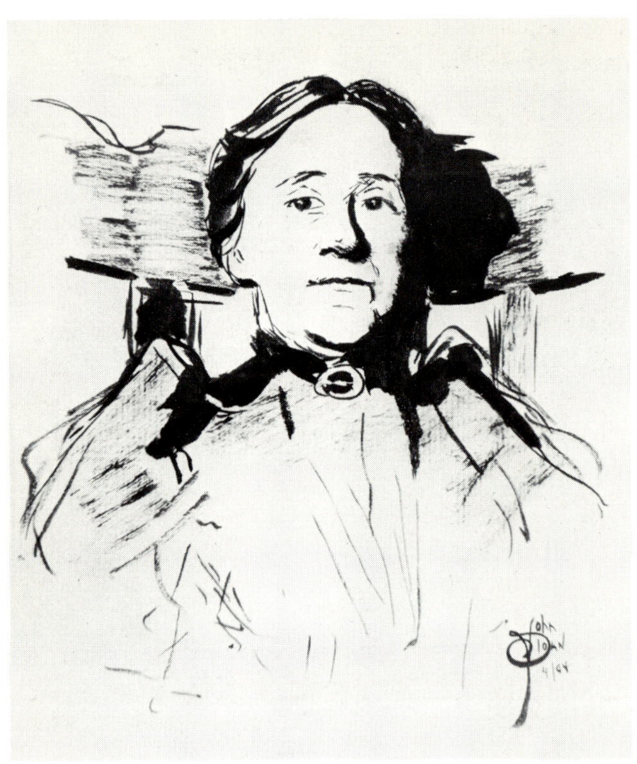

11. *My Mother*. 1894. India ink drawing, 7″ x 5½″.
John Sloan Collection, Delaware Art Museum, Wilmington.

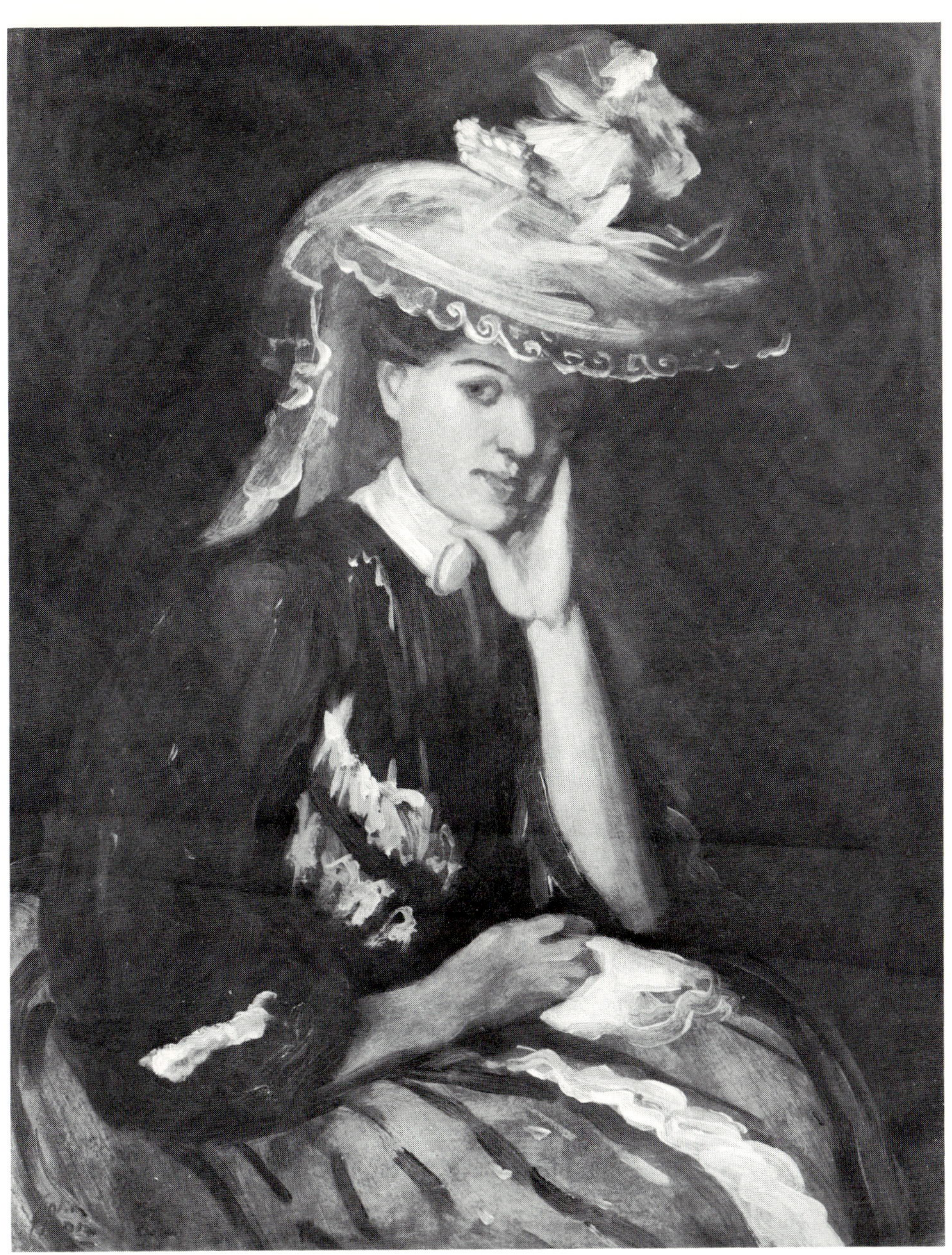

12. *The Model. c.* 1897. Oil on canvas, 32″ x 25″.
Kraushaar Galleries, New York City.
Photo Geoffrey Clements, Staten Island.

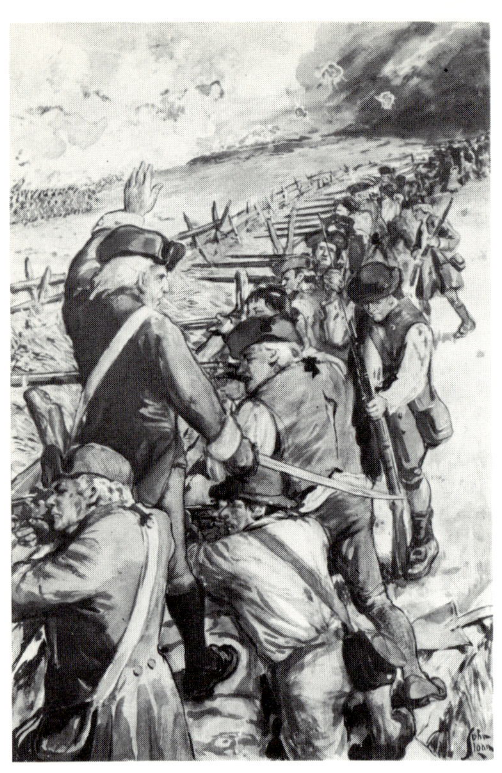

Left

13. *The Battle of Bunker Hill.* 1900. Wash drawing, 20″ x 13″.
John Sloan Collection, Delaware Art Museum, Wilmington.
Photo Lubitsh & Bungarz, Wilmington.

14. *Football Puzzle.* 1901. Reproduced in the *Philadelphia Press.*
John Sloan Collection, Delaware Art Museum, Wilmington.
Photo Geoffrey Clements, Staten Island, New York.

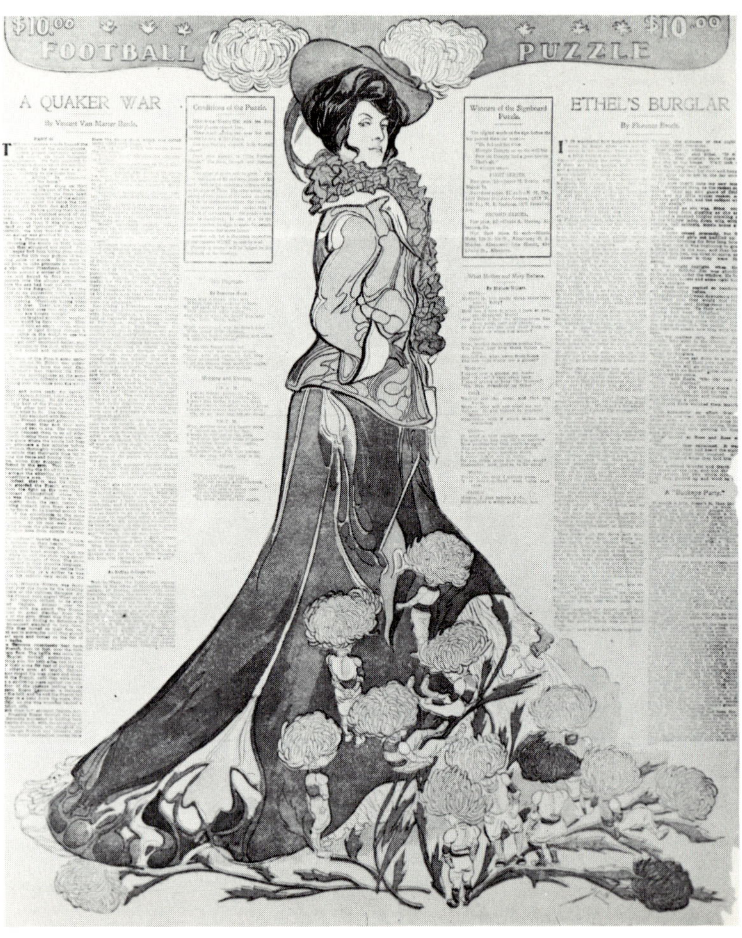

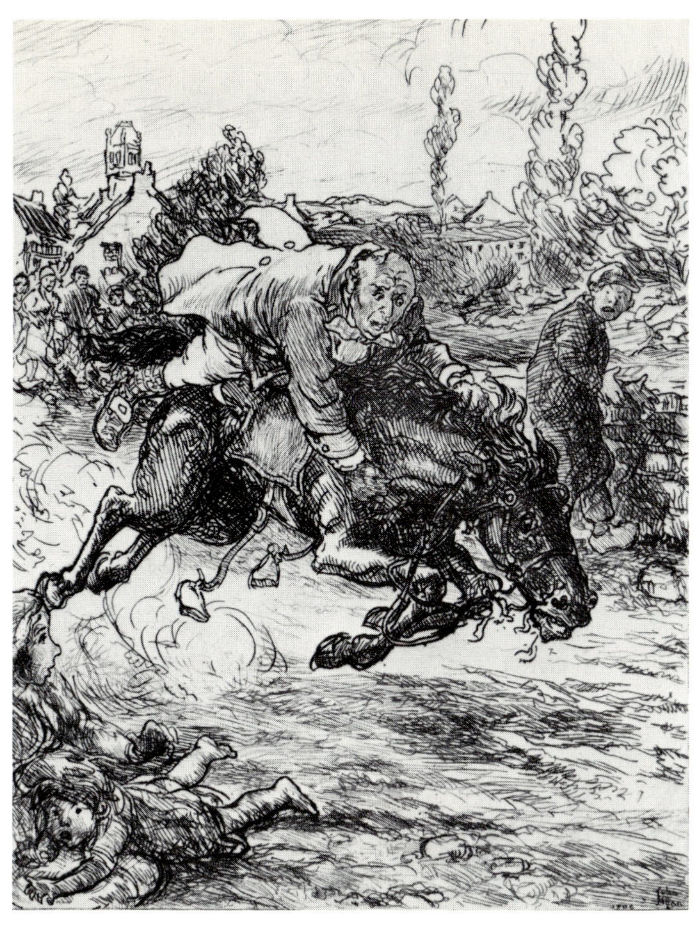

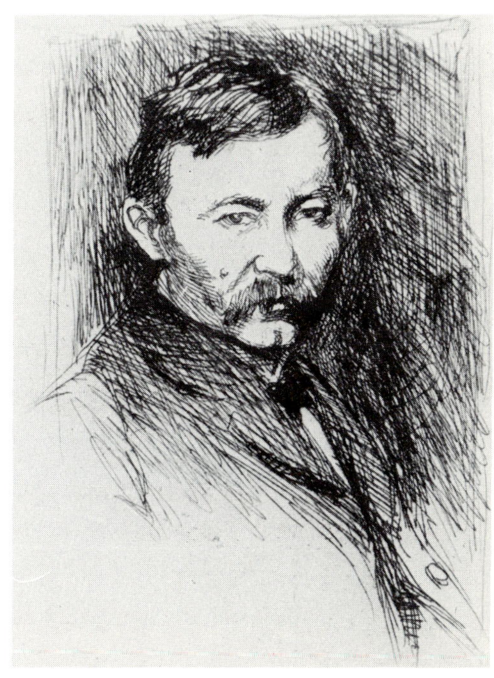

Above

15. *Dupont's Ride.* 1902. Etching, 4¾″ x 3½″. Illustration for Charles Paul de Kock's novel *Monsieur Dupont*. Wilmington Society of the Fine Arts, Delaware Art Museum, Wilmington. *Photo Lubitsch & Bungarz, Wilmington.*

16. *Robert Henri.* 1902. Etching, 6¼″ x 4½″. Wilmington Society of the Fine Arts, Delaware Art Museum, Wilmington.

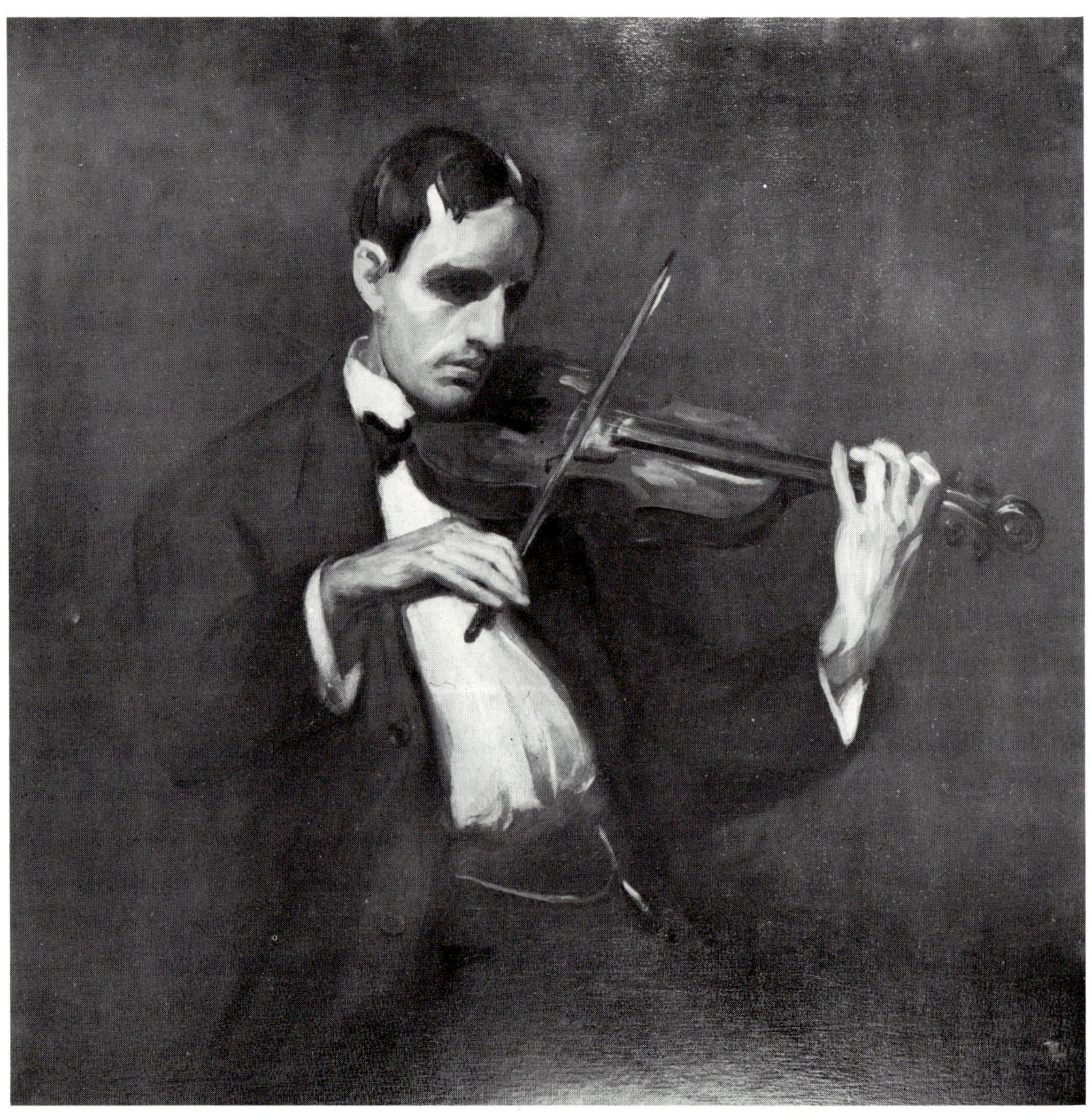

17. *The Violinist (Will Bradner)*. 1903. Oil on canvas, 37″ x 37″.
Wilmington Society of the Fine Arts, Delaware Art Museum, Wilmington.
Photo Lubitsh & Bungarz, Wilmington.

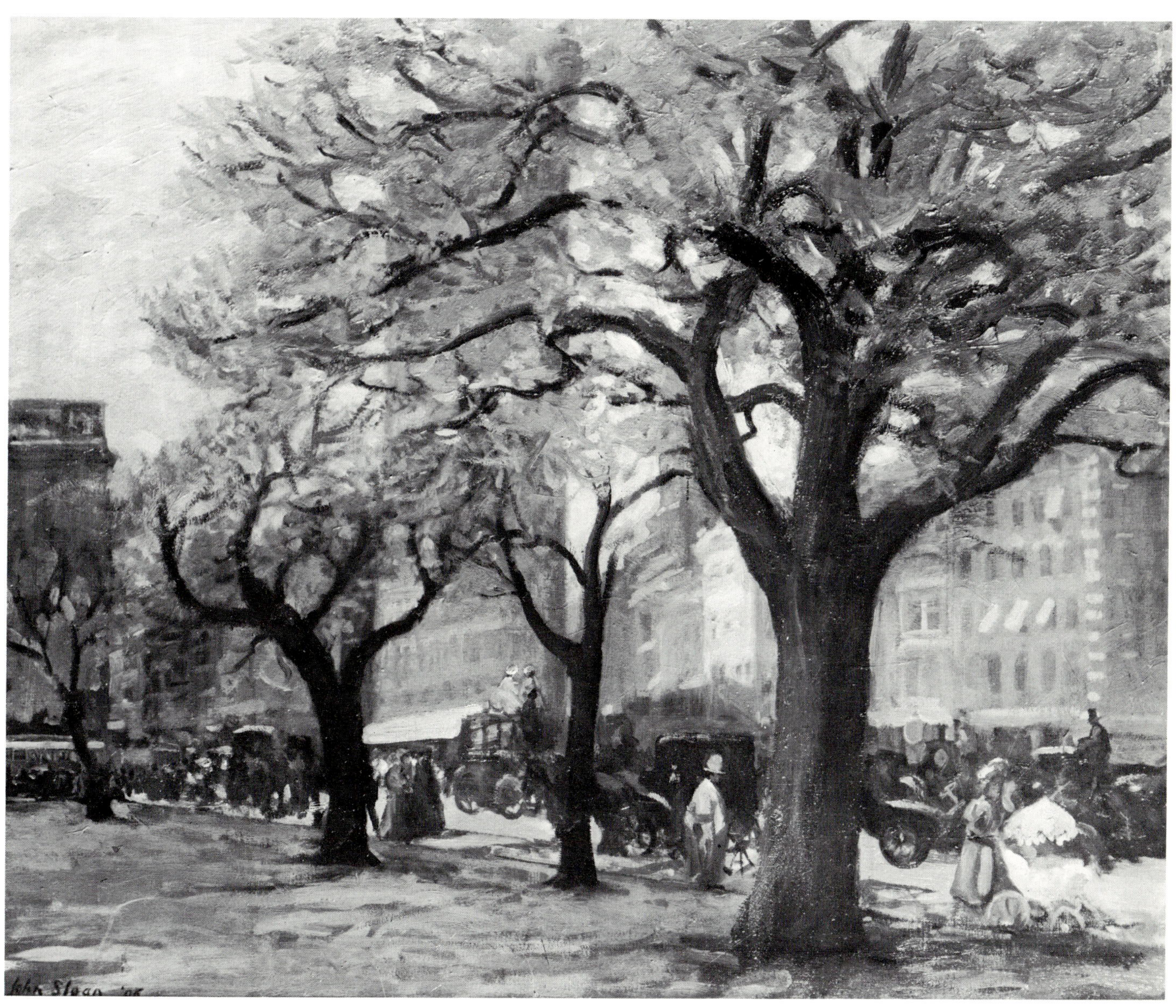

18. *Spring, Madison Square*. 1905. Oil on canvas, 29½″ x 35½″.
Elvehjem Art Center, University of Wisconsin, Madison: Humanistic Foundation
Purchase, 1957. *Photo Peter A. Juley & Son, New York*.

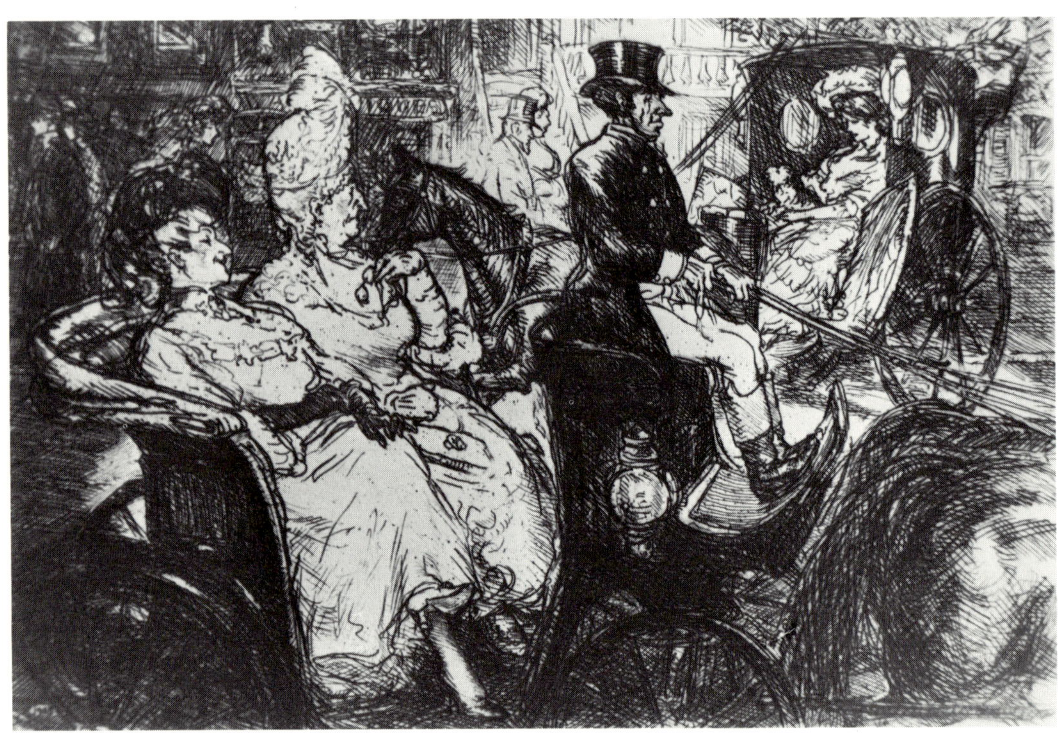

19. *Fifth Avenue Critics*. 1905. Etching, 5″ x 7″.
Wilmington Society of the Fine Arts, Delaware Art Museum, Wilmington.

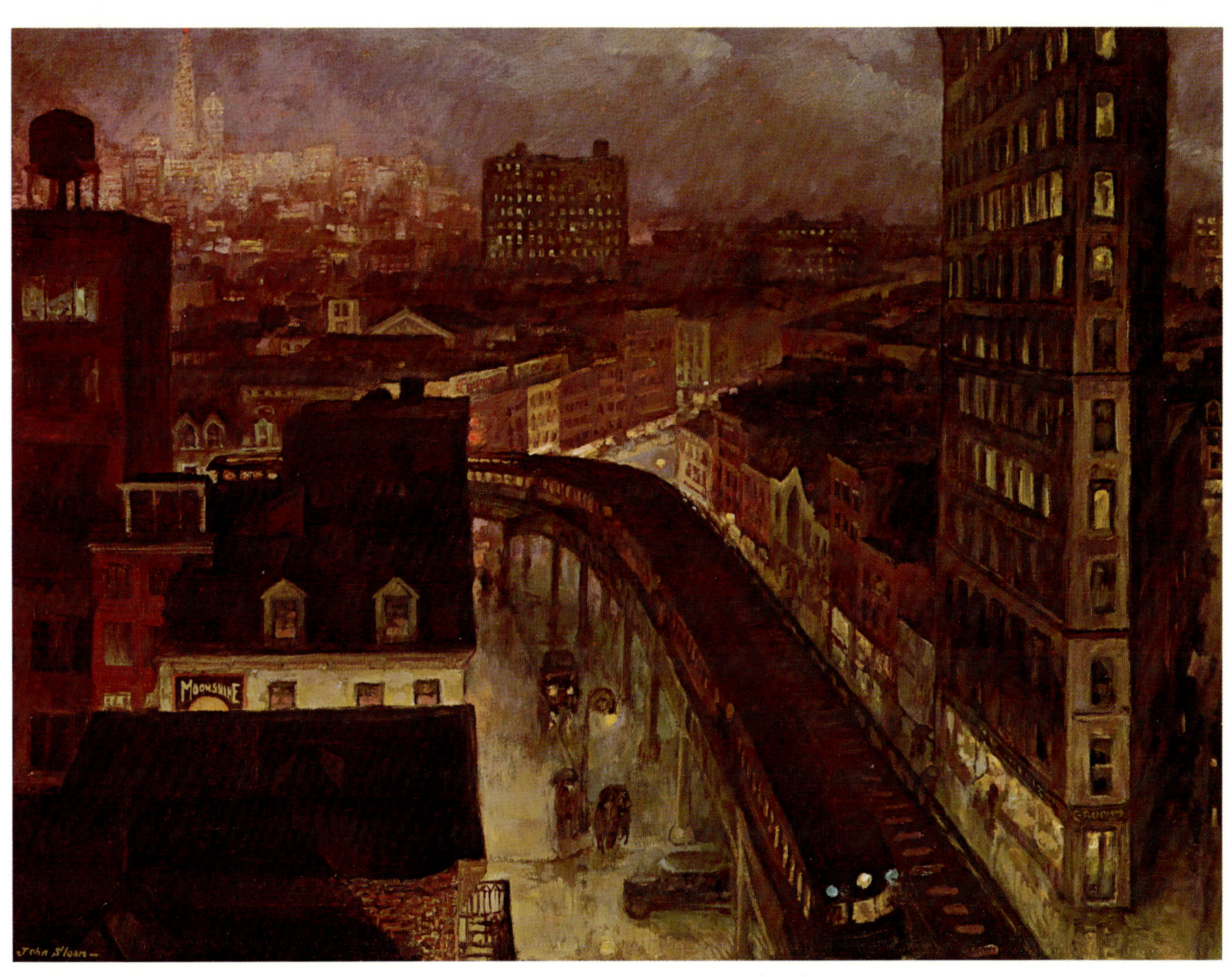

PLATE VII. *The City from Greenwich Village*. 1922. Oil on canvas, 26″ x 40″.
National Gallery of Art, Washington, D.C.; Gift of Helen Farr Sloan.

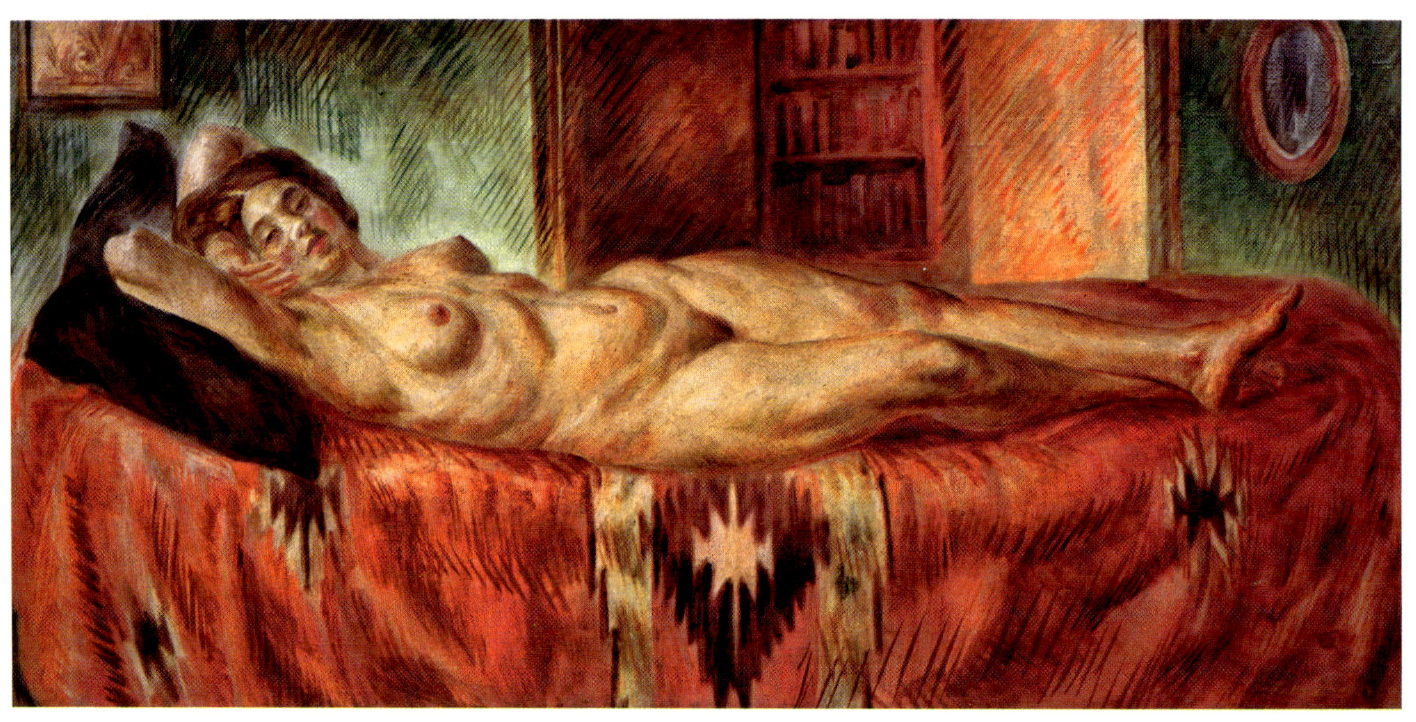

PLATE VIII. *Nude on Navajo Blanket*. 1929. Oil on canvas, 24″ x 48″.
Kraushaar Galleries, New York.

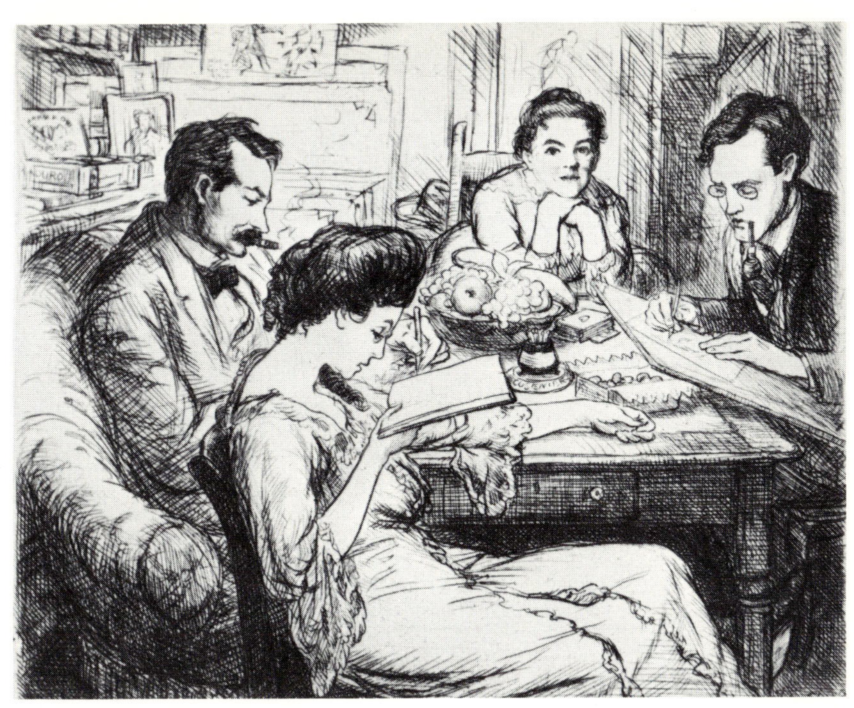

20. *Memory.* 1906. Etching, 7½″ x 9″.
Wilmington Society of the Fine Arts, Delaware Art Museum, Wilmington.

Left
21. *My Dad.* 1906. Pencil drawing, 7″ x 3¾″.
Wilmington Society of the Fine Arts, Delaware Art Museum, Wilmington.

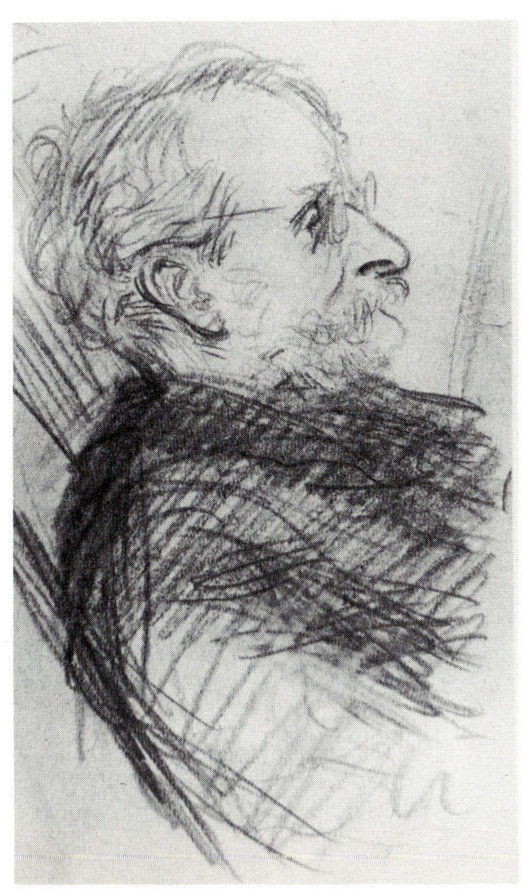

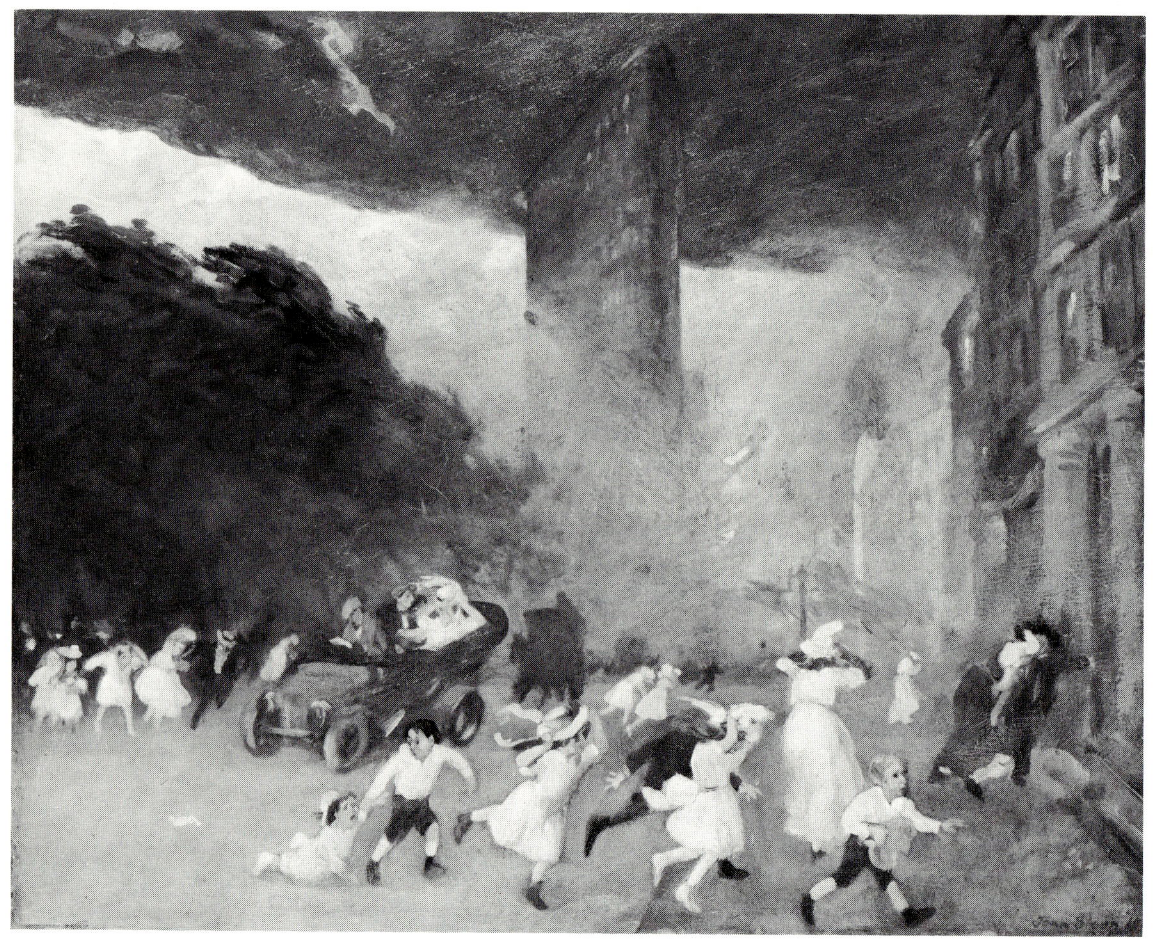

22. *Dust Storm, Fifth Avenue.* 1906. Oil on canvas, 22″ x 27″.
The Metropolitan Museum of Art, New York: George A. Hearn Fund, 1921.

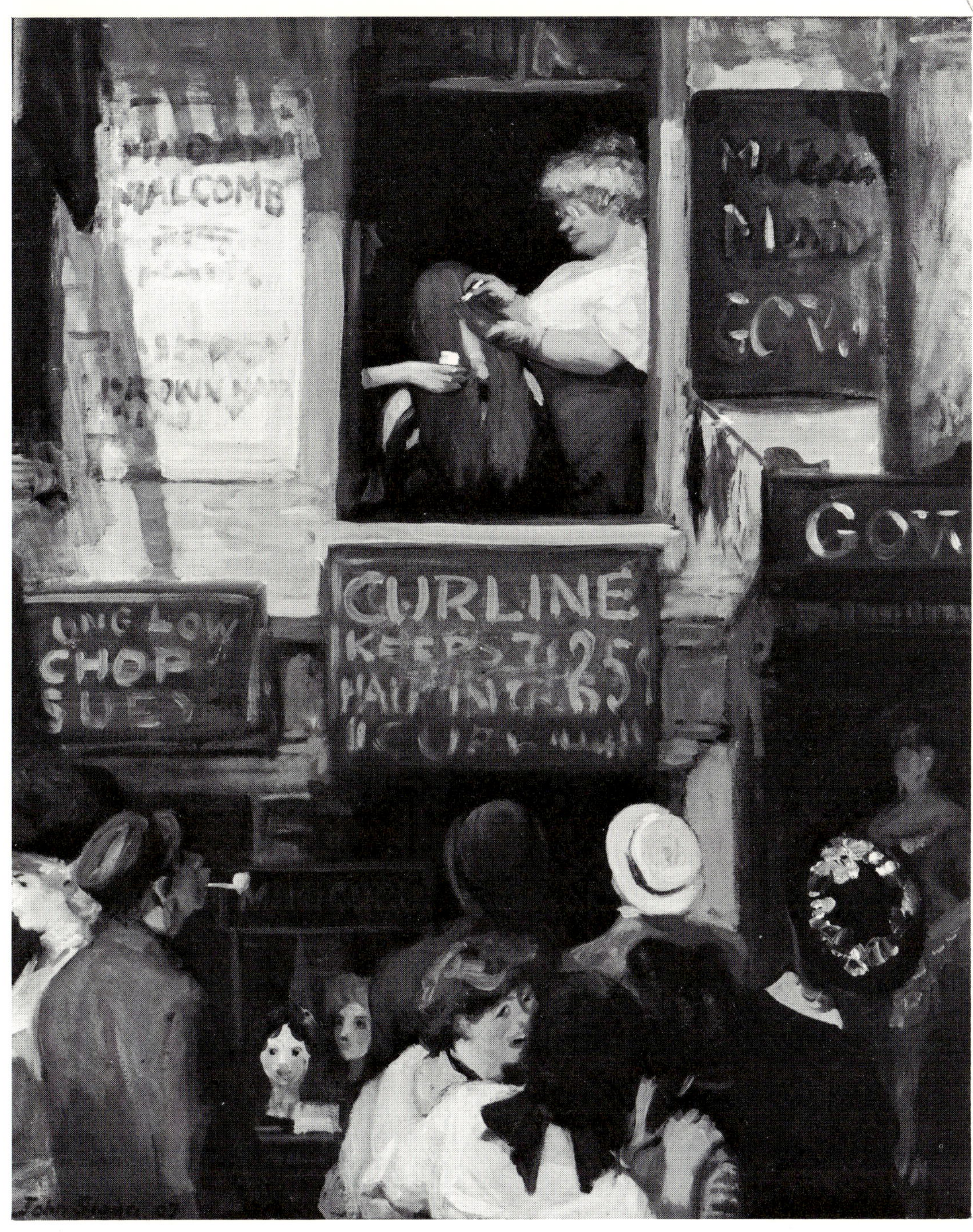

23. *Hairdresser's Window*. 1907. Oil on canvas, 31⅞″ x 26″.
Courtesy Wadsworth Atheneum, Hartford, Connecticut:
Ella Gallup Sumner and Mary Catlin Sumner Collection.
Photo E. Irving Blomstrann, New Britain, Connecticut.

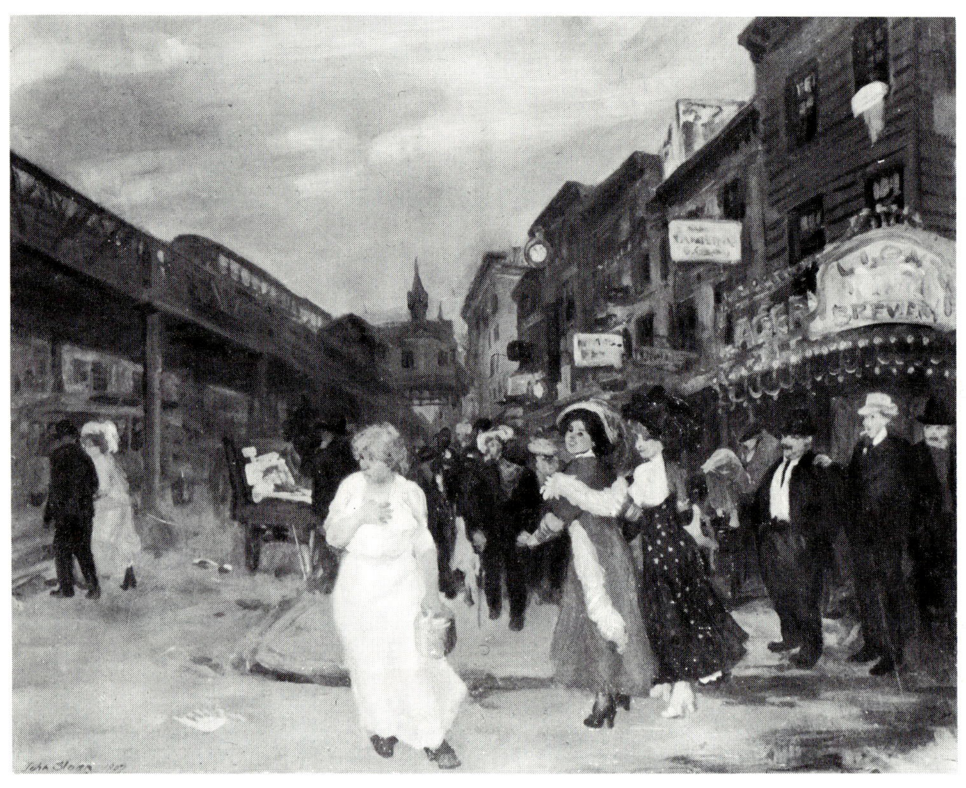

24. *Sixth Avenue and Thirtieth Street*. 1907. Oil on canvas, 26″ x 32″.
Collection of Mr. and Mrs. Meyer P. Potamkin, Philadelphia.
Photo Peter A. Juley & Son, New York.

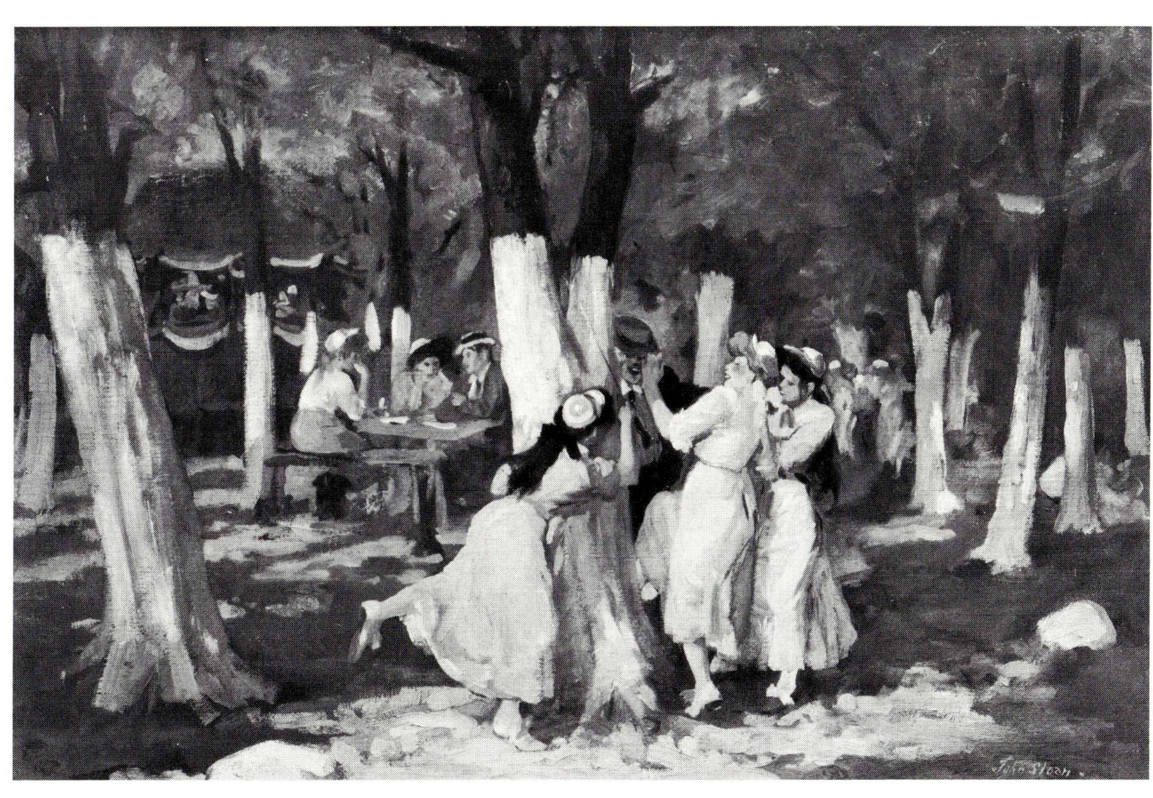

25. *The Picnic Grounds*. 1906–7. Oil on canvas, 24″ x 36″.
Collection Whitney Museum of American Art, New York.
Photo Peter A. Juley & Son, New York.

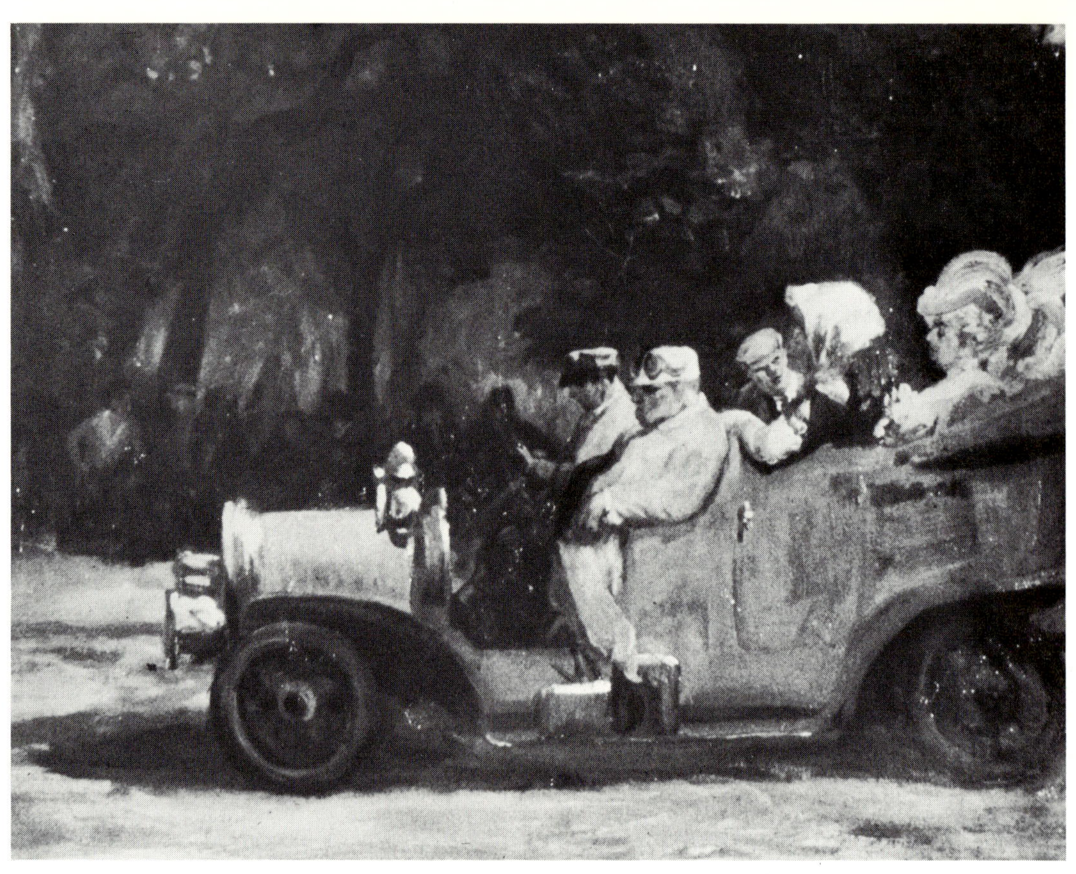

26. *Gray and Brass.* 1907. Oil on canvas, 22″ x 27″.
Collection of Mr. Lincoln Isham, Dorset, Vermont.

27. *The Haymarket*. 1907. Oil on canvas, 26″ x 31⅞″.
In The Brooklyn Museum Collection, New York.

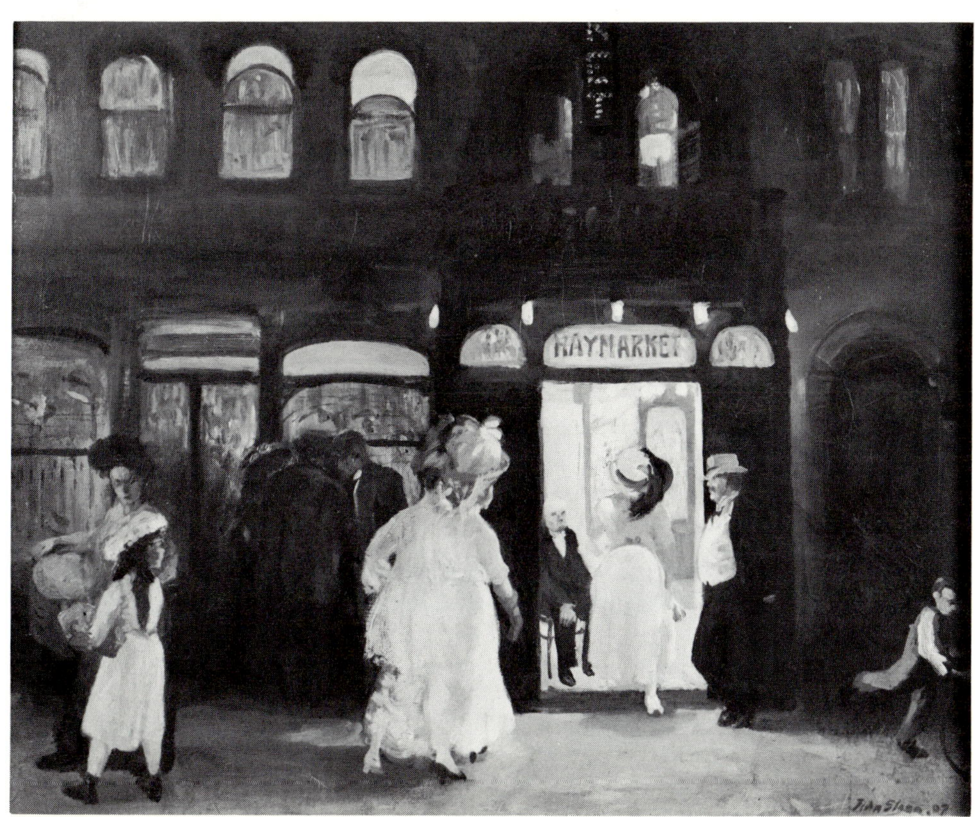

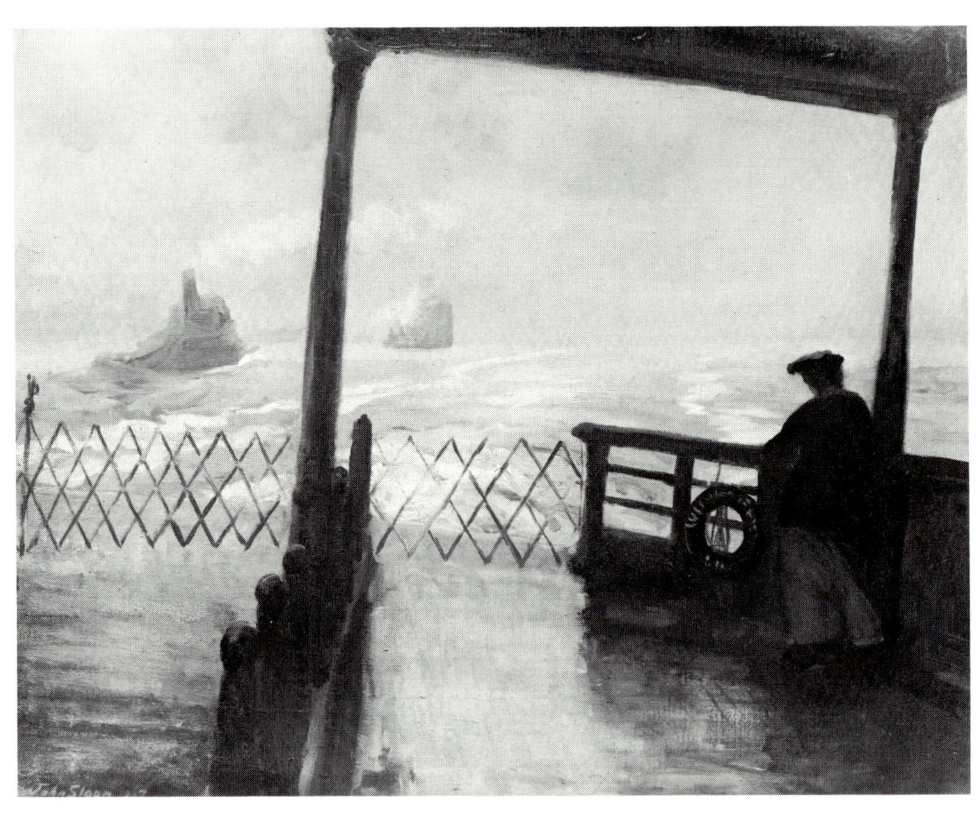

28. *The Wake of the Ferry*. 1907. Oil on canvas, 26″ x 32″.
The Phillips Collection, Washington, D.C.

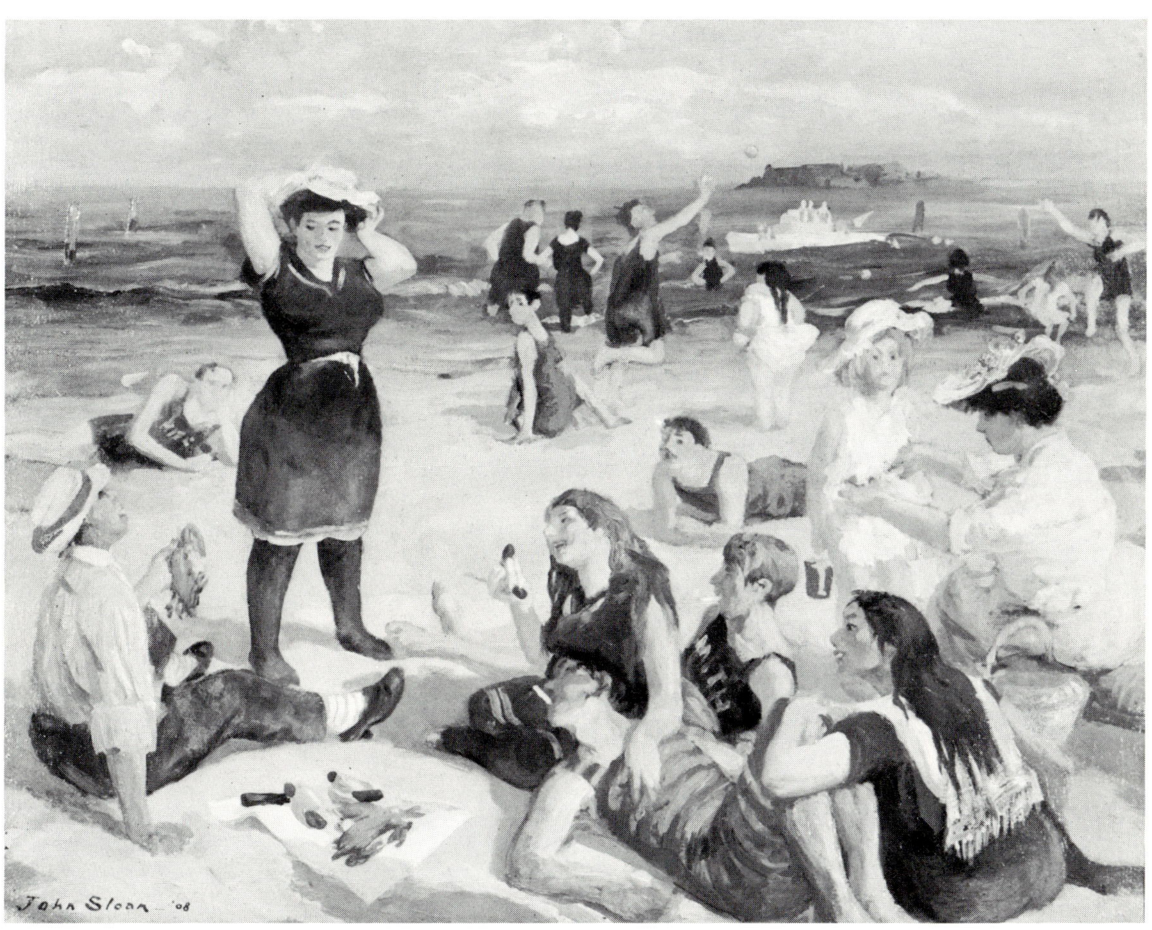

29. *South Beach Bathers*. 1907–8. Oil on canvas, 25⅞″ x 31⅞″.
Walker Art Center, Minneapolis, Minnesota.

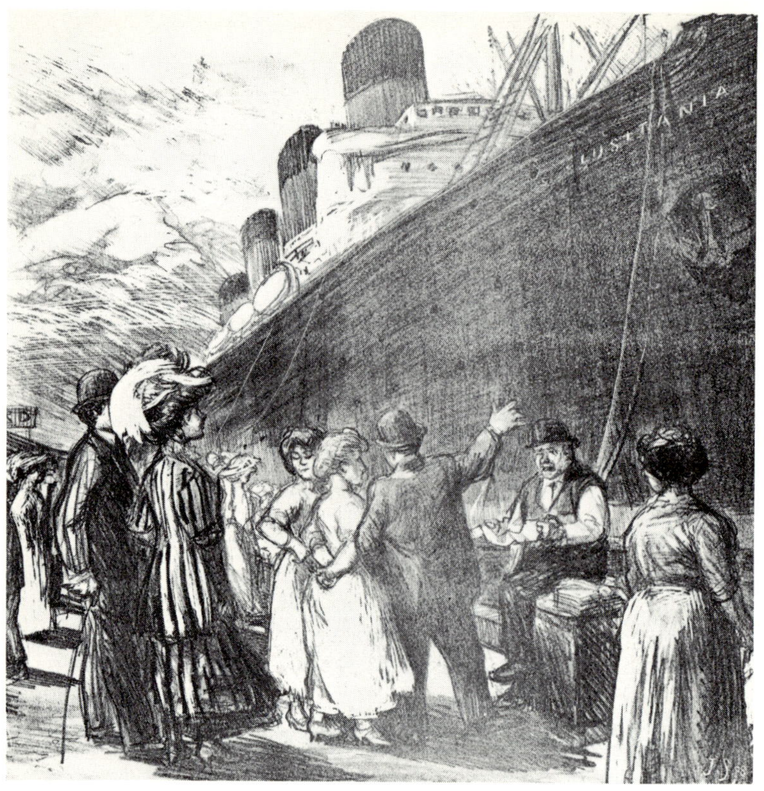

30. *The Lusitania in Dock*. 1908. Lithograph, 14⅜″ x 14⅛″.
Wilmington Society of the Fine Arts, Delaware Art Museum,
Wilmington. *Photo Lubitsh & Bungarz, Wilmington.*

Right
31. *Sixth Avenue and Thirtieth Street*. 1908. Lithograph, 14″ x
11″. Wilmington Society of the Fine Arts, Delaware Art Museum,
Wilmington. *Photo Lubitsh & Bungarz, Wilmington.*

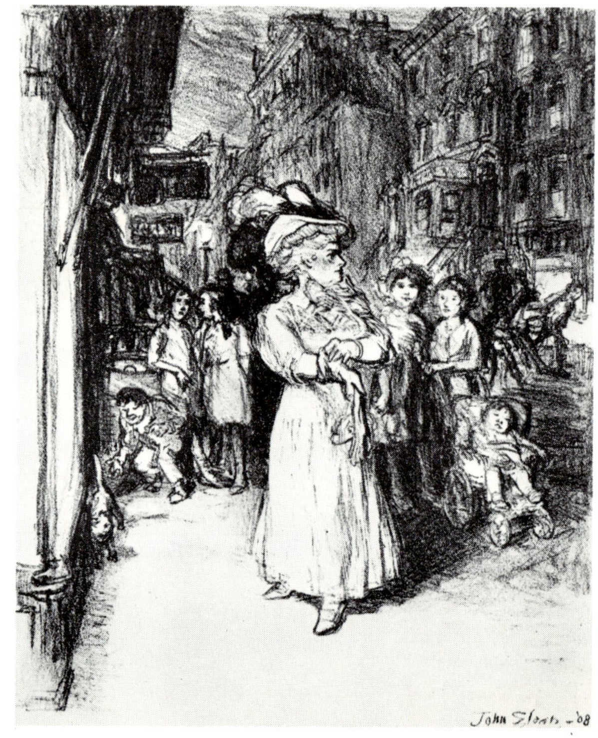

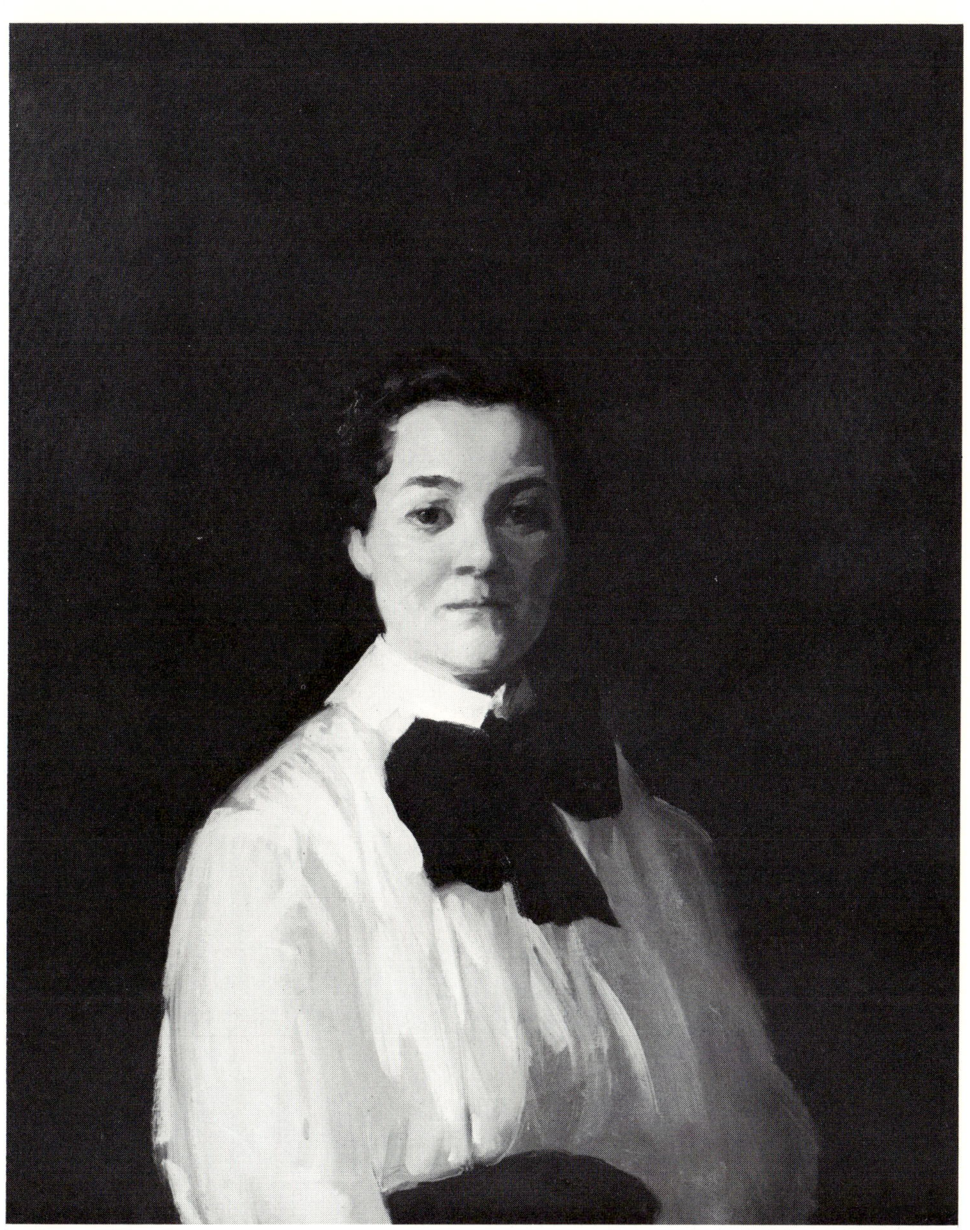

32. *Dolly with a Black Bow*. 1909. Oil on canvas, 32″ x 26″.
Collection Whitney Museum of American Art, New York:
Gift of Amelia Elizabeth White.
Photo Geoffrey Clements, New York.

33. *Fifth Avenue*. 1909. Oil on canvas, 32″ x 26″.
Collection of Mrs. John F. Kraushaar, New York.

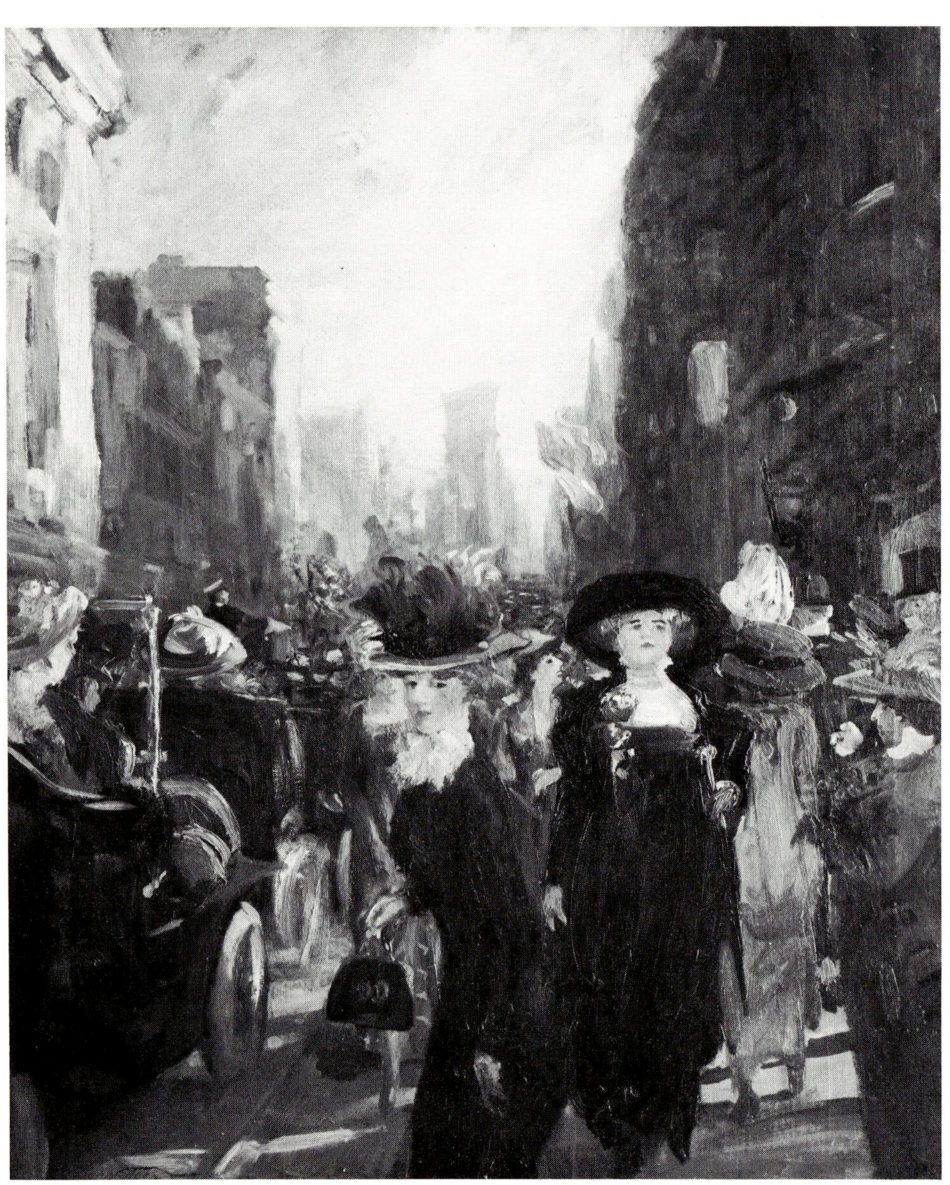

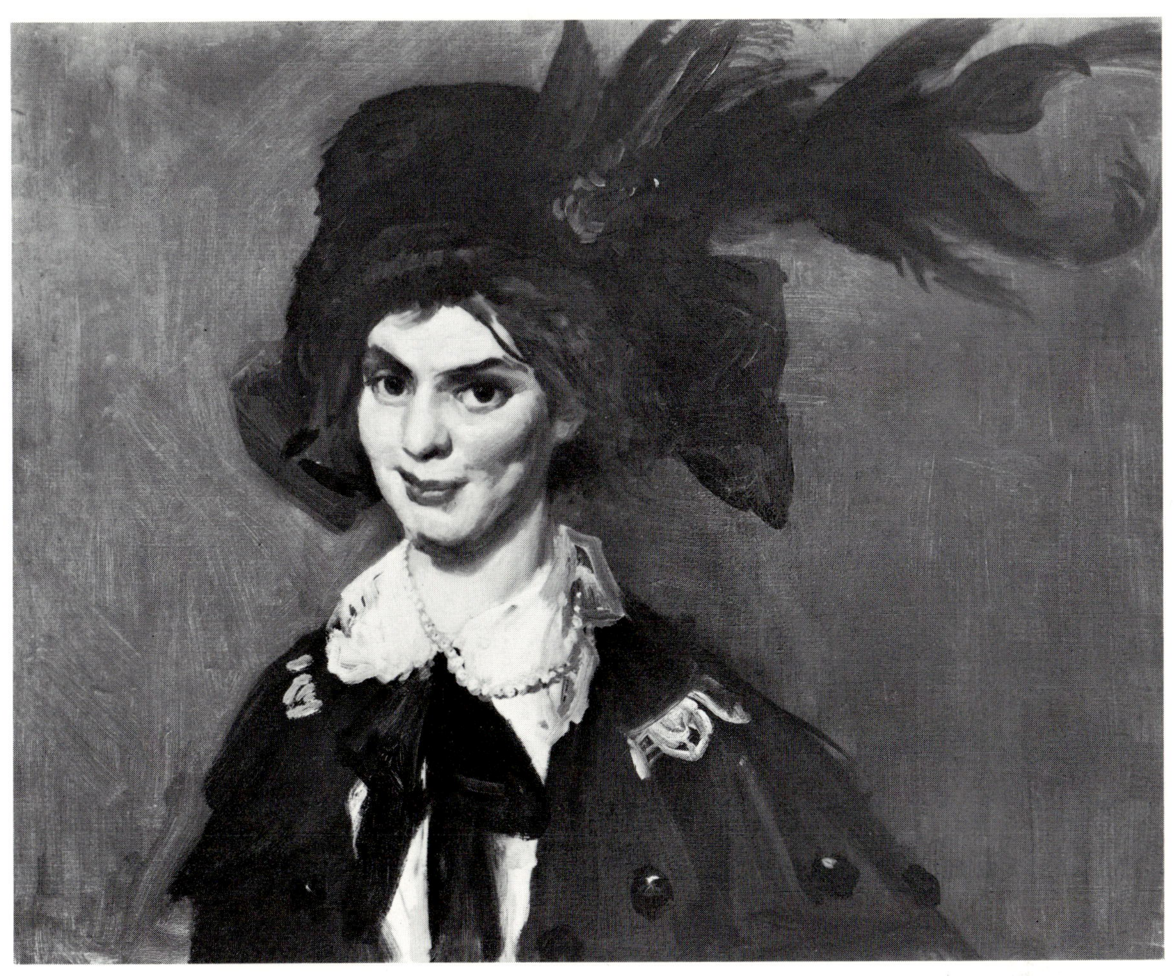

34. *Yolande in the Large Hat*. 1910. Oil on canvas, 26″ x 32″.
John Sloan Trust.

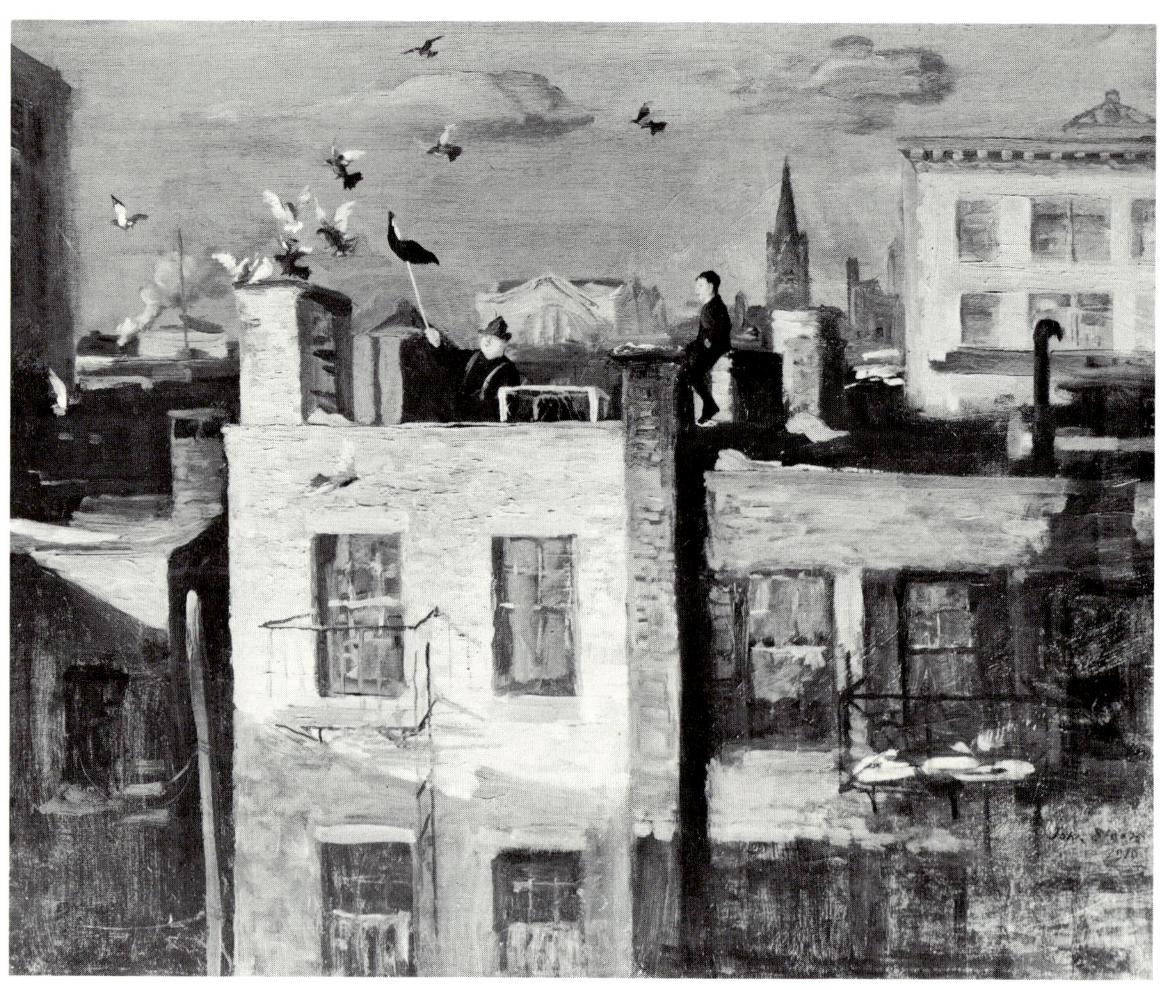

35. *Pigeons.* 1910. Oil on canvas, 26″ x 32″.
Courtesy Museum of Fine Arts, Boston: Hayden Collection.

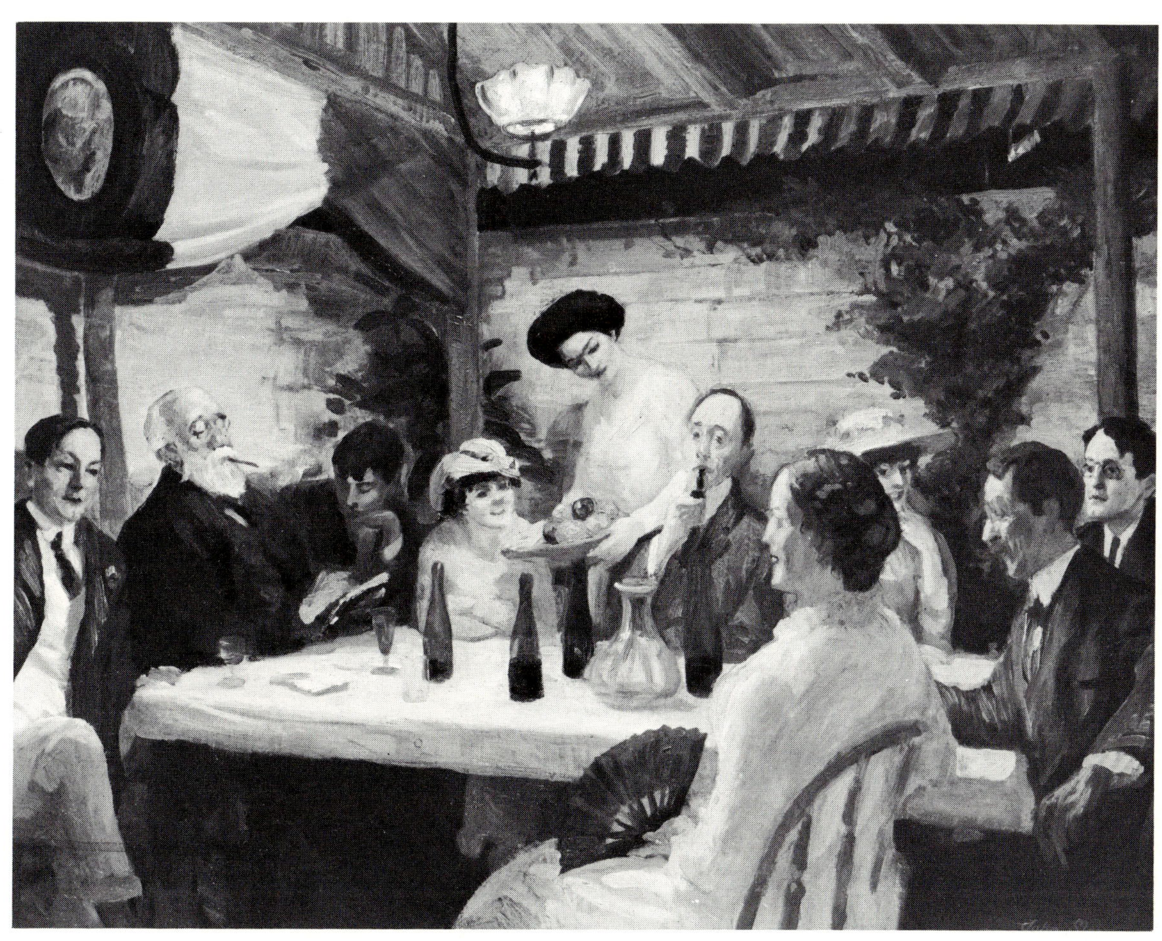

36. *Yeats at Petitpas'*. 1910. Oil on canvas, 26⅜″ x 32¼″.
The Corcoran Gallery of Art, Washington, D.C.

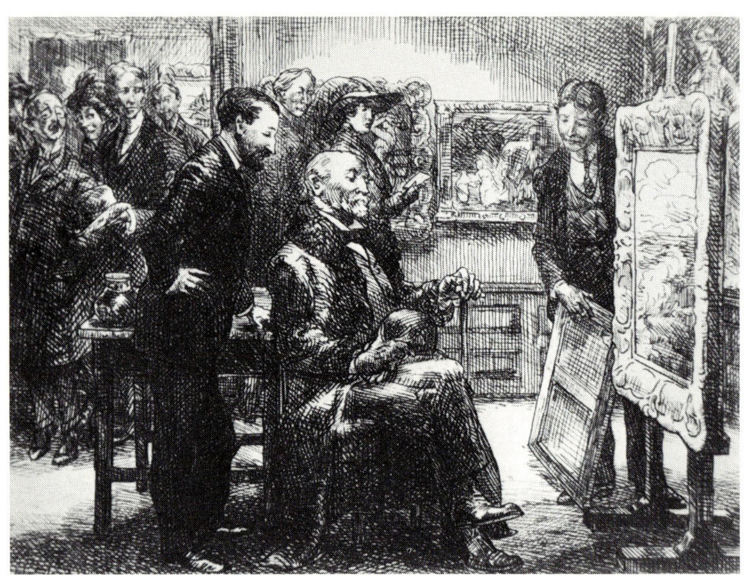

37. *The Picture Buyer*. 1911. Etching, 5¼″ x 7″.
Wilmington Society of the Fine Arts, Delaware Art Museum, Wilmington.

Below
38. Preliminary drawing for *Woman's Work*. 1911. Pencil, 7½″ x 9″.
John Sloan Collection, Delaware Art Museum, Wilmington.
Photo Lubitsh & Bungarz, Wilmington.

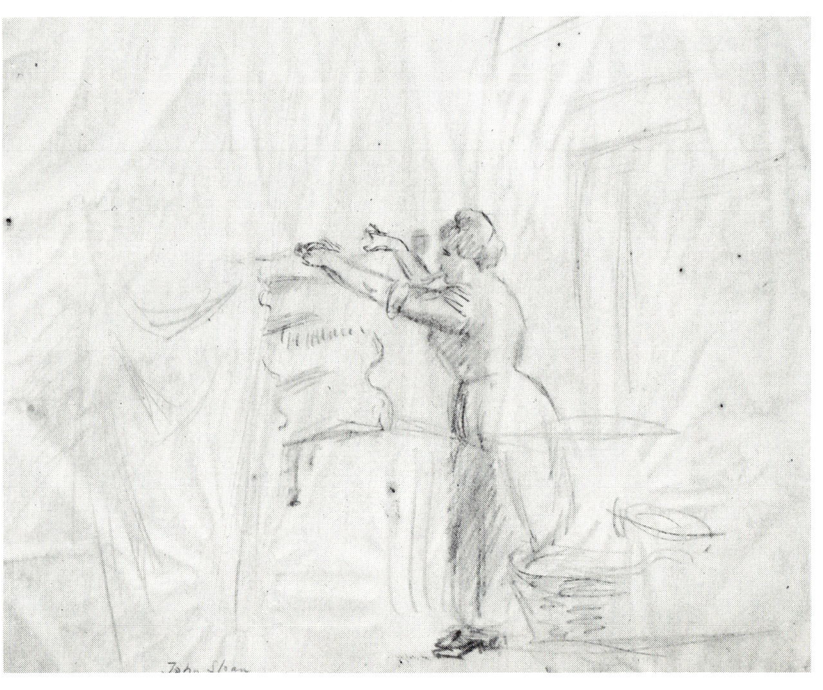

39. *Woman's Work*. 1911. Oil on canvas, 31⅝″ x 25¾″.
The Cleveland Museum of Art: Gift of Amelia Elizabeth White.

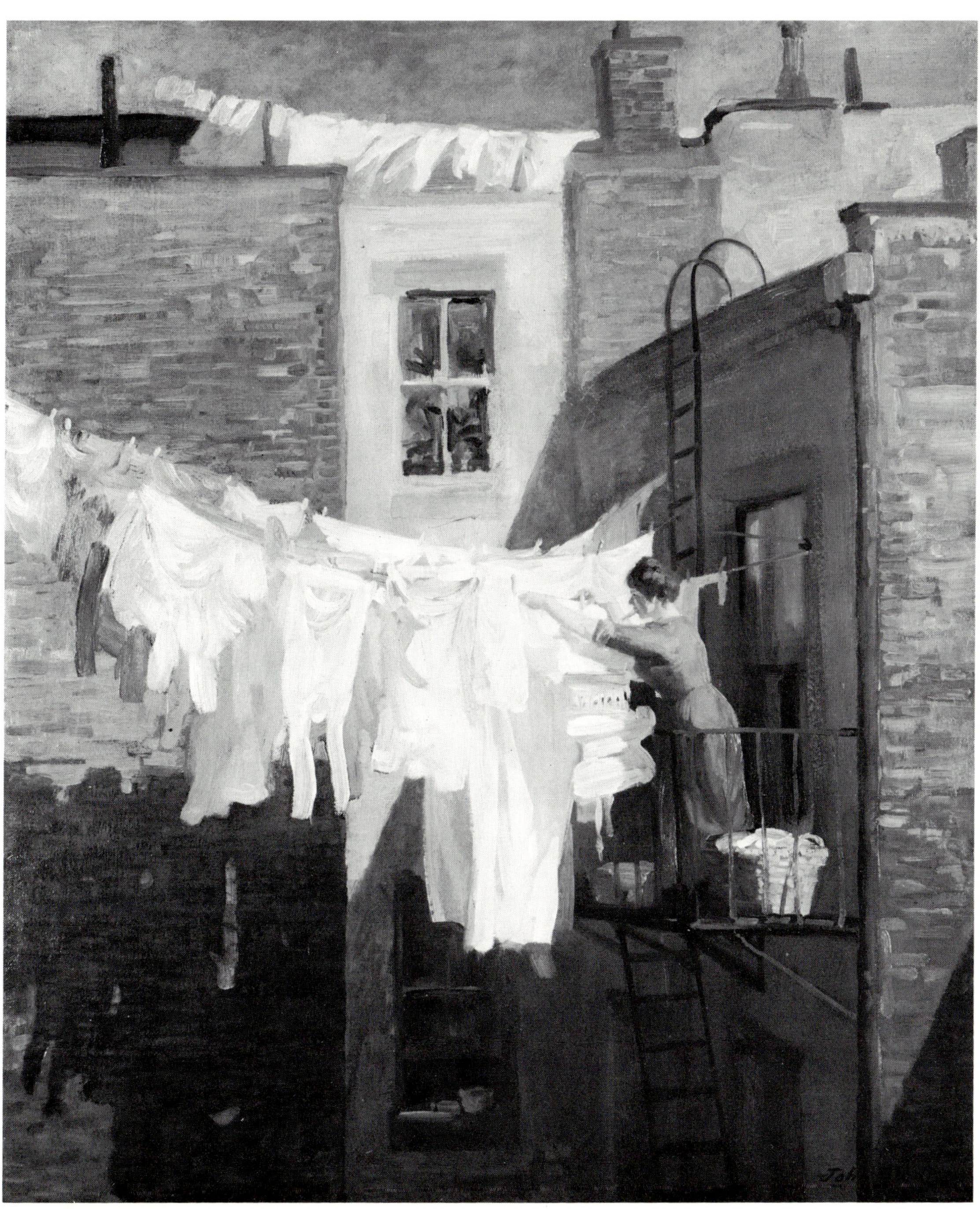

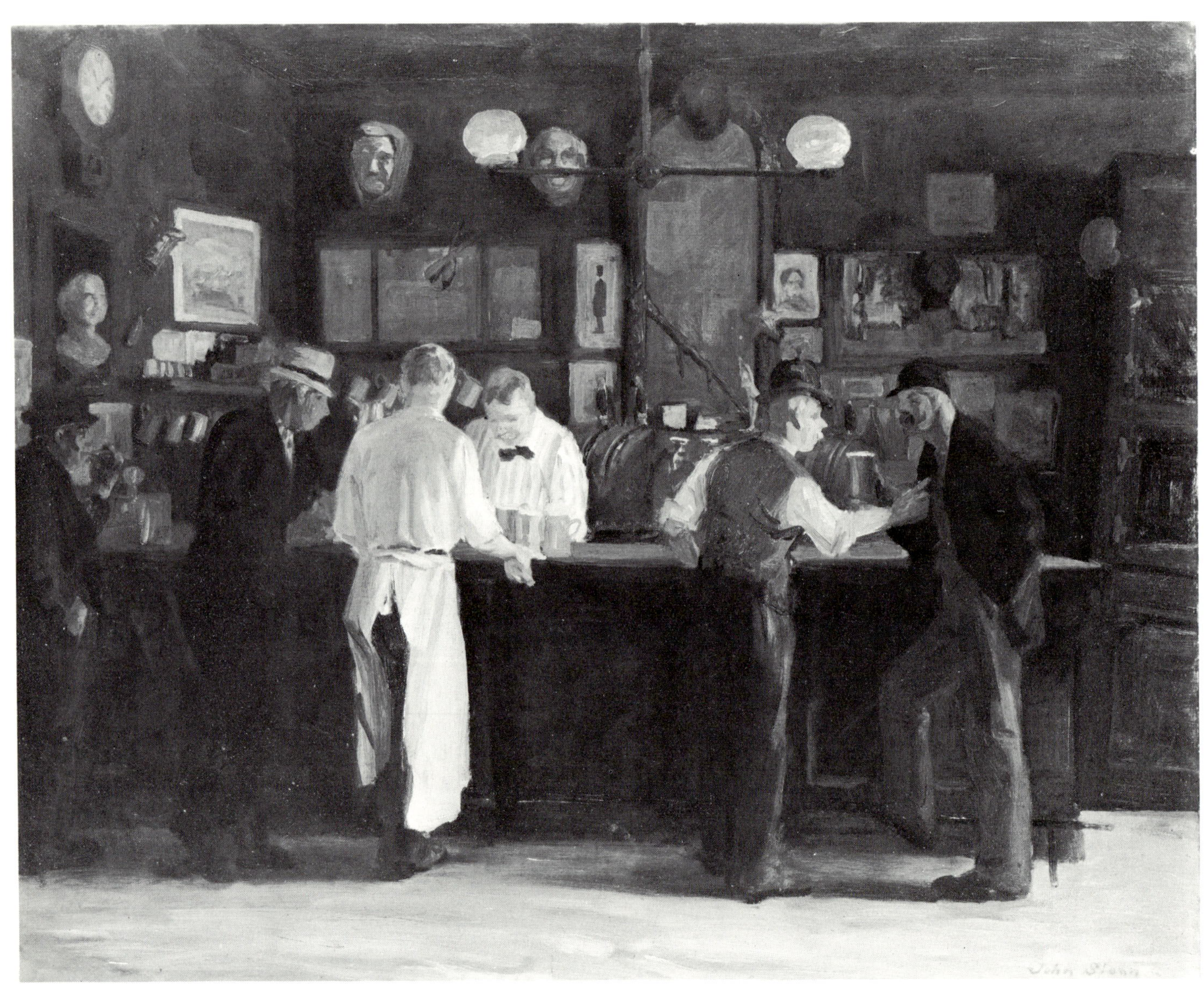

40. *McSorley's Ale House*. 1912. Oil on canvas, 26″ x 32″.
Courtesy of The Detroit Institute of Arts.

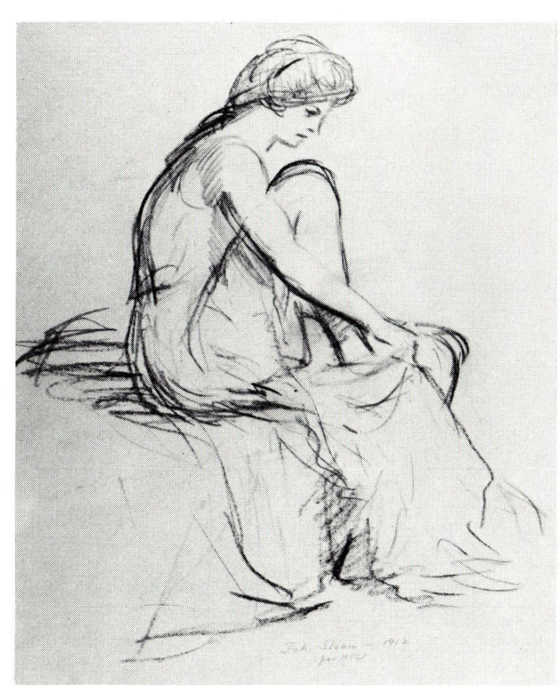

41. *Seated Woman*. 1912. Red chalk drawing, 9″
x 8″. John Sloan Collection, Delaware Art Museum, Wilmington.

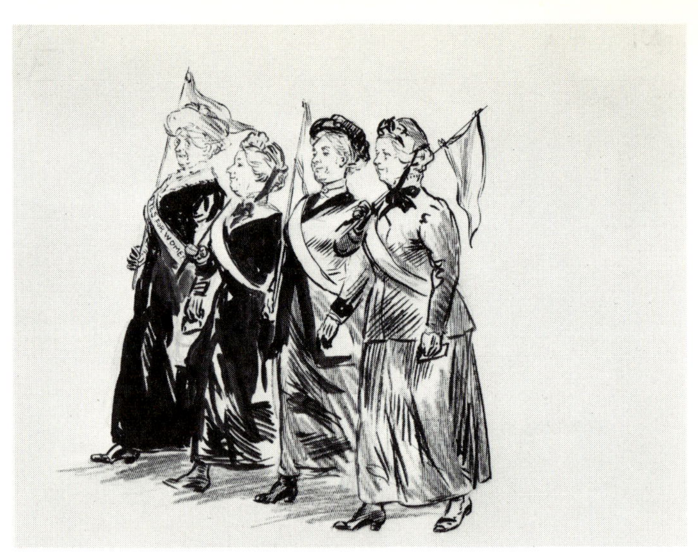

42. *The Four Suffragettes*. 1912. Pencil drawing, 6½″ x 7″.
Illustration for "Women March," *Collier's*, May 18, 1912.
Collection of the University of Michigan Museum of Art, Ann
Arbor. *Photo Oliver Baker Associates, Inc., New York*.

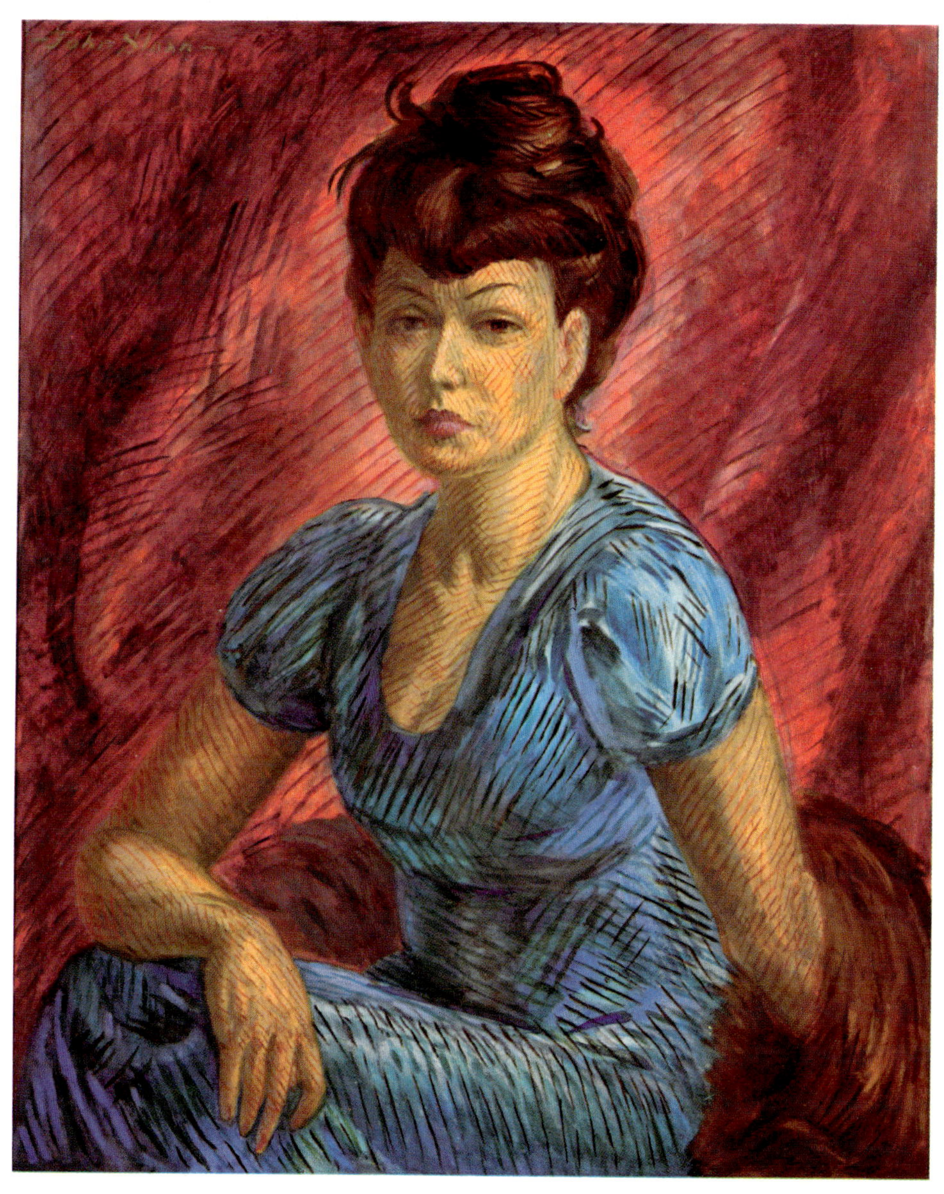

PLATE IX. *Jeanne Dubinsky*. 1940. Oil on canvas, 30″ x 24″.
Kraushaar Galleries, New York.

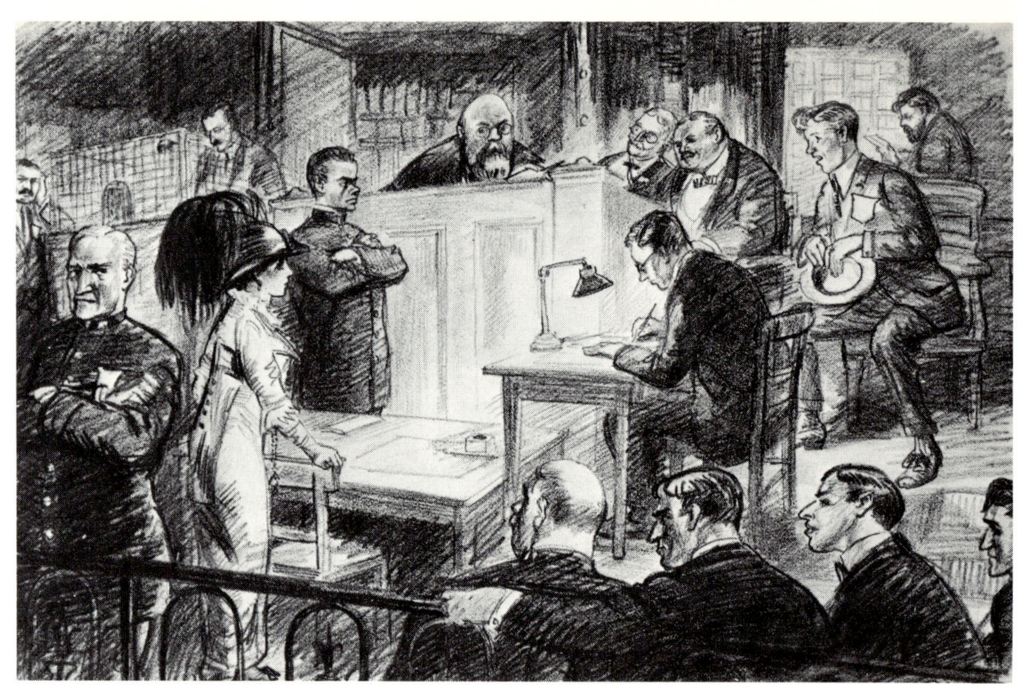

44. *Before Her Makers and Her Judge.* 1913. Crayon, 16½″ x 25″. Illustration for *The Masses,* August, 1913. Collection Whitney Museum of American Art, New York. *Photo Geoffrey Clements, Staten Island, New York.*

Left
45. *Reverence.* 1913. Crayon drawing, 17″ x 12¾″. Illustration for *The Masses,* December, 1913. Collection of Philip and Muriel Berman, Allentown, Pennsylvania.

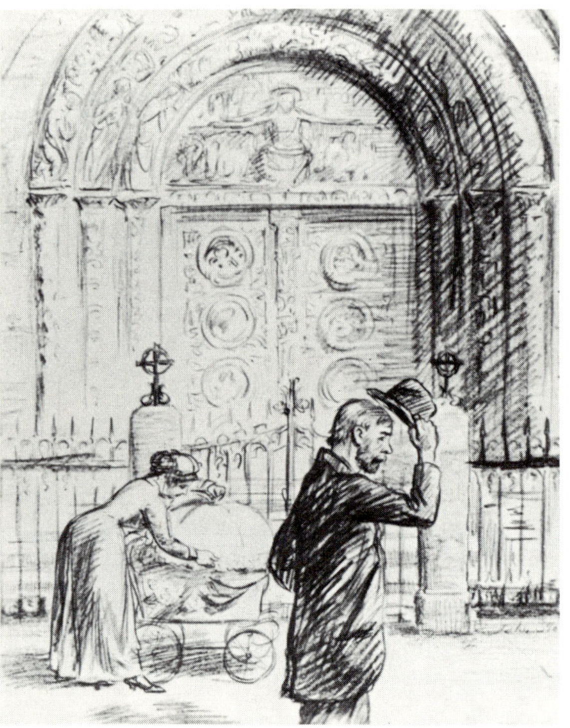

46. *The Unemployed.* 1914. Crayon drawing, 19″ x 28″.
Illustration for *The Masses,* March, 1914.
Collection of Dr. and Mrs. Martin Cherkasky, New York.
Photo Geoffrey Clements, Staten Island, New York.

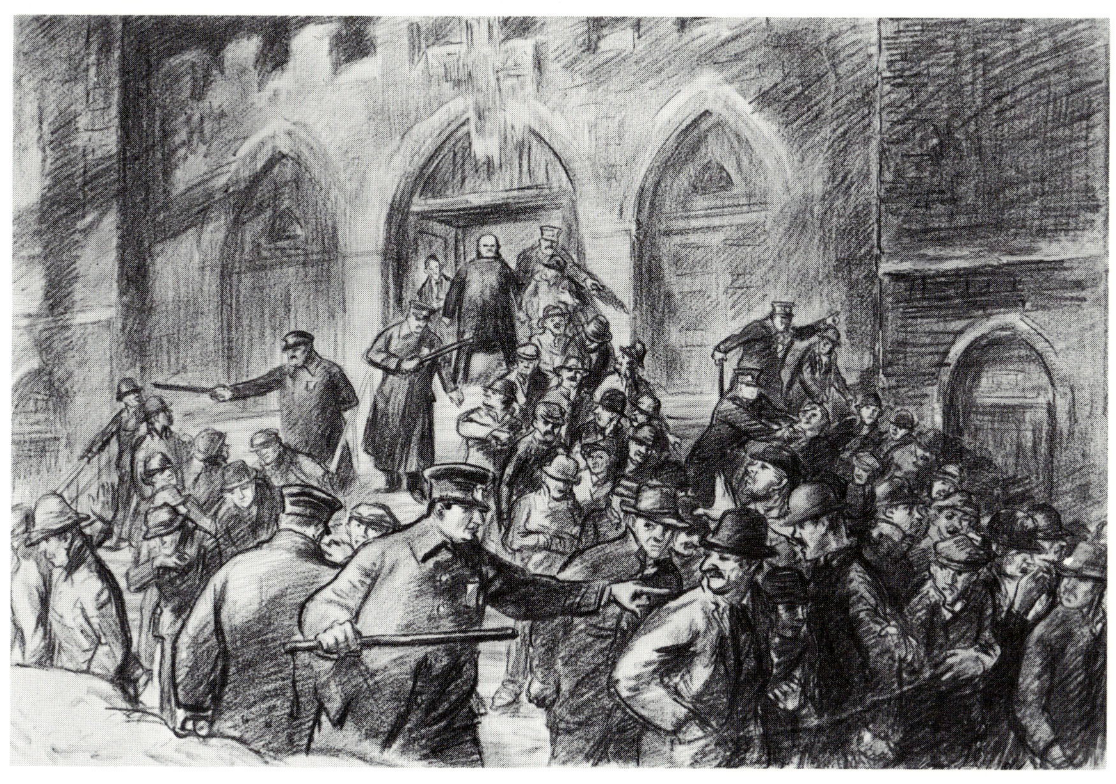

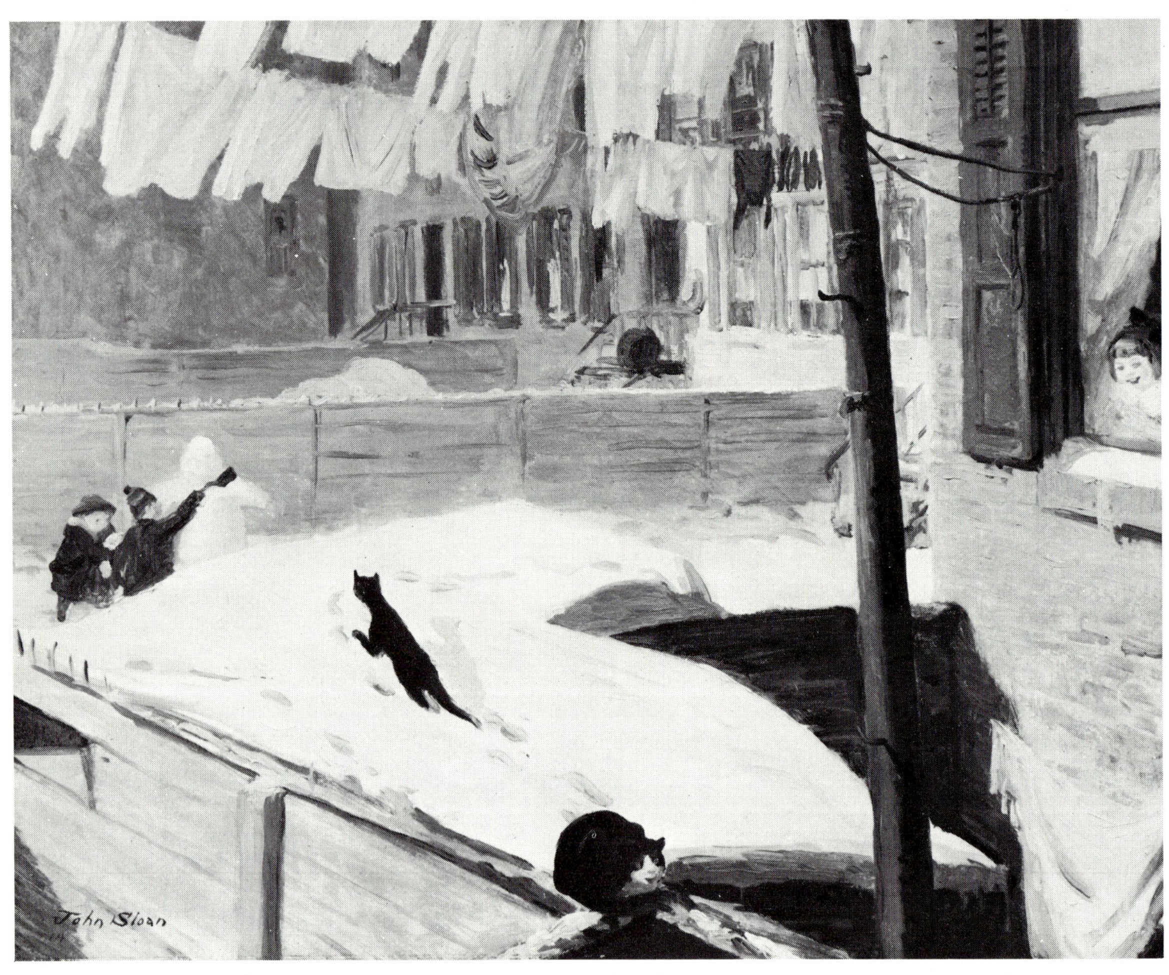

47. *Backyards, Greenwich Village.* 1914. Oil on canvas, 26″ x 32″.
Collection Whitney Museum of American Art, New York.
Photo Geoffrey Clements, Staten Island, New York.

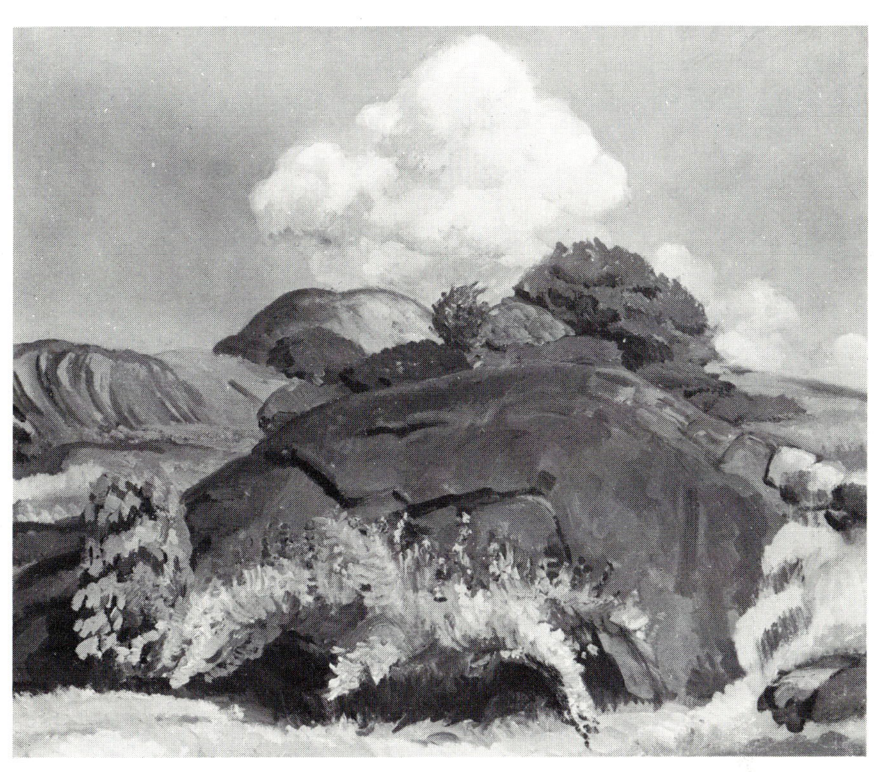

48. *White Cloud and Rocks*. 1915. Oil on canvas, 20″ x 24″.
Kraushaar Galleries, New York.
Photo Geoffrey Clements, Staten Island, New York.

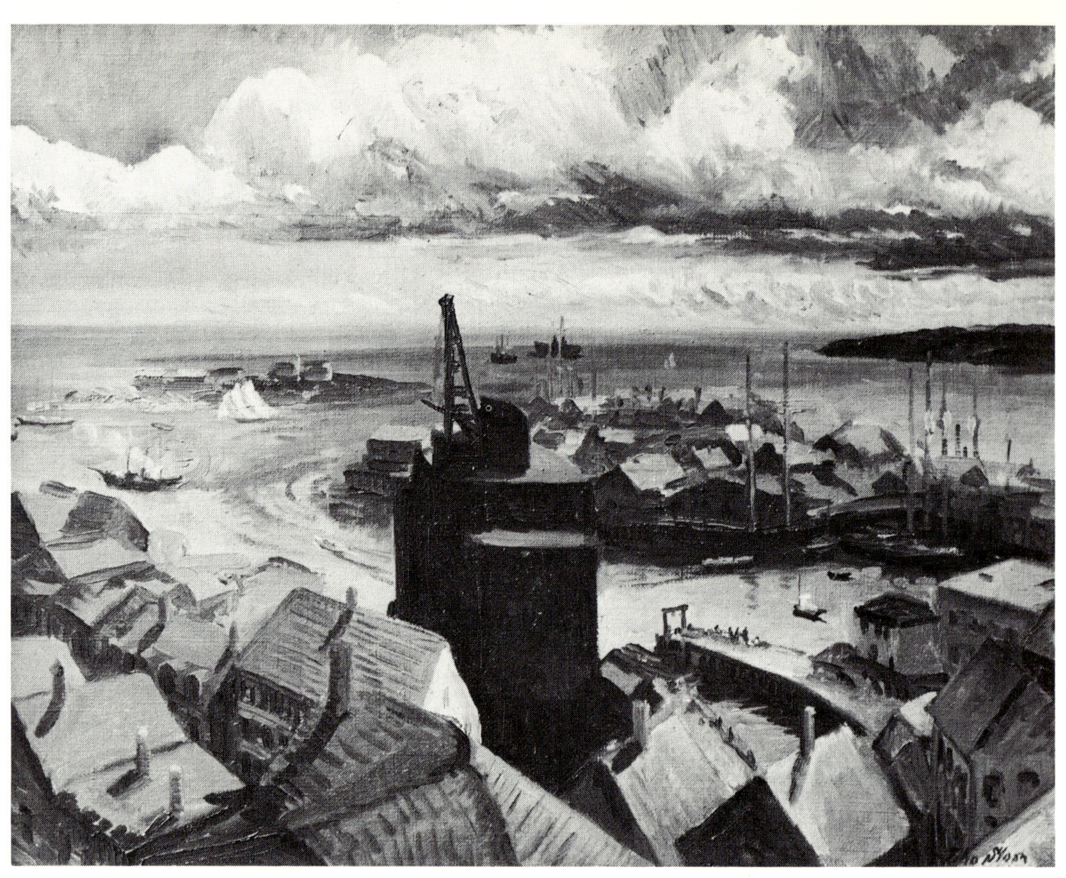

49. *Gloucester Harbor*. 1916. Oil on canvas, 26″ x 32″.
Collection Syracuse University, New York.

50. *House by the Road Along the Harbor.* 1916. Oil on canvas, 26″ x 32″.
Collection of Dr. and Mrs. Fletcher H. McDowell, New York.

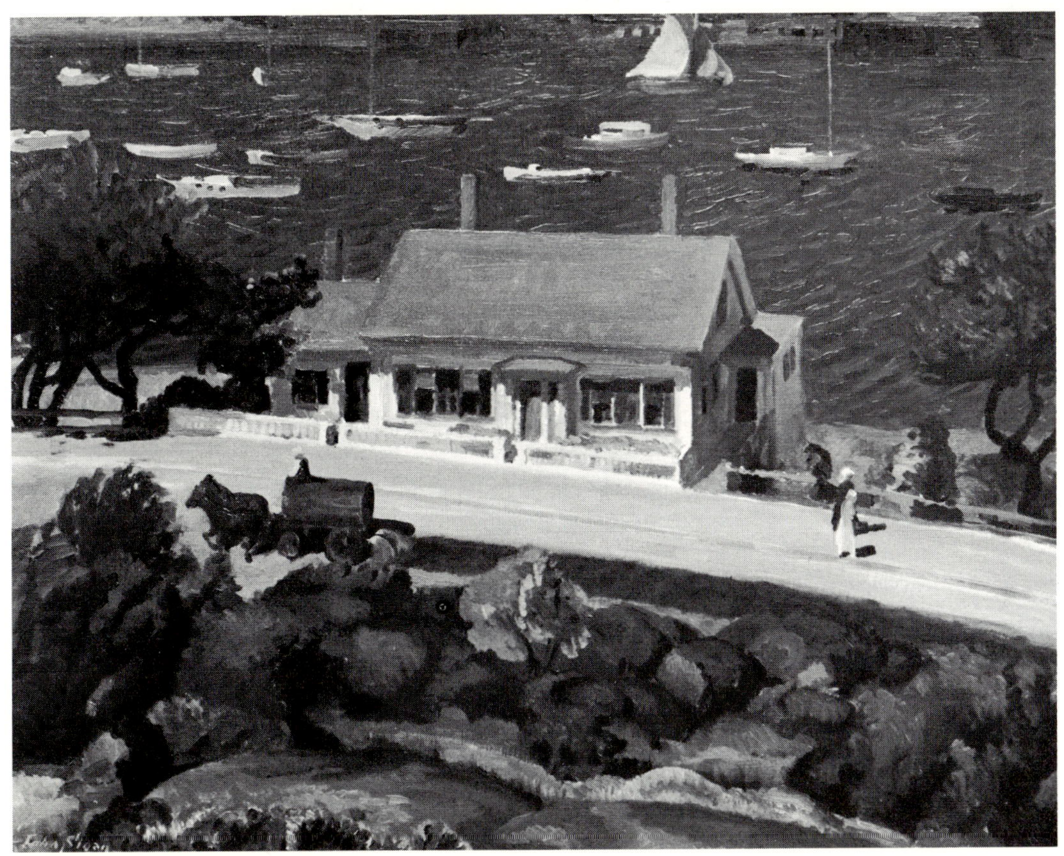

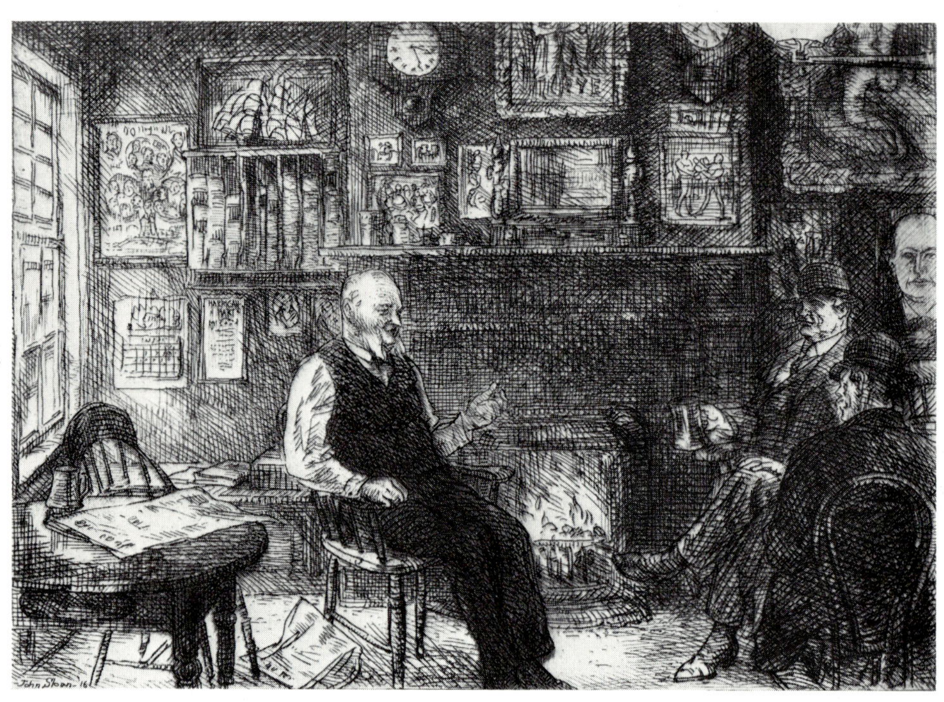

51. *McSorley's Back Room.* 1916. Etching, 5¼″ x 7⅛″.
Wilmington Society of the Fine Arts, Delaware Art Museum, Wilmington.

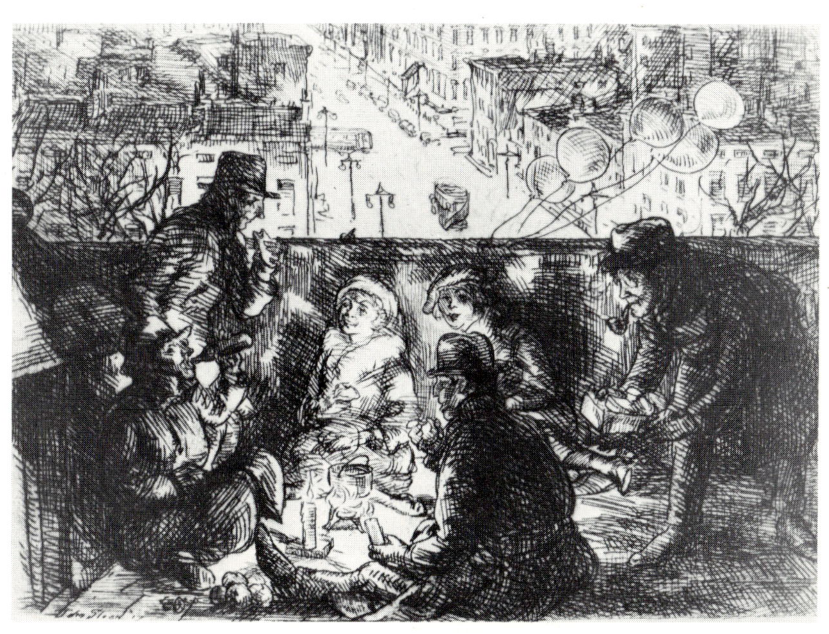

52. *Arch Conspirators*. 1917. Etching, 4¼″ x 6″.
Wilmington Society of the Fine Arts, Delaware Art Museum, Wilmington.

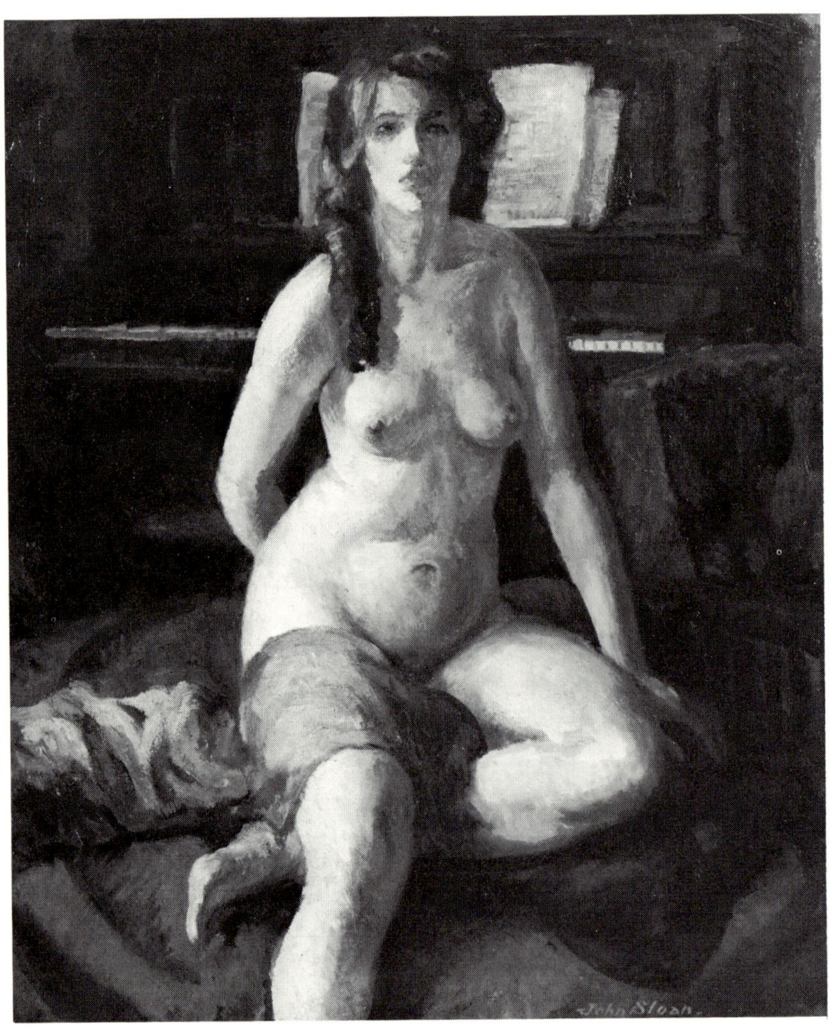

53. *Blonde Nude, Rose Scarf*. 1918. Oil on canvas, 24″ x 20″.
Collection of Dr. and Mrs. Harold Rifkin, Bronx, New York.
Photo Oliver Baker Associates, Inc., New York.

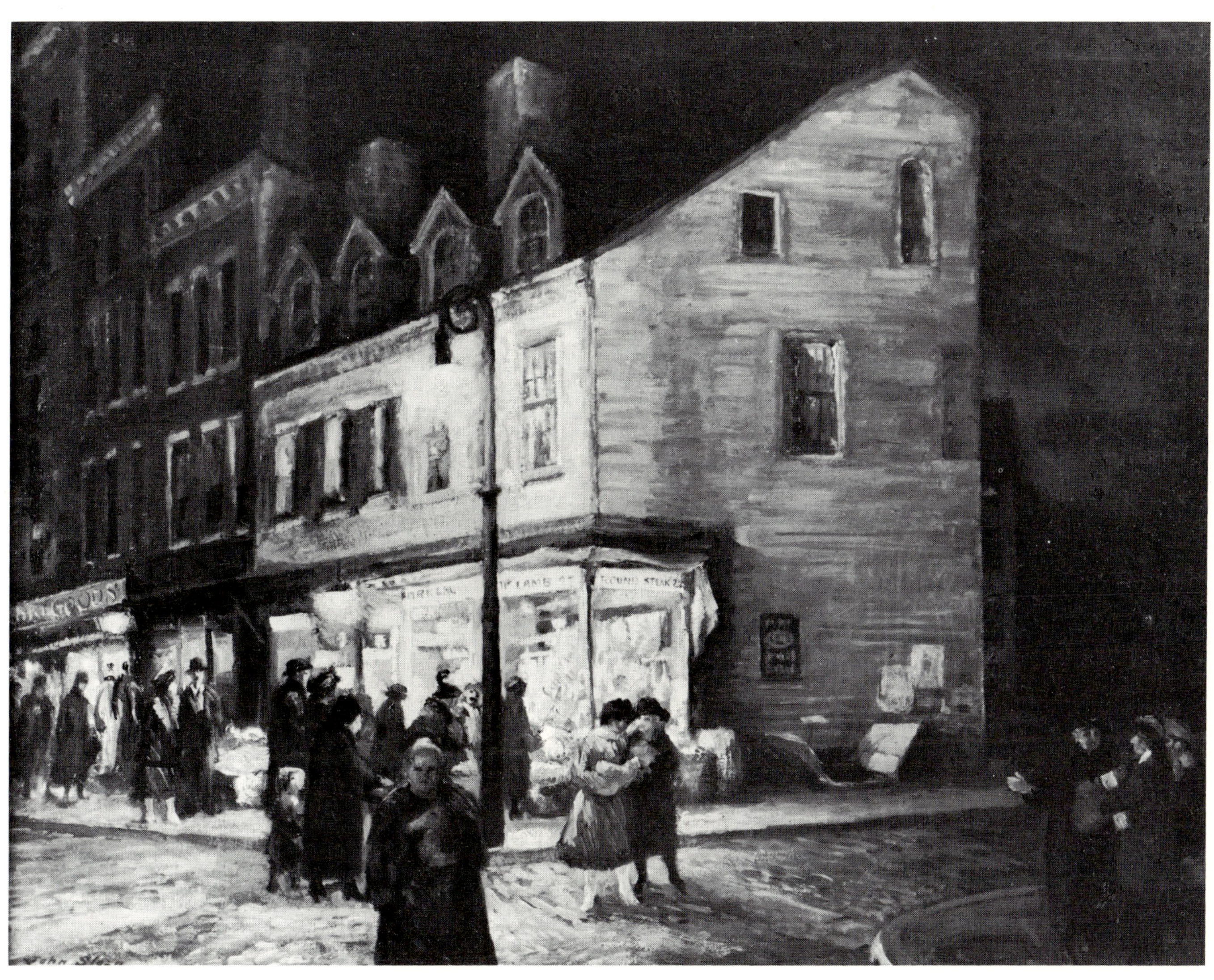

54. *Bleecker Street, Saturday Night.* 1918. Oil on canvas, 26″ x 32″.
Collection of the IBM Corporation, New York.

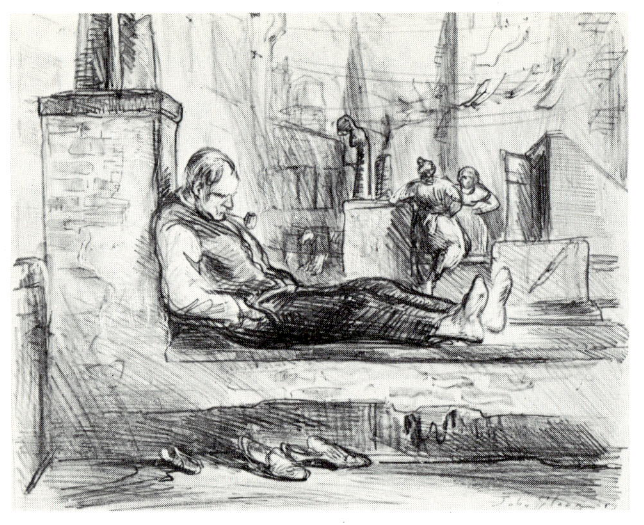

55. *Saturday Afternoon on the Roof.* 1919. Lithograph, 10½″ x 13″. Wilmington Society of the Fine Arts, Delaware Art Museum, Wilmington. *Photo Lubitsh & Bungarz, Wilmington.*

56. *Juliana Force.* 1919 and 1950. Oil on canvas, 32″ x 26″. John Sloan Trust.

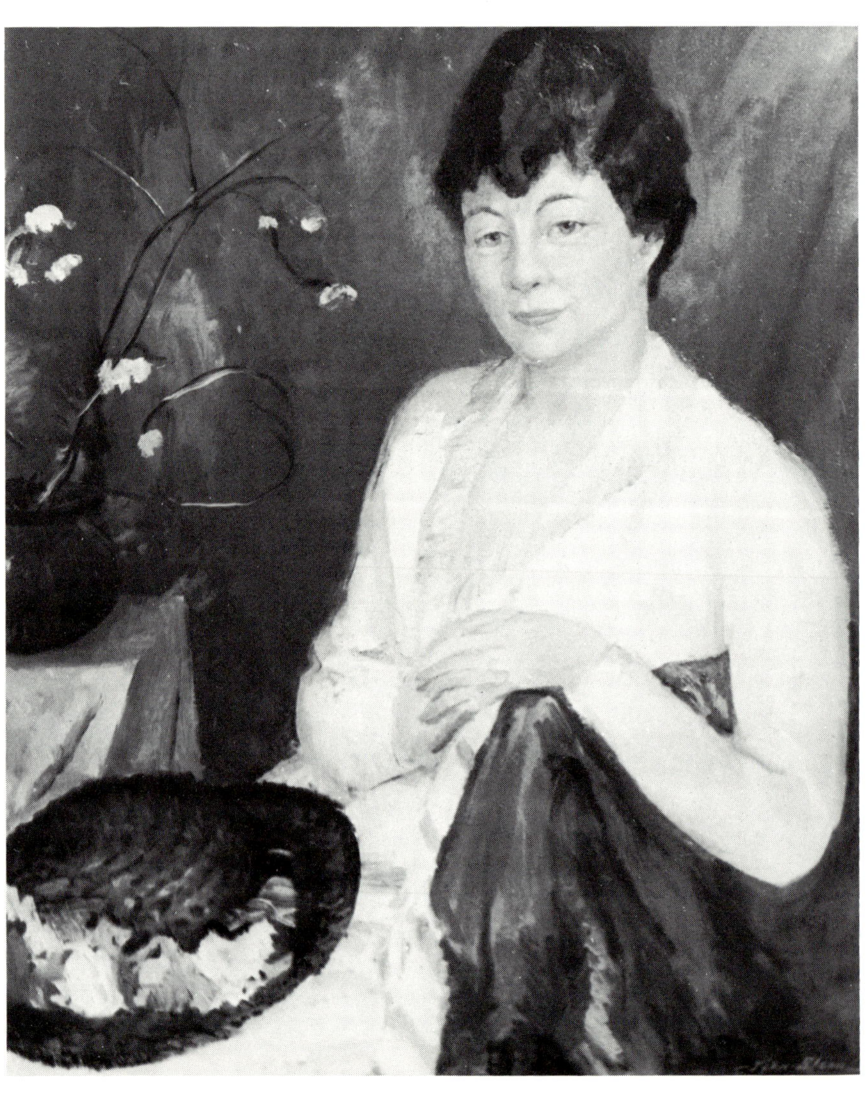

57. *Hotel Dance, Santa Fe.* 1919. Oil on canvas, 20″ x 24″.
Collection of Mr. and Mrs. Harold J. Goldman, Bellaire, Texas.

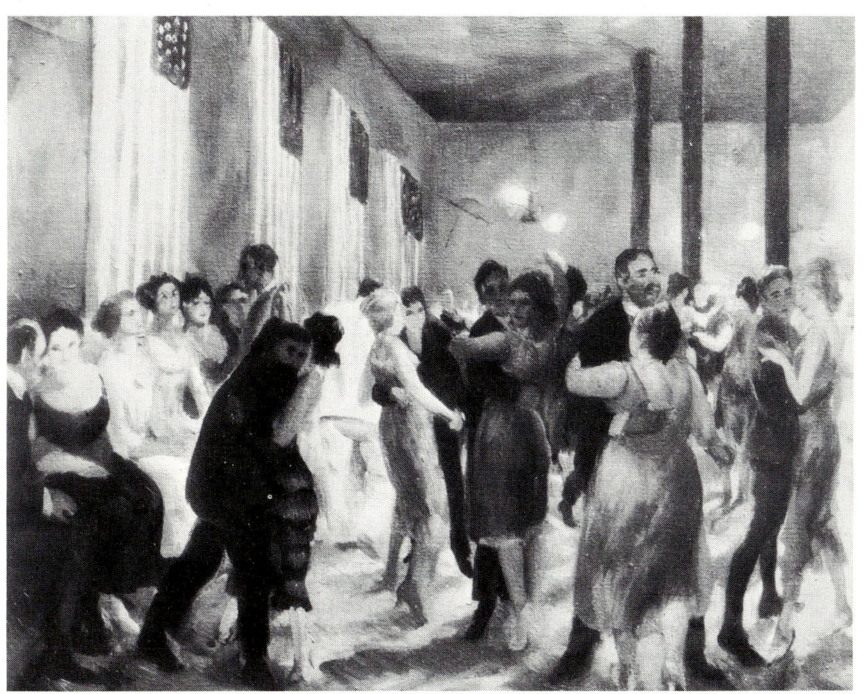

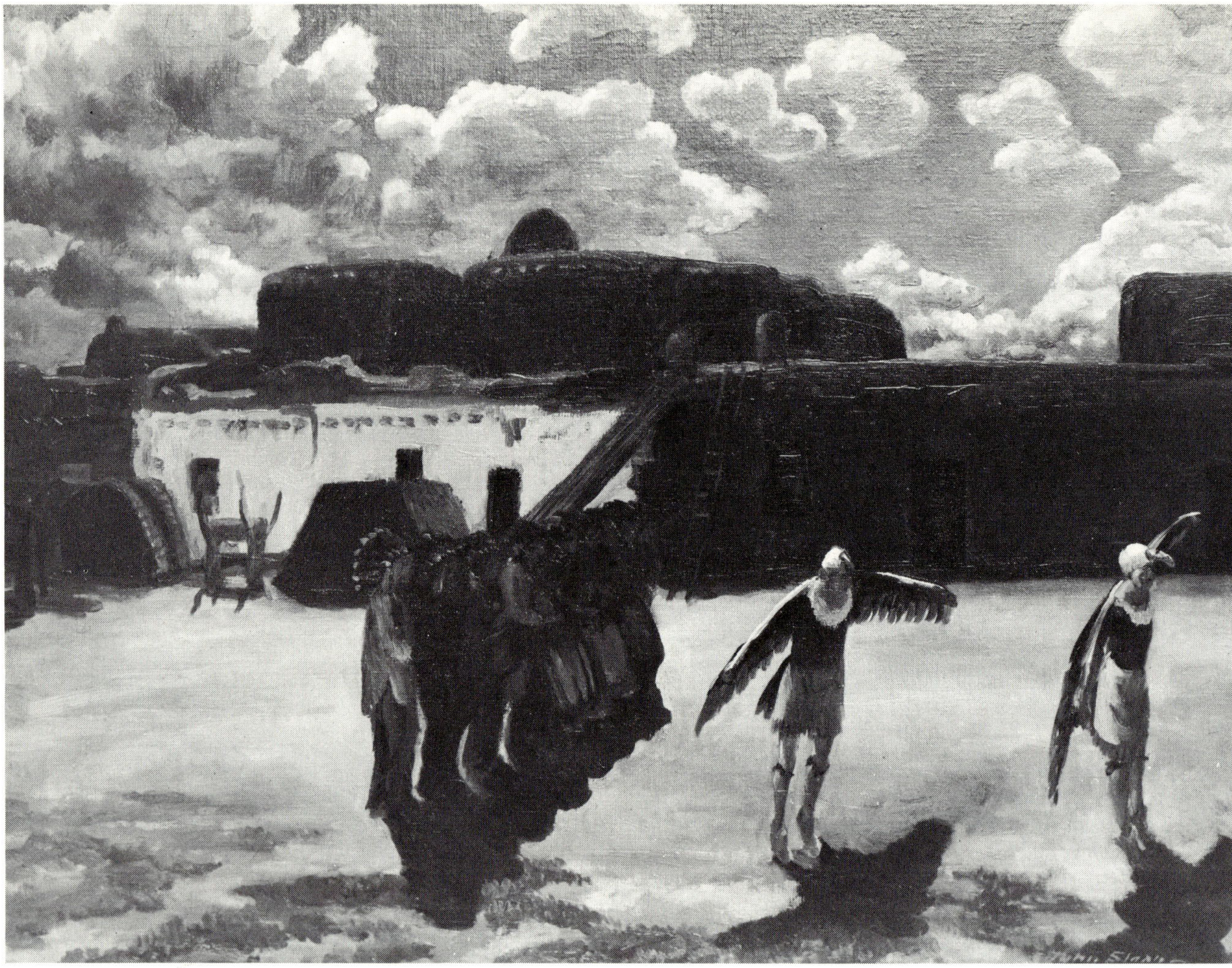

58. *Eagles of Tesuque*. 1921. Oil on canvas, 26″ x 34″.
Collection Colorado Springs Fine Arts Center, Colorado Springs.

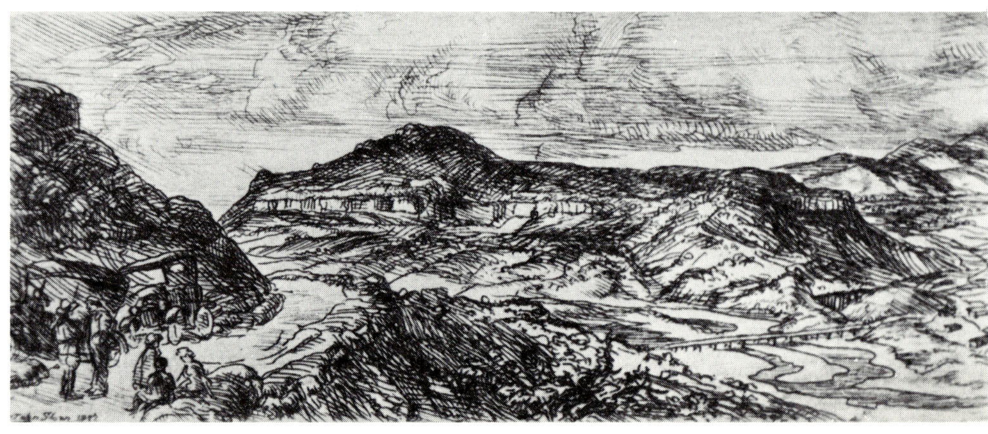

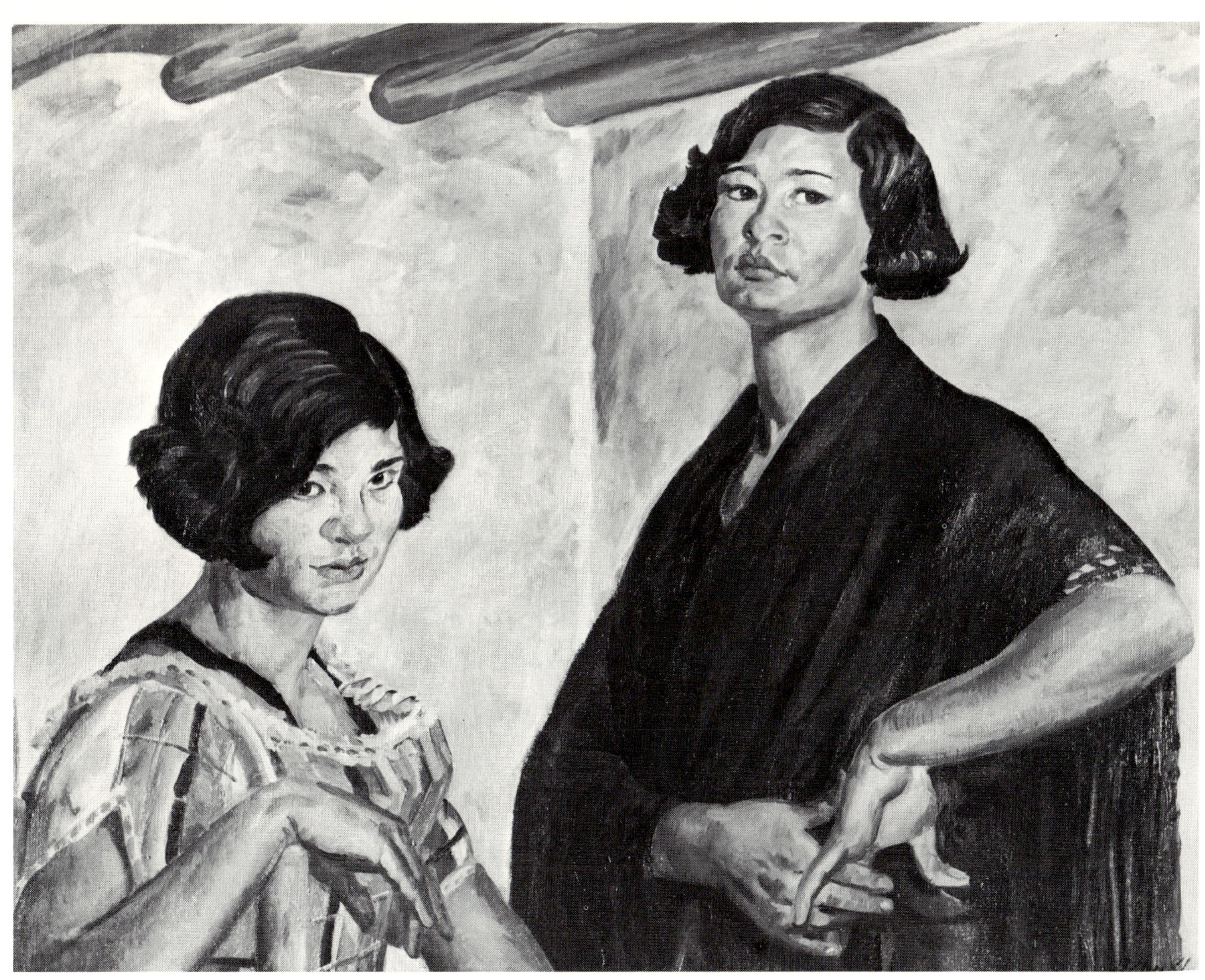

59. *Two Sisters*. 1925. Oil on canvas, 30″ x 40″.
John Sloan Trust.

Left
60. *Dragon of the Rio Grande*. 1922. Etching, 2¼″ x 5¼″.
Wilmington Society of the Fine Arts, Delaware Art Museum, Wilmington.

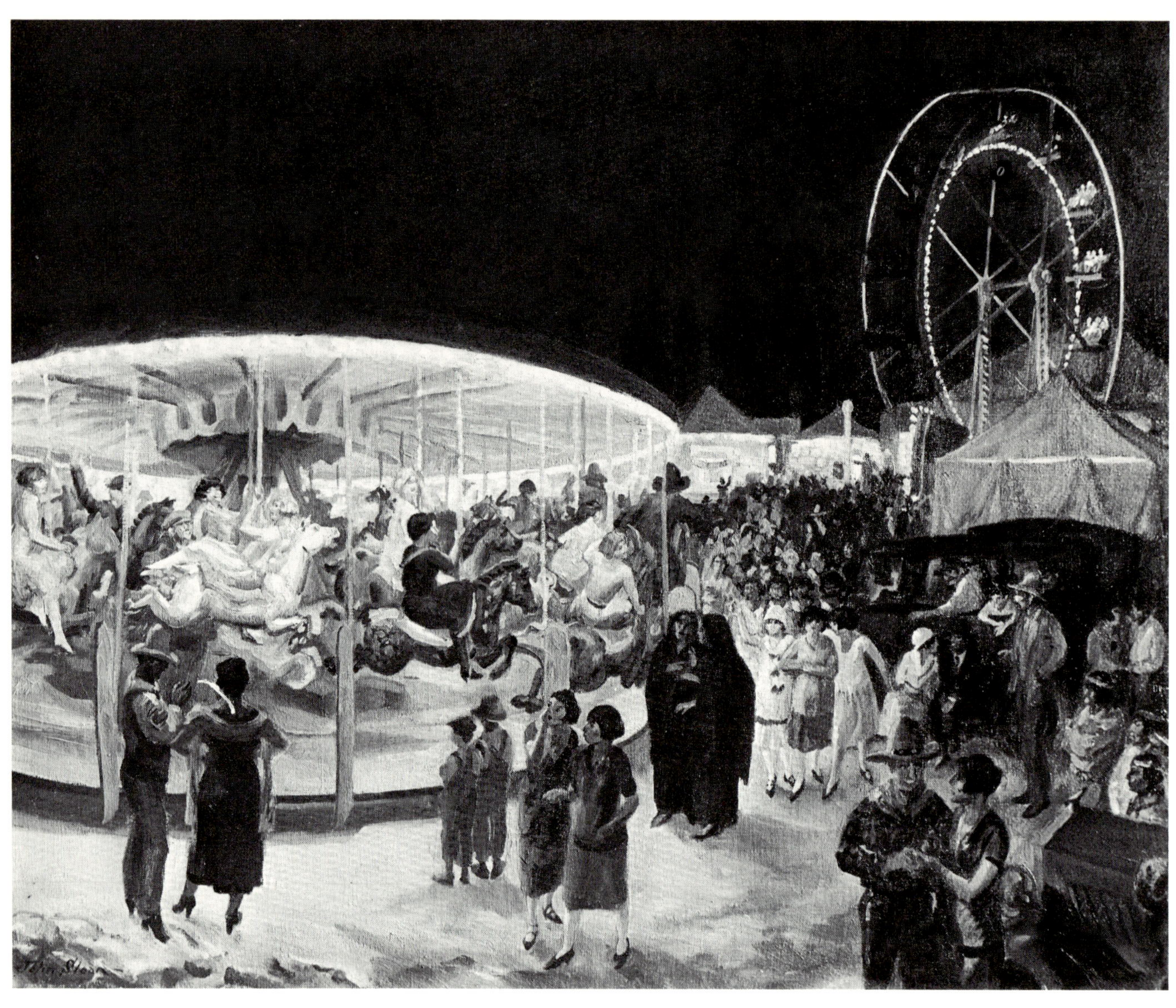

64. *Galvin Tent Show*. 1924. Oil on canvas, 26″ x 32″.
John Sloan Trust.

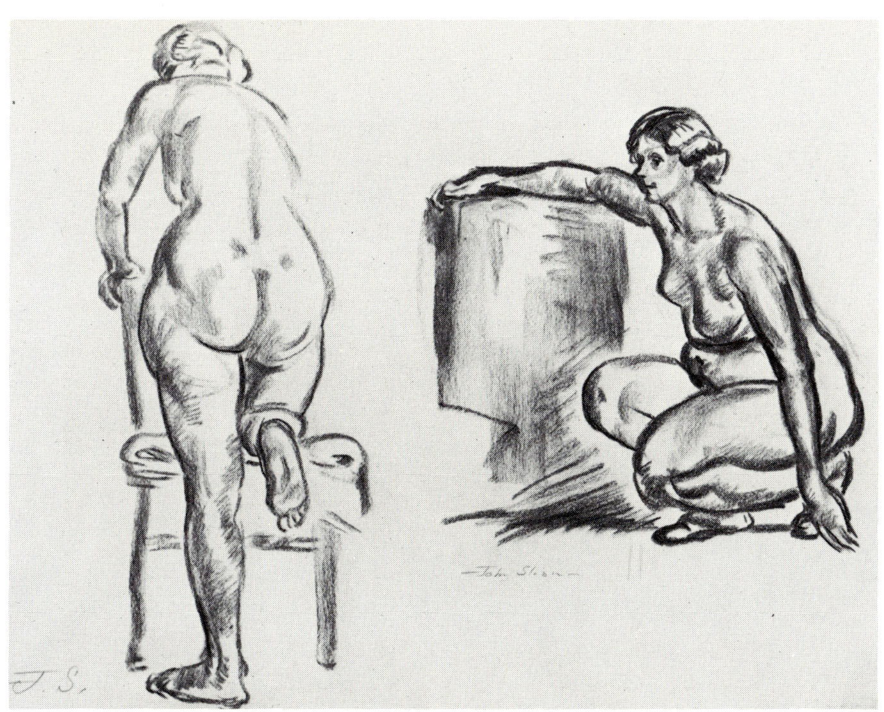

65. *Two Nudes*. 1924. Charcoal drawing, 14¼″ x 18⅞″.
John Sloan Collection, Delaware Art Museum, Wilmington.
Photo Lubitsh & Bungarz, Wilmington.

Right
66. *Snowstorm in the Village*. 1925. Etching, 7″ x 5″.
Wilmington Society of the Fine Arts, Delaware Art Museum, Wilmington.

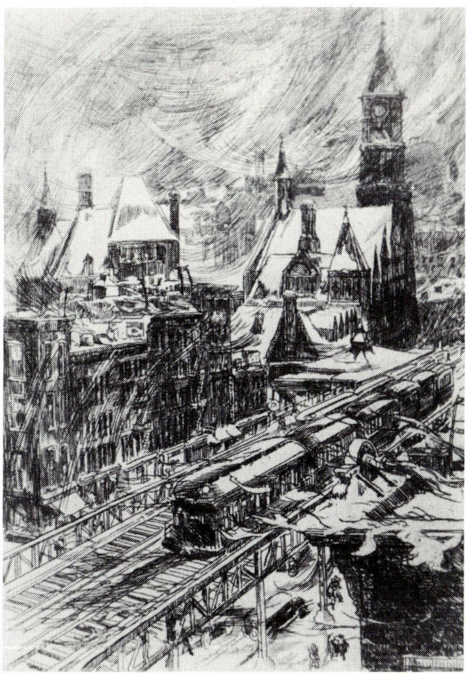

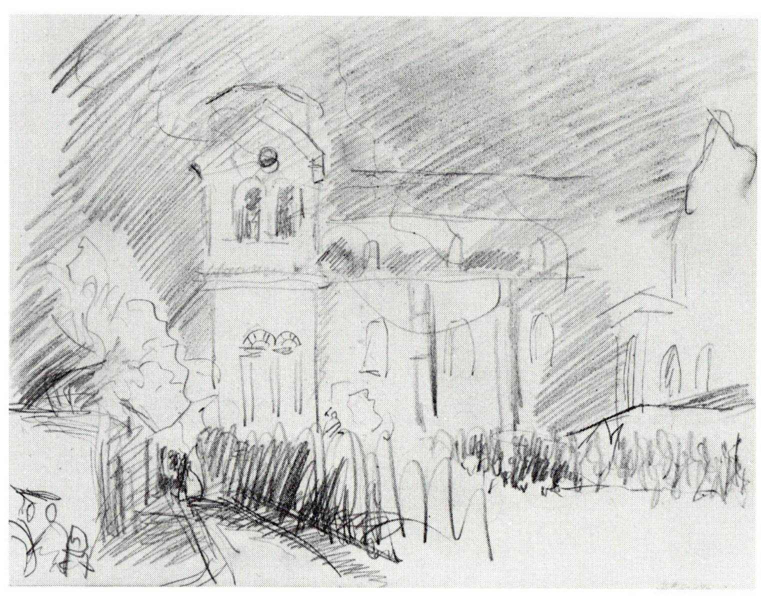

67. Preparatory drawing for *The Eve of St. Francis, Santa Fe.* 1925. Pencil, 5″ x 7″. John Sloan Trust. *Photo Lubitsh & Bungarz, Wilmington.*

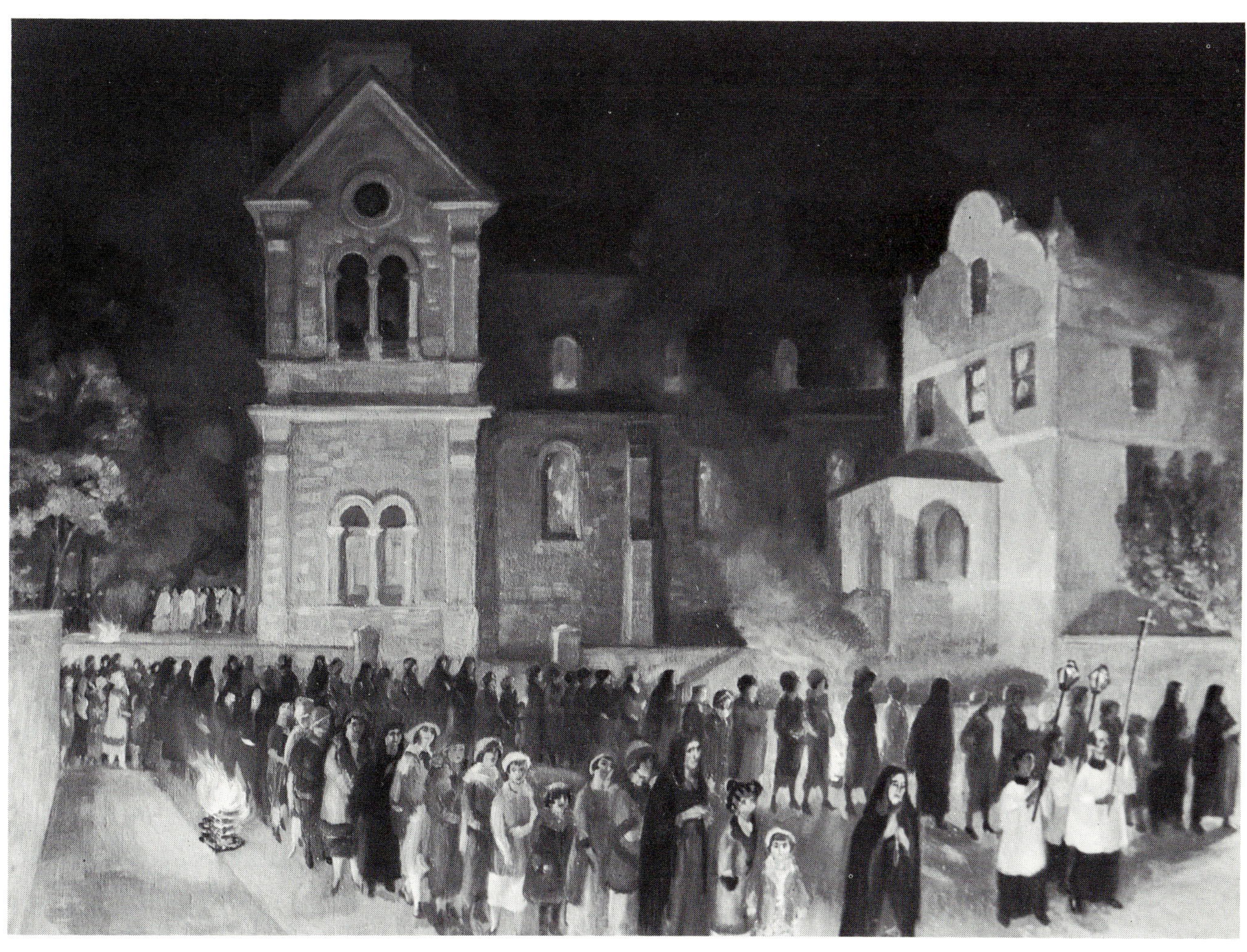

68. *The Eve of St. Francis, Santa Fe.* 1925. Oil on canvas, 30″ x 40″.
Wichita Art Museum, Wichita, Kansas: Roland P. Murdock Collection.

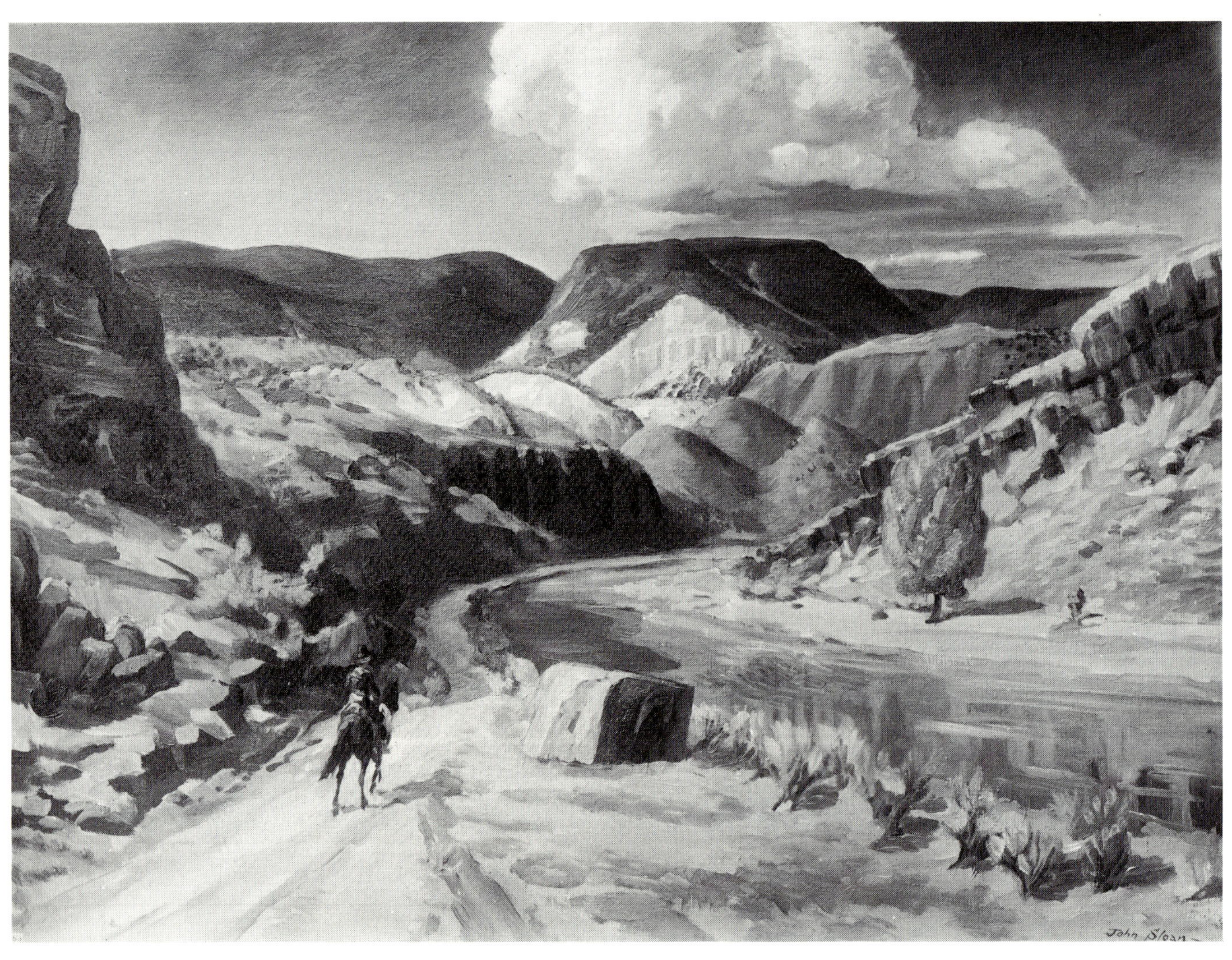

69. *Chama Running Red*. 1925. Oil on canvas, 30″ x 40″.
Collection of Miss Ruth Martin, New York.
Photo W. Coulbourn Brown, Philadelphia.

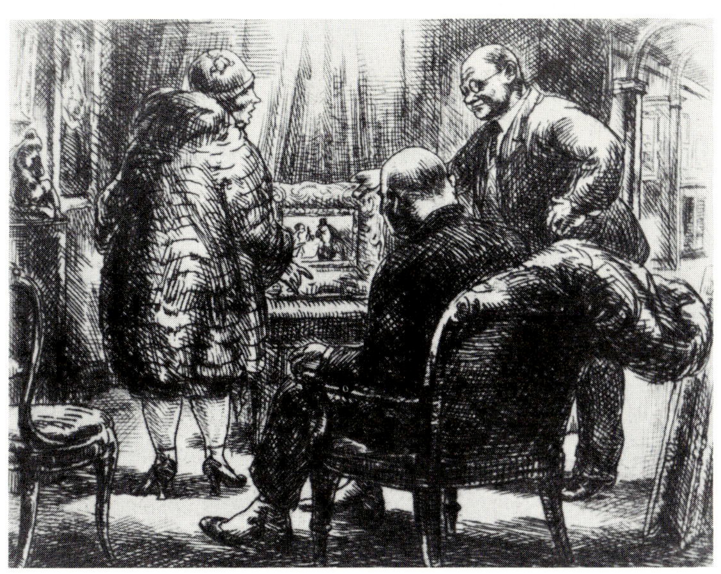

70. *Kraushaar's*. 1926. Etching, 4″ x 5″. Wilmington Society of the Fine Arts, Delaware Art Museum, Wilmington.

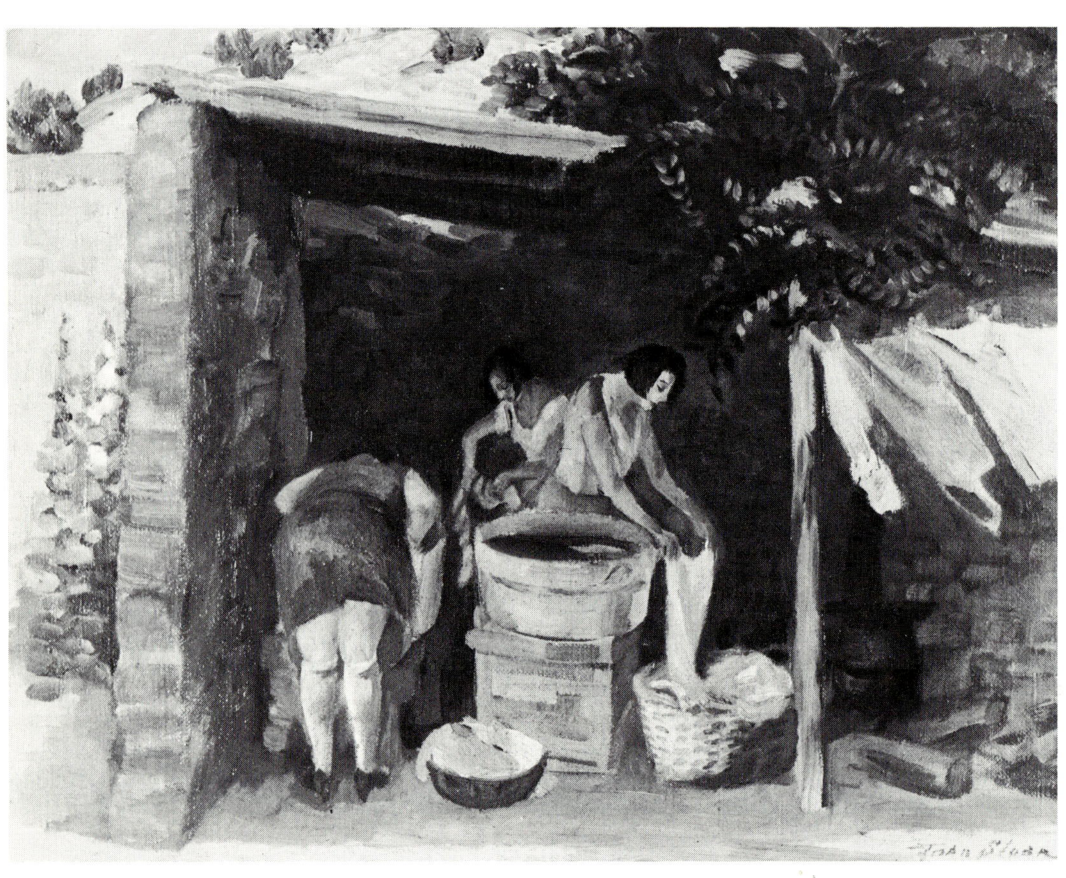

71. *Wash Day, Santa Fe.* 1926. Oil on canvas, 16″ x 20″.
John Sloan Trust.

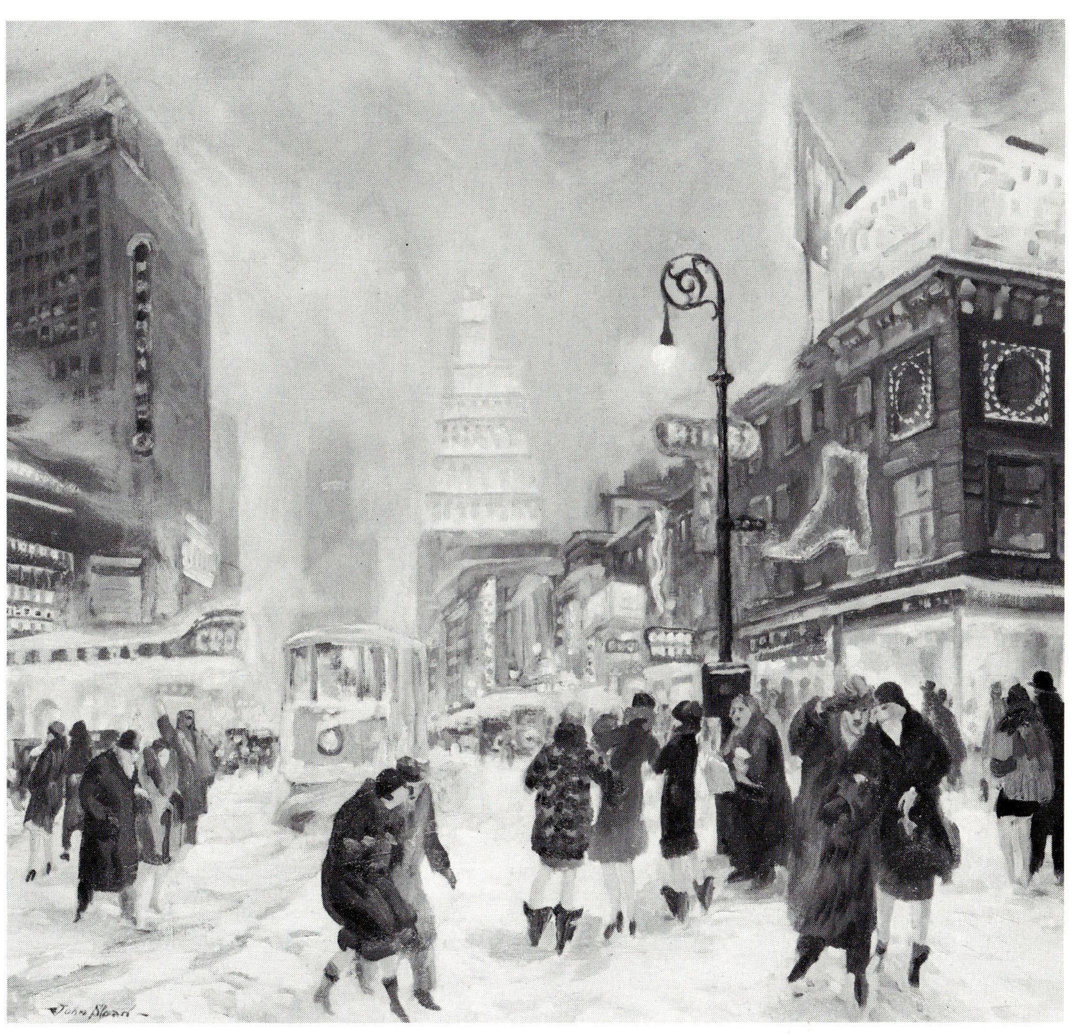

72. *The White Way.* 1926 and 1927. Oil on canvas, 30″ x 32″.
Collection of the Philadelphia Museum of Art.

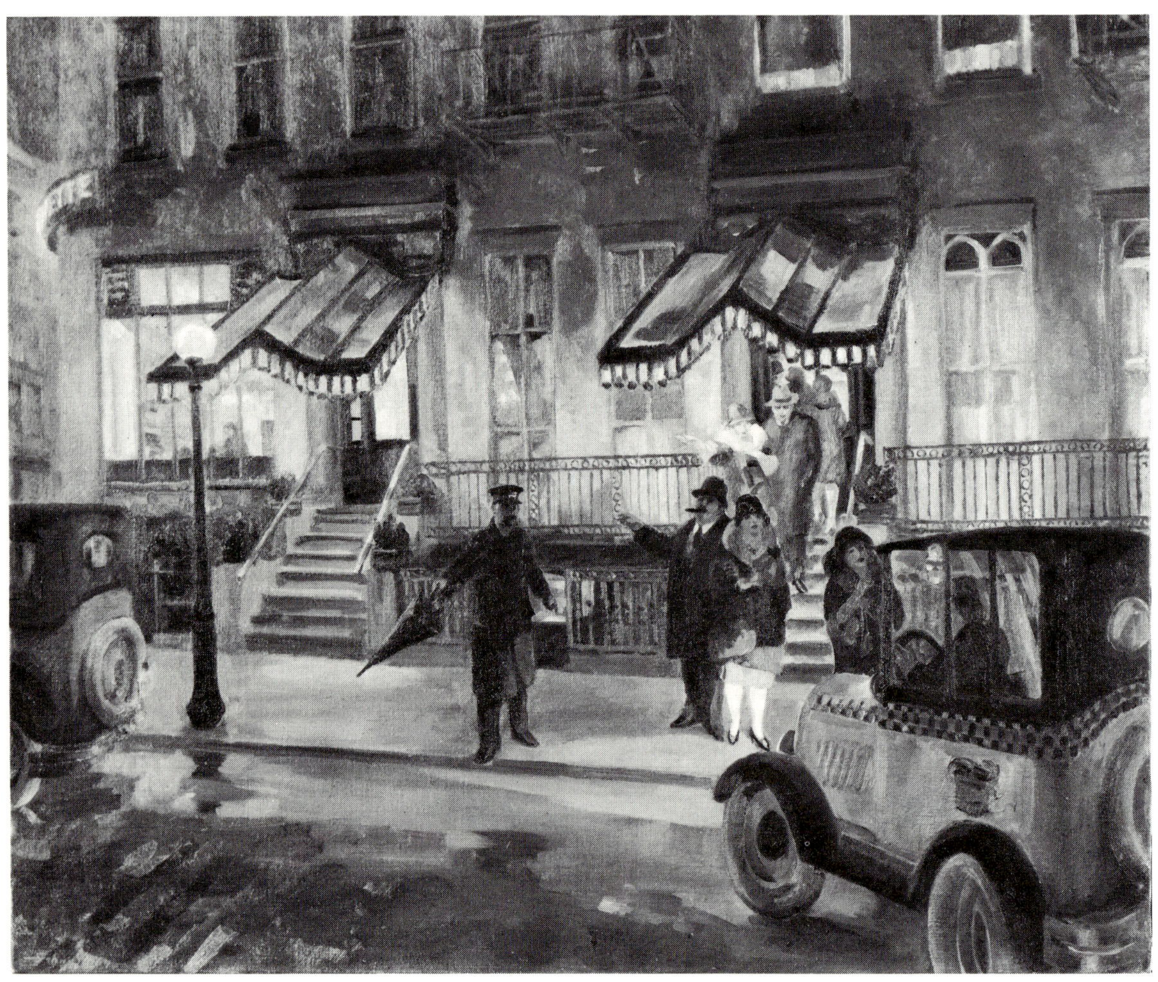

73. *The Lafayette Hotel.* 1927. Oil on canvas, 30½″ x 36⅛″.
The Metropolitan Museum of Art, New York: Gift of the Friends of John Sloan, 1928.

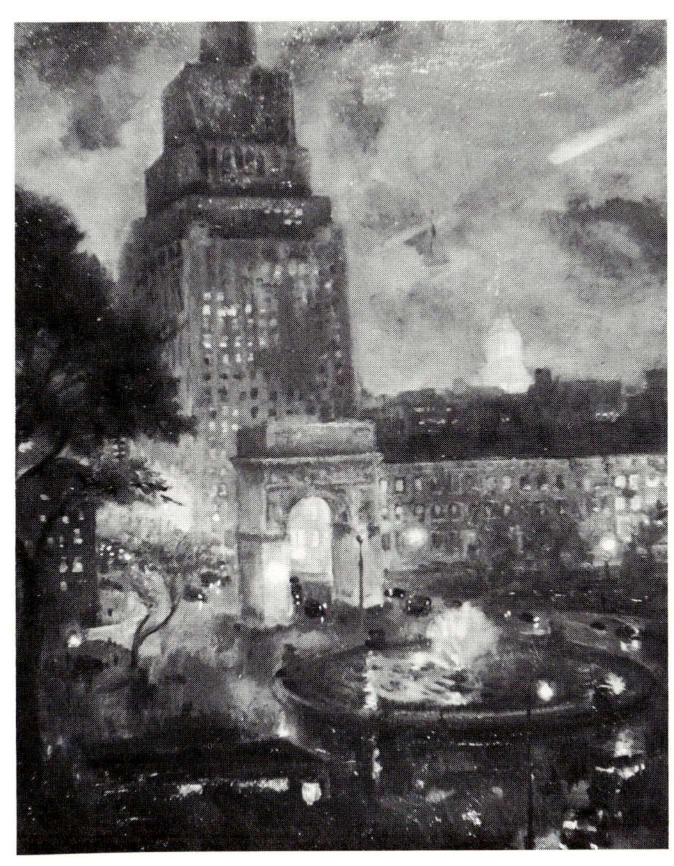

74. *Wet Night, Washington Square.* 1928. Oil on canvas, 26″ x 20″.
John Sloan Trust.

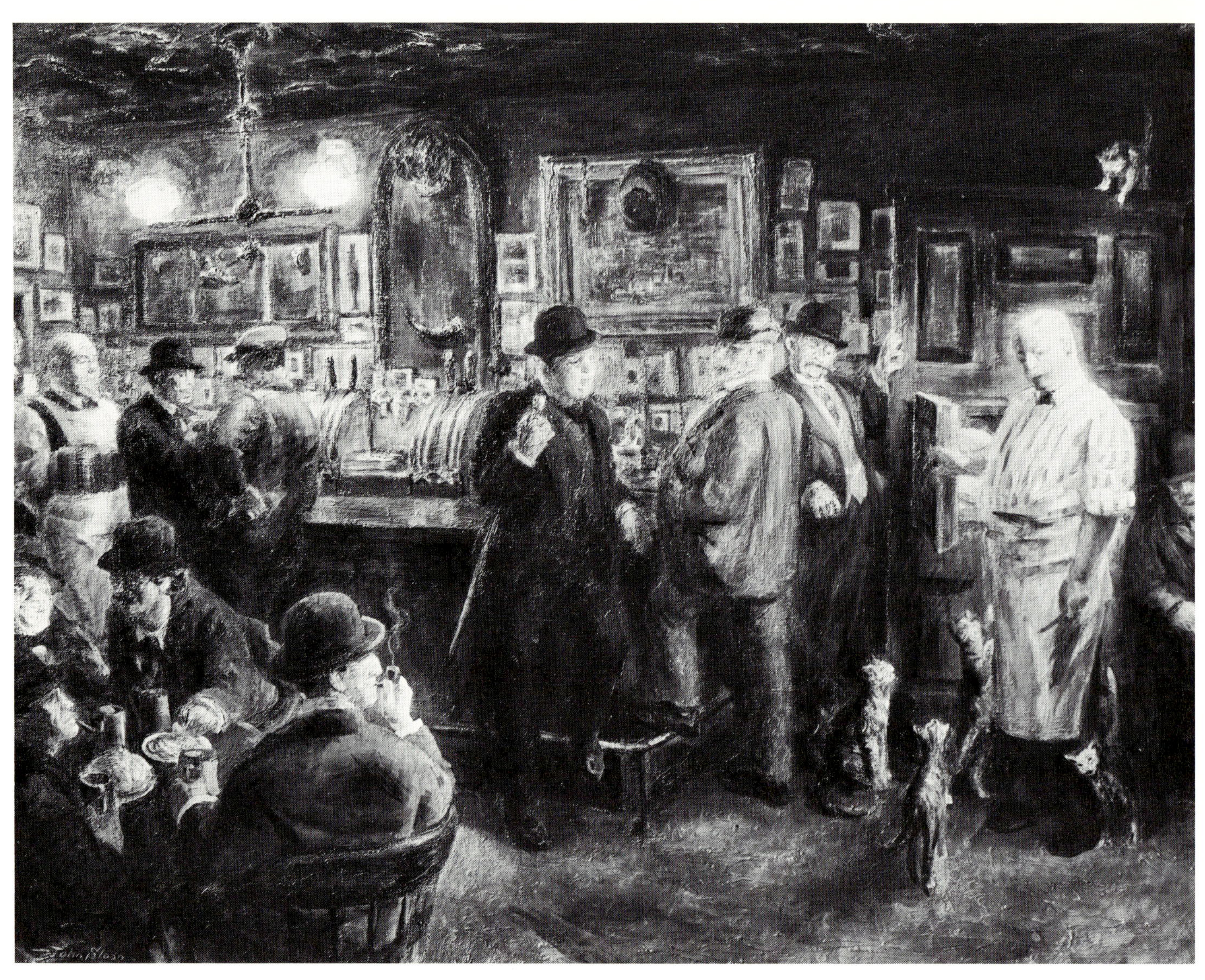

75. *McSorley's Cats.* 1929. Oil on canvas, 35⅛″ x 45⅛″.
John Sloan Trust.
Photo Soichi Sunami, New York.

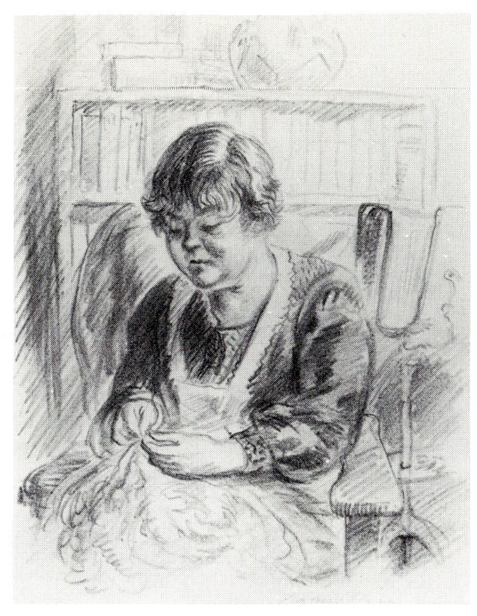

Left
76. *Dolly Sewing*. 1930. Crayon drawing, 11½″ x 8″.
John Sloan Collection, Delaware Art Museum, Wilmington.

Below
77. *Vagis the Sculptor*. 1930. Oil on canvas, 24″ x 30″.
John Sloan Trust.
Photo Peter A. Juley & Son, New York.

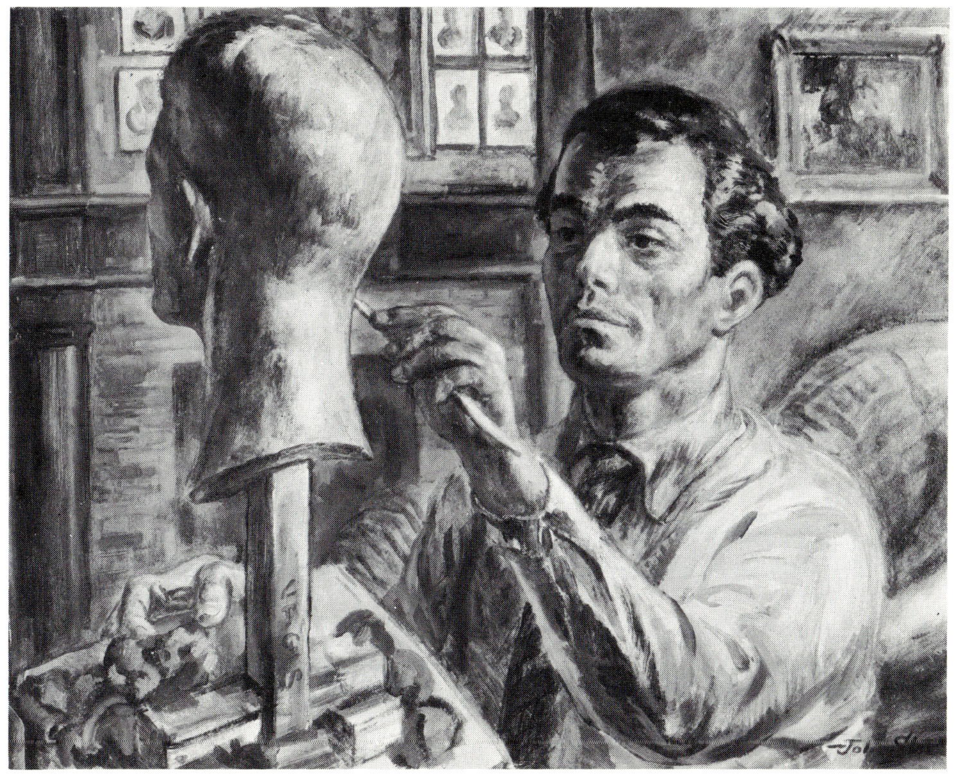

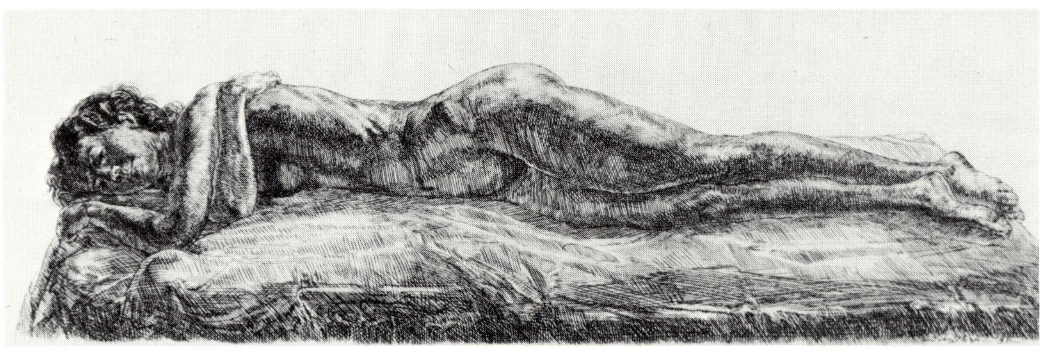

78. *Long Prone Nude*. 1931. Etching, 4¼″ x 12¾″.
Wilmington Society of the Fine Arts, Delaware Art Museum, Wilmington.

Below
79. *Reclining Nude*. 1931. Colored crayon drawing, 9″ x 12″.
John Sloan Collection, Delaware Art Museum, Wilmington.
Photo Lubitsh & Bungarz, Wilmington.

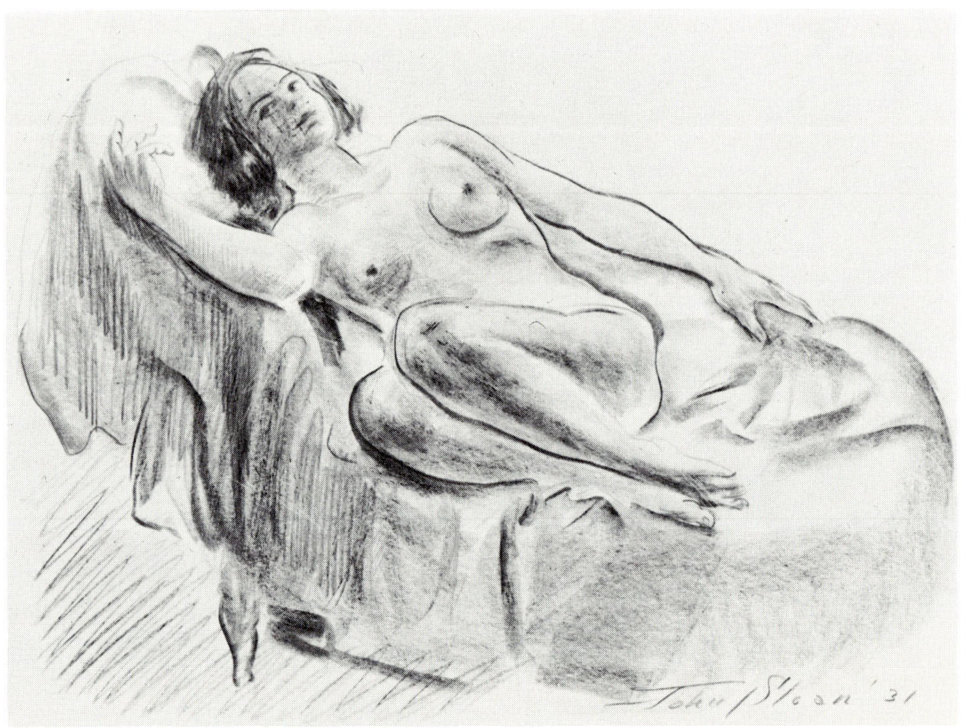

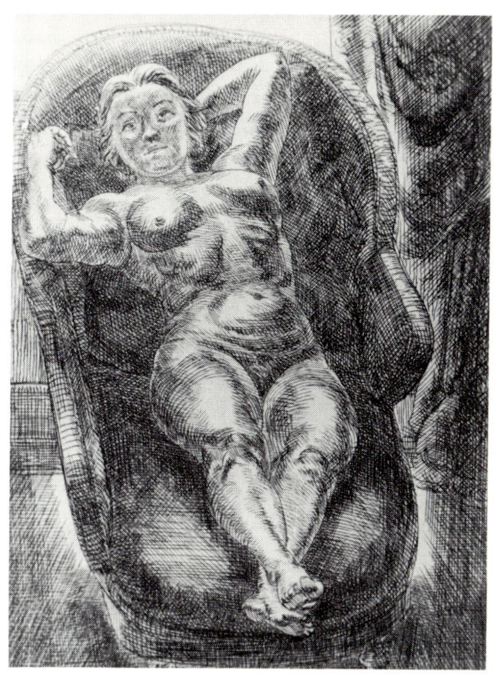

80. *Nude Foreshortened*. 1933. Etching, 7″ x 5″. Wilmington Society of the Fine Arts, Delaware Art Museum, Wilmington.

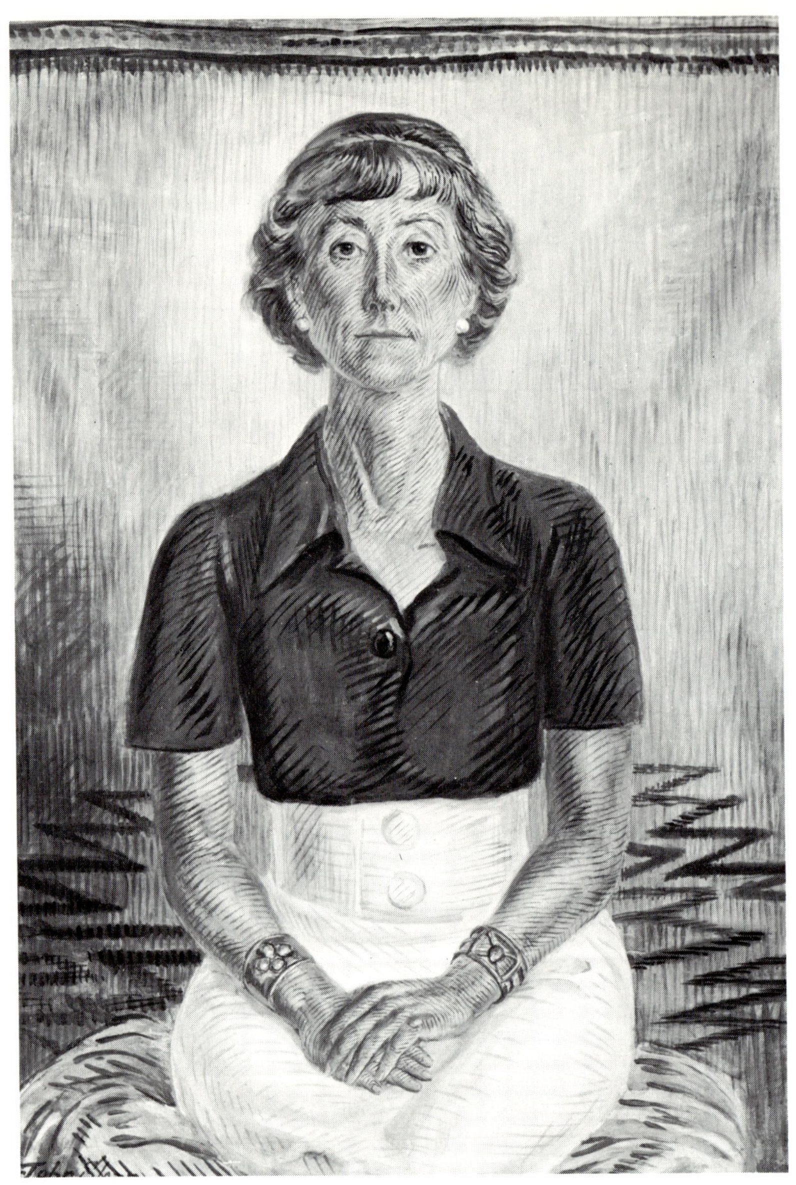

81. *Amelia Elizabeth White*. 1934–35. Oil and tempera on wood, 36″x24″. Collection Whitney Museum of American Art, New York: Gift of Miss Amelia Elizabeth White. *Photo Oliver Baker, New York*.

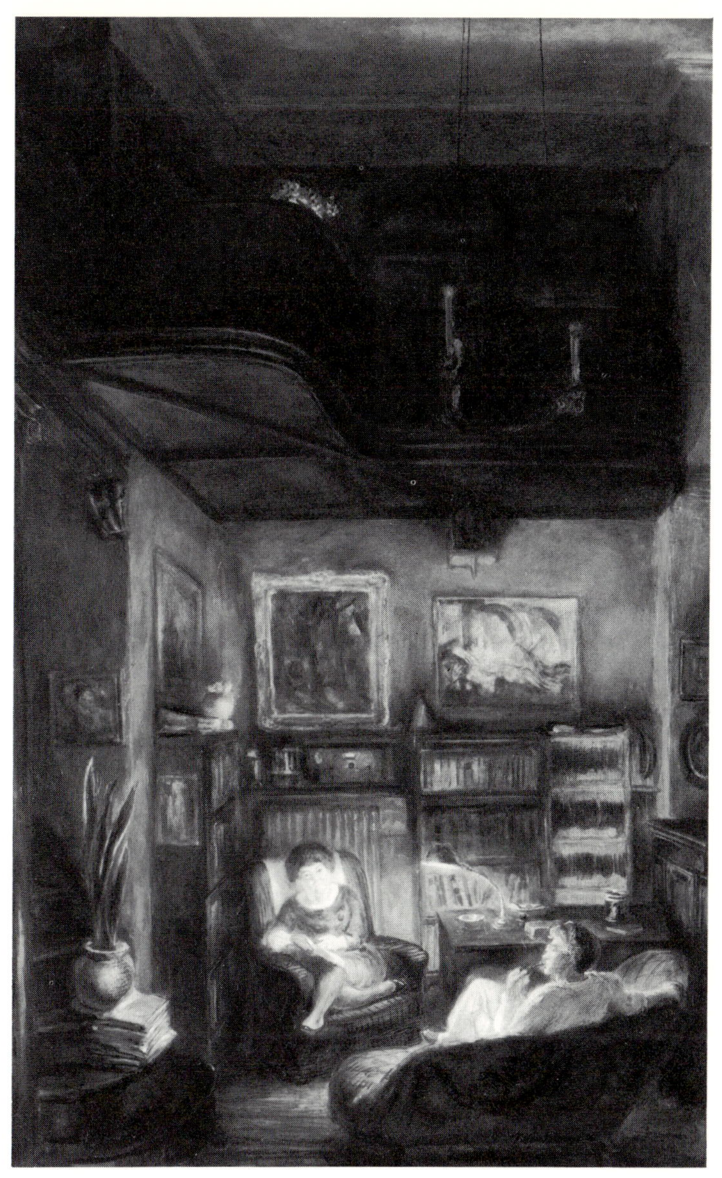

82. *Our Corner of the Studio*. 1935. Oil on canvas. 36″ x 22¾″.
John Sloan Trust.
Photo Peter A. Juley & Sons, New York.

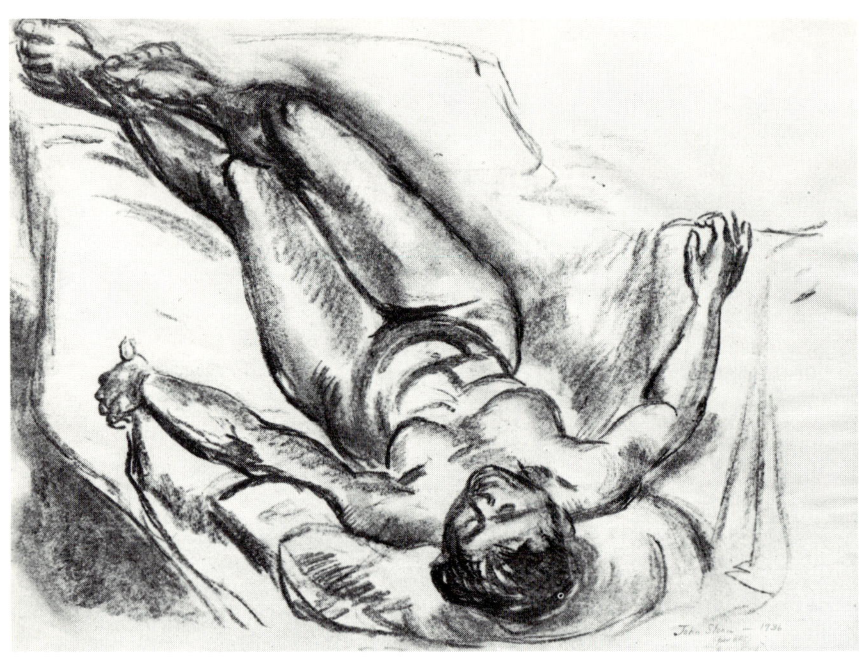

83. *Nude Foreshortened* (study for *Realization*). 1936. Charcoal drawing, 12″ x 16″.
John Sloan Collection, Delaware Art Museum, Wilmington.

84. *Romany Marye in Christopher Street, 1922.* 1936.
Etching, 6″ x 8″. Wilmington Society of the Fine
Arts, Delaware Art Museum, Wilmington.

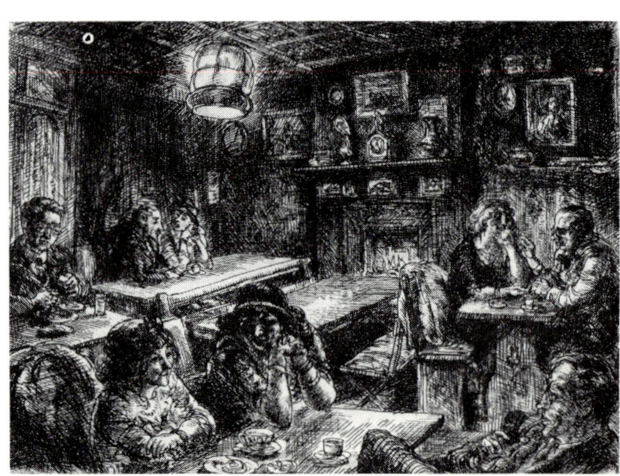

85. *Nude and Nine Apples.* 1937. Tempera and oil on composition board, 24″ x 30″.
Collection Whitney Museum of American Art, New York.
Photo Peter A. Juley & Son, New York.

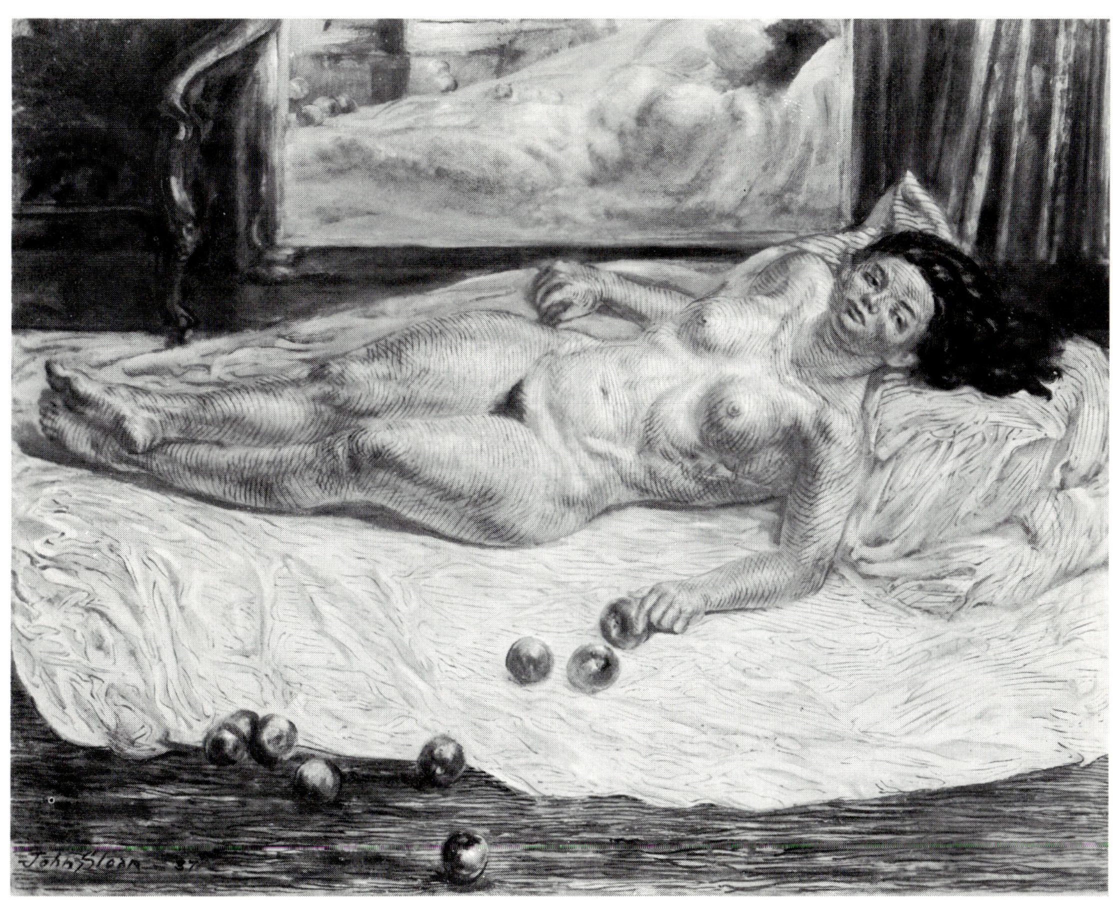

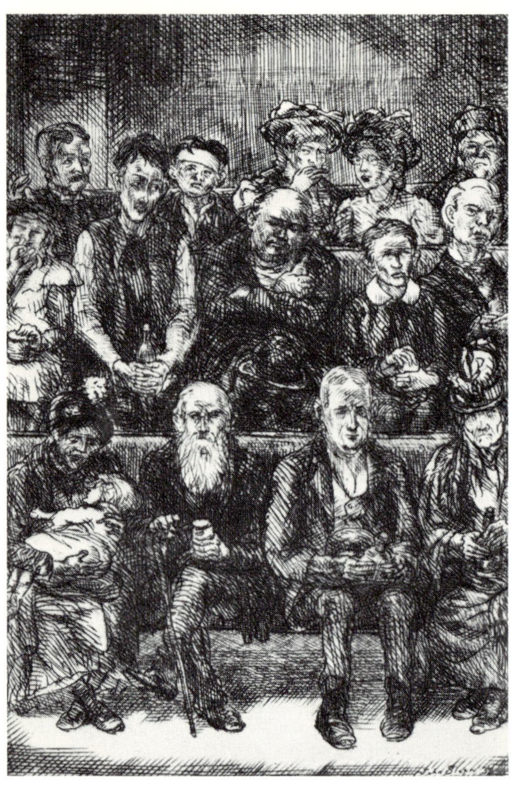

86. *The Clinic*. 1937. Etching, 6″ x 4″. Illustration for W. Somerset Maugham's novel *Of Human Bondage*. Wilmington Society of the Fine Arts, Delaware Art Museum, Wilmington.

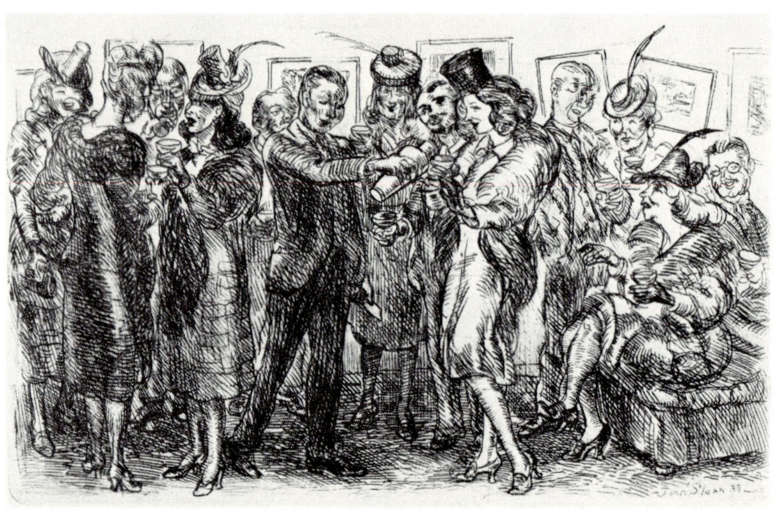

87. *A Thirst for Art*. 1939. Etching, 4″ x 6″. Wilmington Society of the Fine Arts, Delaware Art Museum, Wilmington.

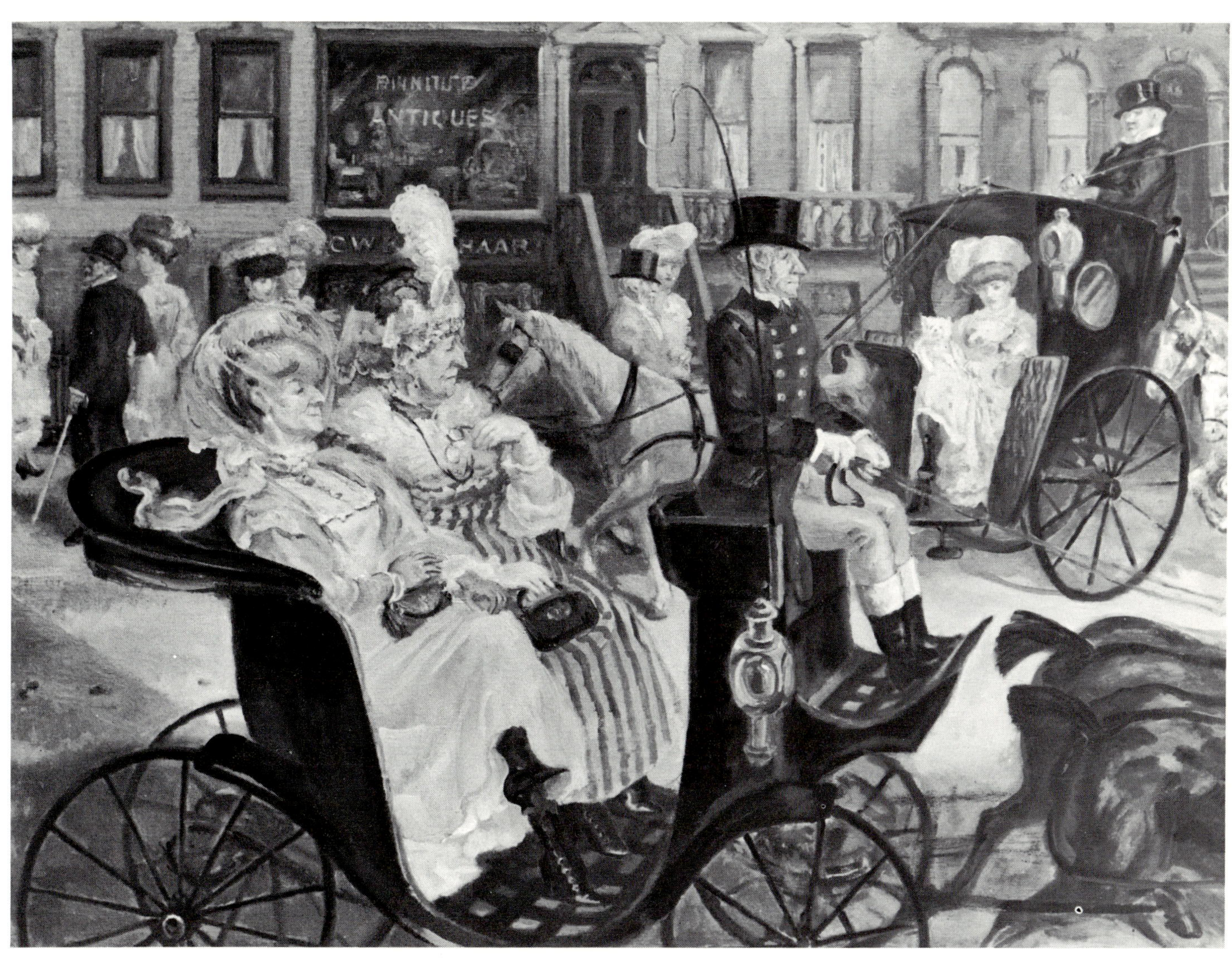

88. *Fifth Avenue Critics, 1905.* 1940. Oil on canvas, 36″ x 45″.
Collection of Miss Ruth Martin, New York.

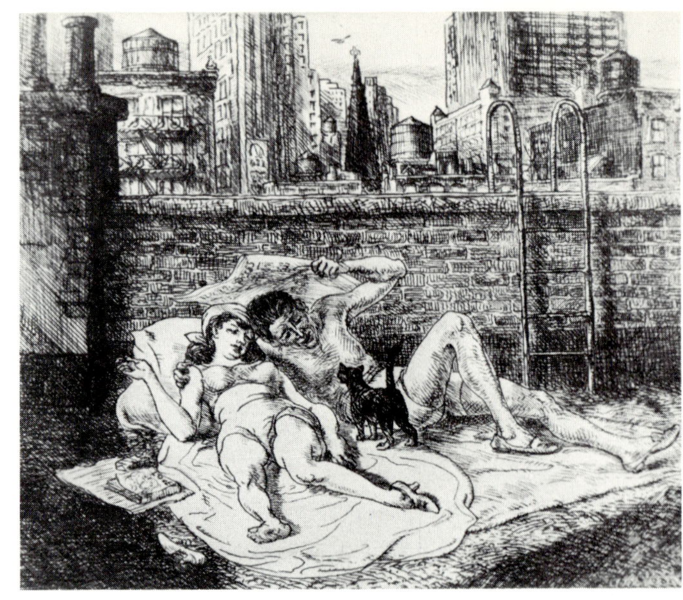

Right
89. *Sunbathers on the Roof*. 1941. Etching, 6″ x 7″. Wilmington Society of the Fine Arts, Delaware Art Museum, Wilmington.

90. *Roof Chats*. 1944. Oil on canvas, 16″ x 20″.
John Sloan Trust.
Photo Geoffrey Clements, Staten Island, New York.

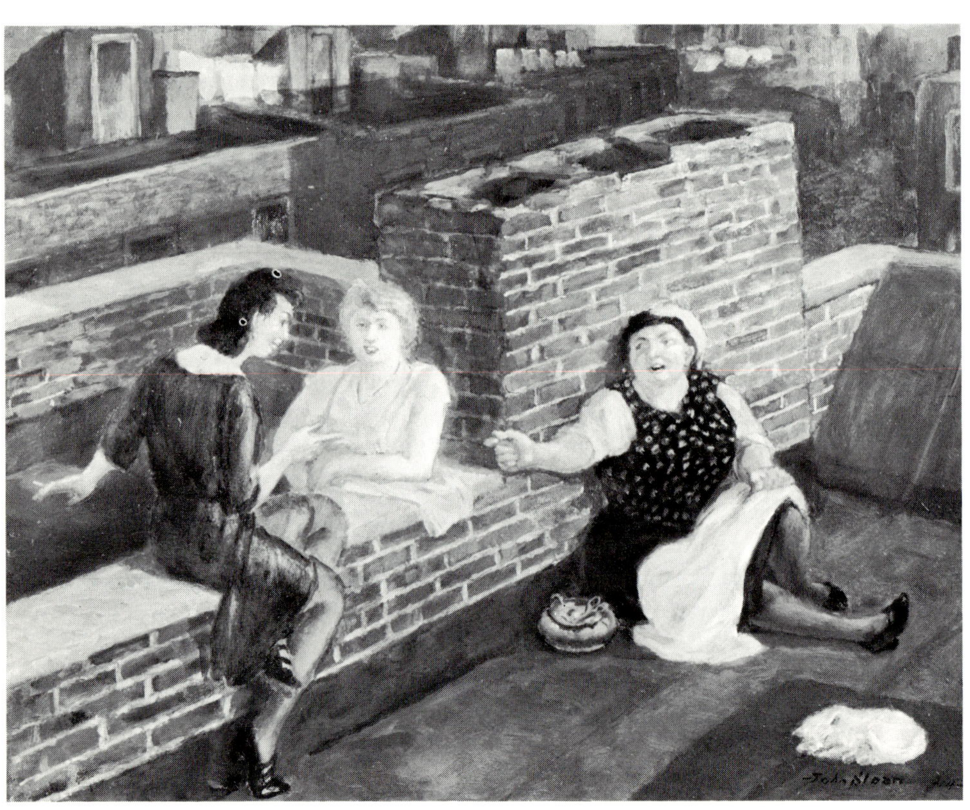

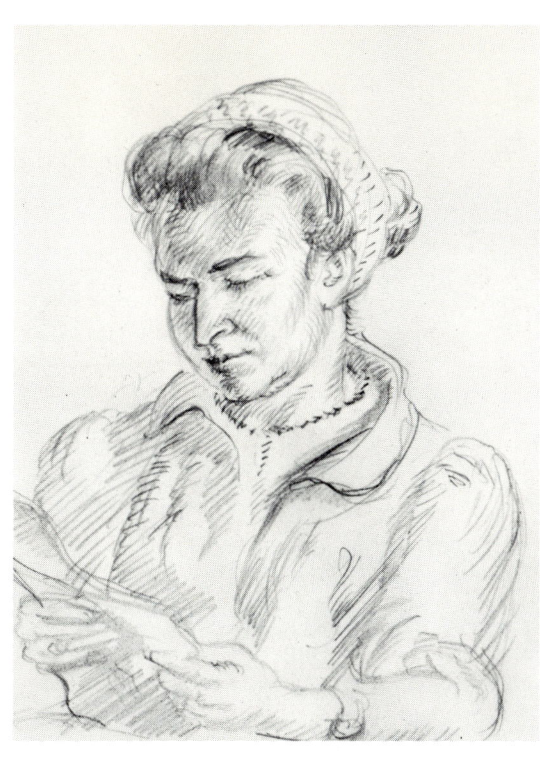

Left
91. *Helen at Sinagua*. 1944. Pencil drawing, 8½″ x 6″.
John Sloan Collection, Delaware Art Museum, Wilmington.
Photo Lubitsh & Bungarz, Wilmington.

92. *Seated Nude* (study for *Realization*). 1945. Green chalk drawing,
11″ x 14½″. John Sloan Collection, Delaware Art Museum, Wilmington. *Photo Lubitsh & Bungarz, Wilmington.*

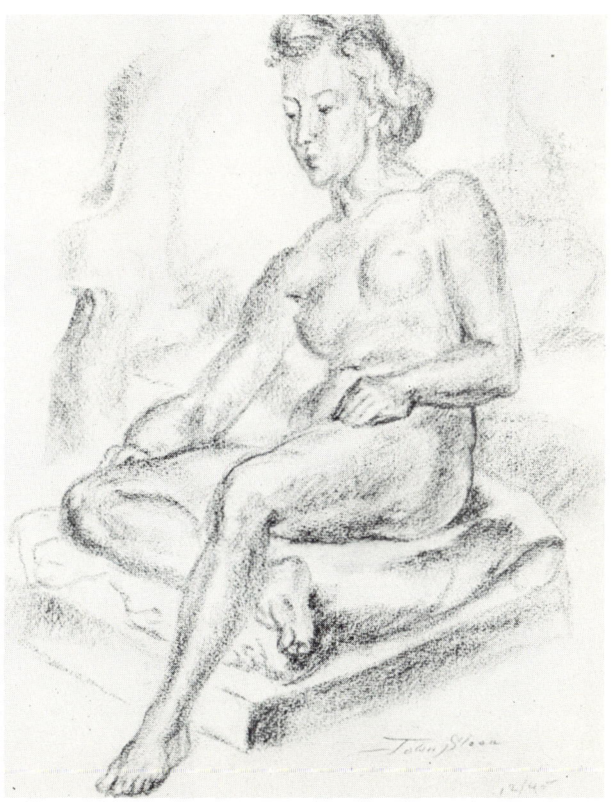

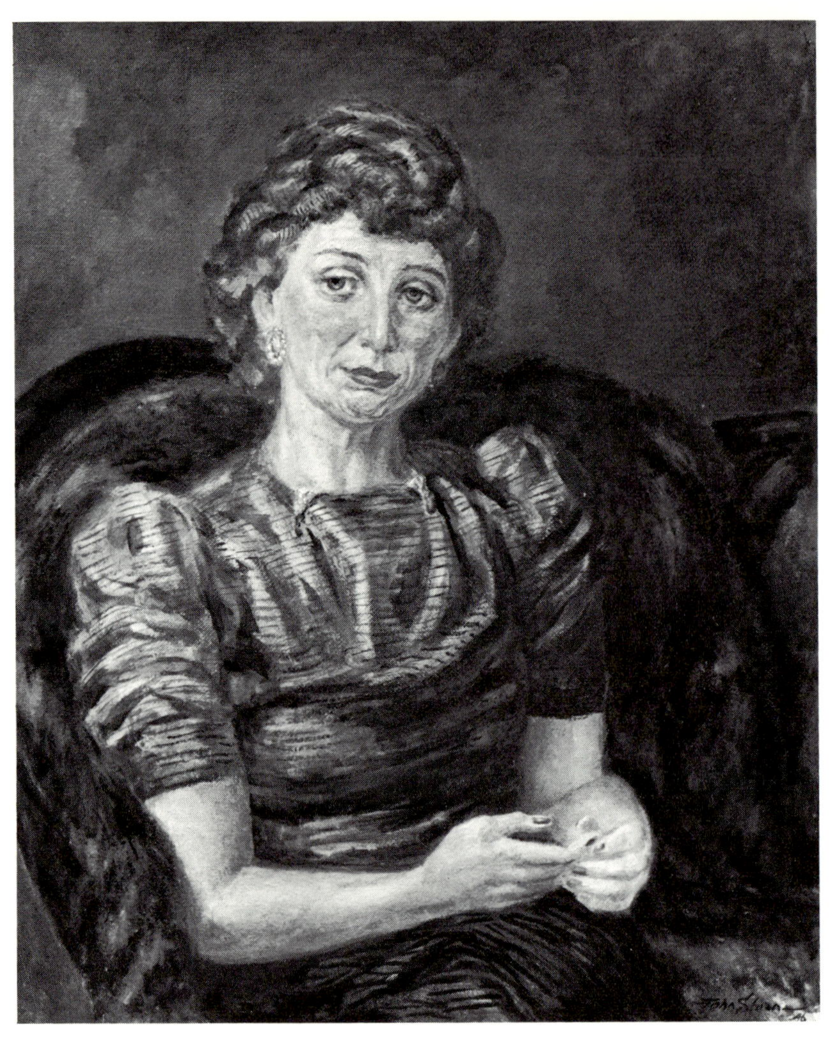

93. *Yolande van R.* 1946. Oil on canvas, 29″ x 23½″.
John Sloan Trust.
Photo Colten, New York.

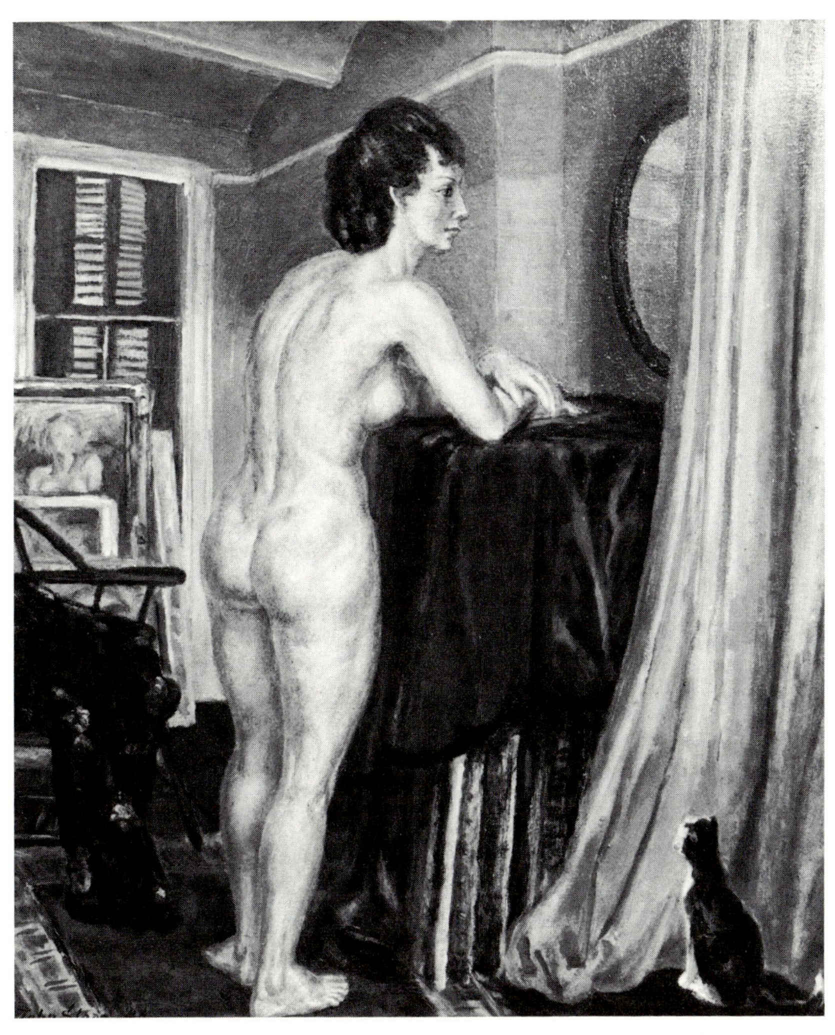

94. *Gladys with a Black Cat.* 1946. Oil on canvas, 28¾″ x 23½″.
John Sloan Trust.

95. *Tea for One*. 1948. Oil on canvas, 32″ x 26″.
John Sloan Trust.

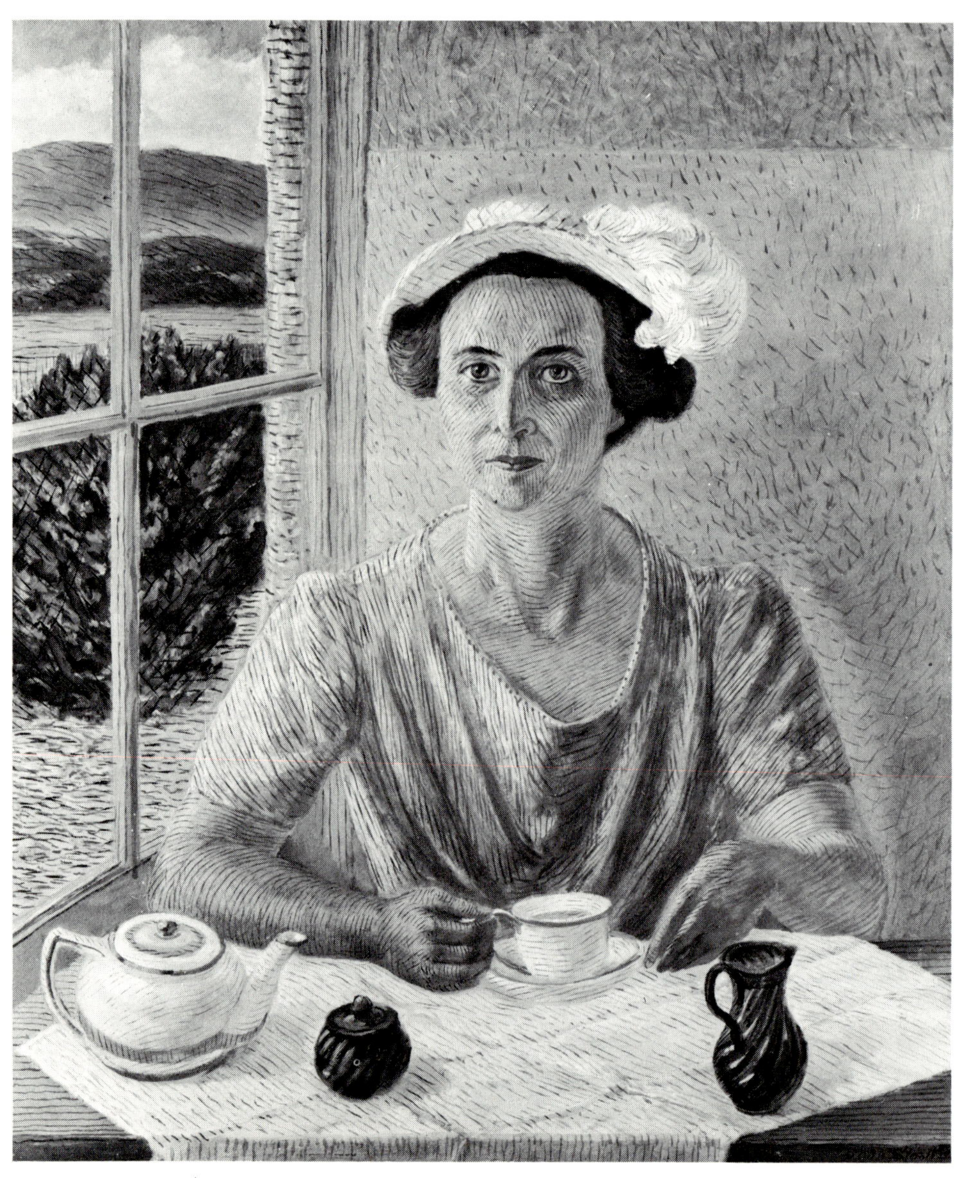

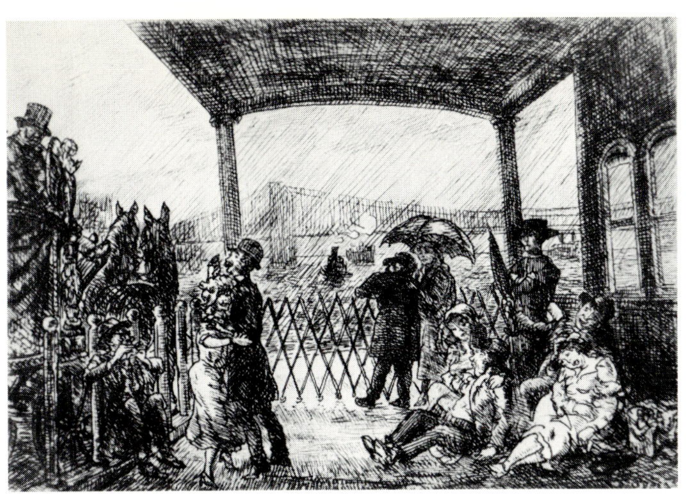

96. *Wake on the Ferry*. 1949. Etching, 5″ x 7″. Wilmington Society of the Fine Arts, Delaware Art Museum, Wilmington.

97. *Charlotte with Parasol*. 1950. Oil on canvas, 28″ x 20″. Collection American Academy of Arts and Letters, New York. *Photo Oliver Baker, New York.*

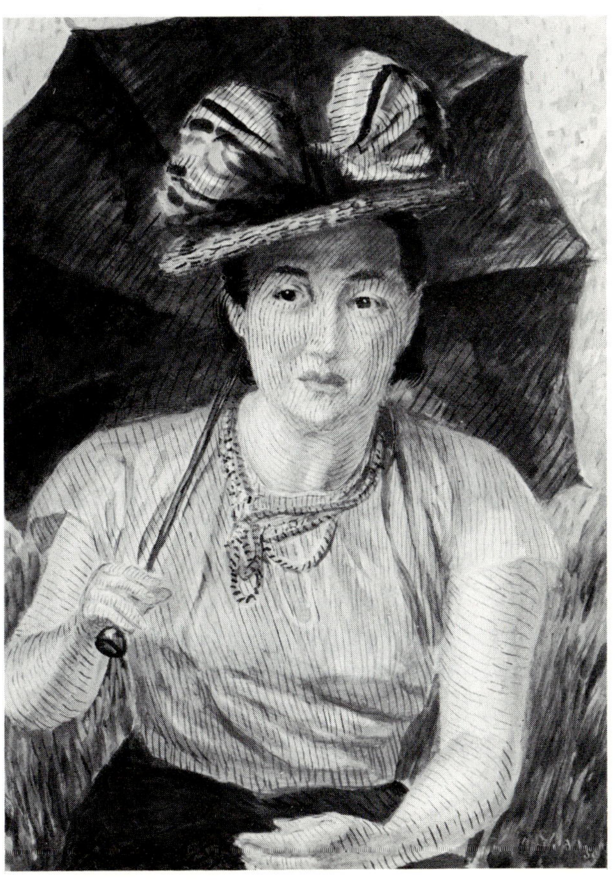

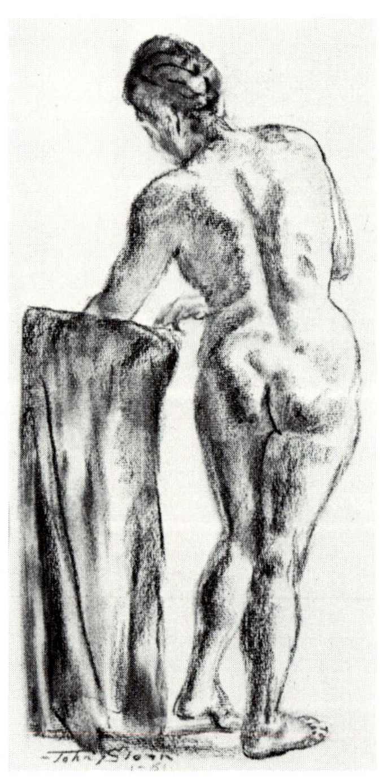

98. *Standing Nude.* 1951. Charcoal drawing, 16″ x 8″.
John Sloan Collection, Delaware Art Museum, Wilmington.
Photo Lubitsh & Bungarz, Wilmington.

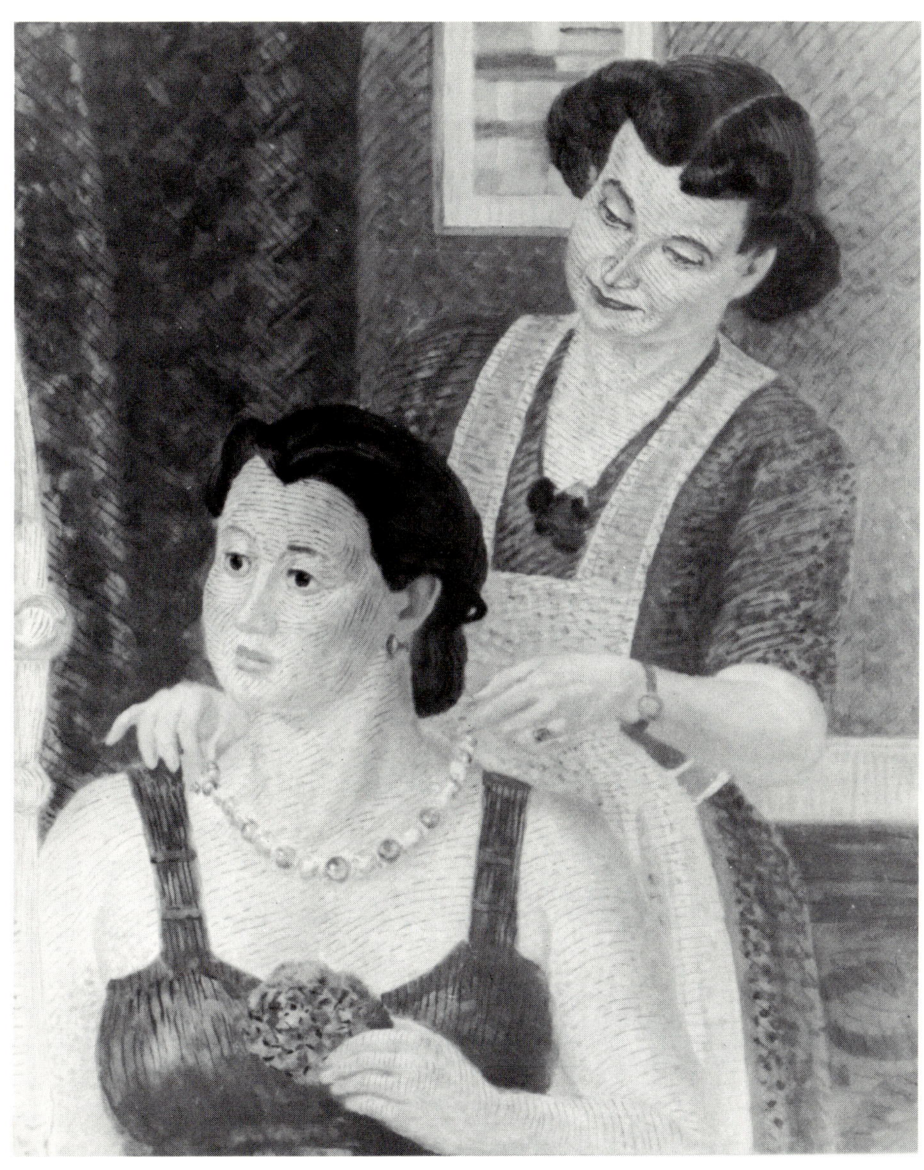

99. *The Necklace*. 1951. Oil on canvas, 30½″ x 26″.
John Sloan Trust.

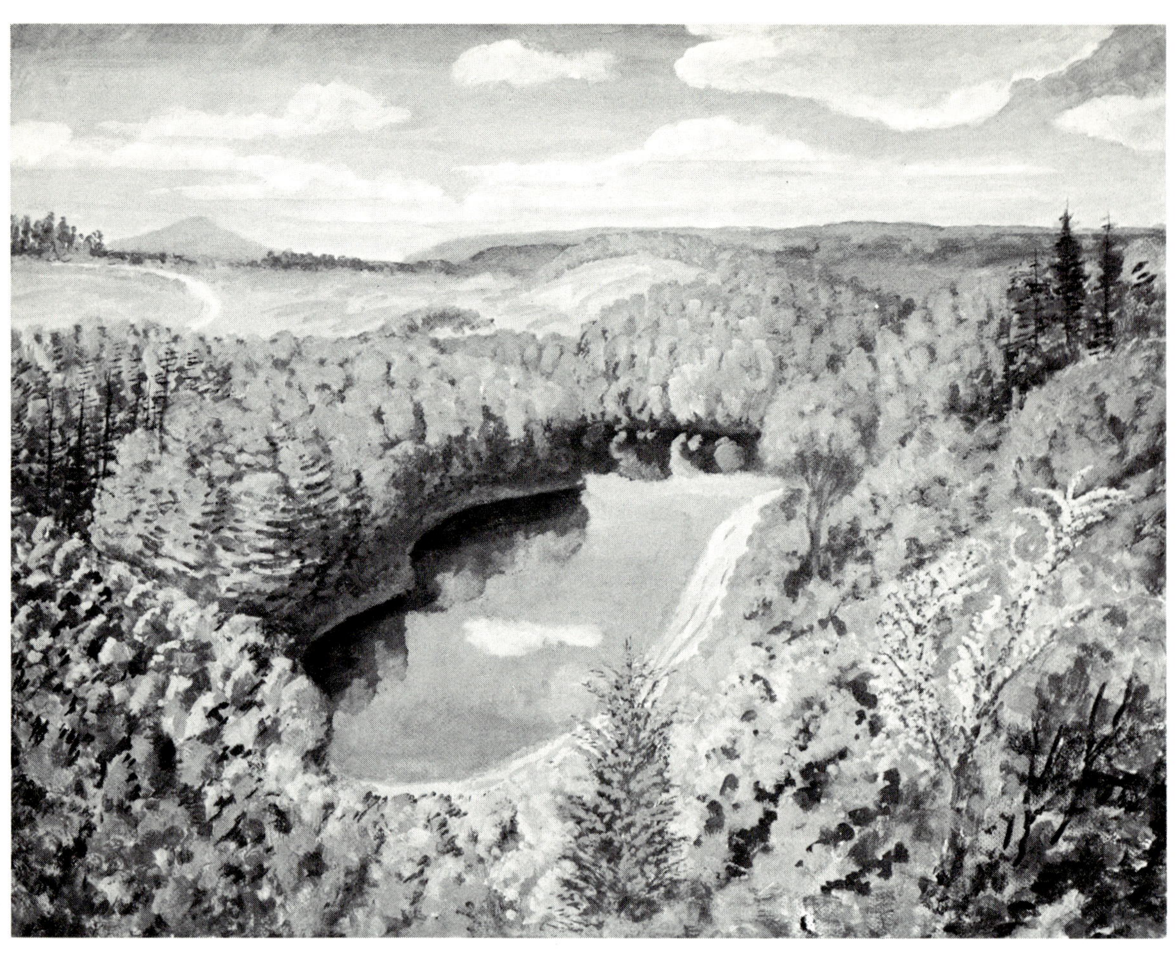

100. *Mink Brook*. 1951. Oil on canvas, 24″ x 30″.
John Sloan Trust.
Photo Colten, New York.

APPENDIX

Selected Comments from *Gist of Art*

By JOHN SLOAN

The numbers in parentheses refer to the pages on which the quotations appear.

ON PAINTING

". . . the artist who paints for himself is an amateur. In that sense I am proud to be an amateur. So was Rembrandt and so, too, Van Gogh." *(34)*

"An artist can be independent as an artist. He can't be independent as a human individual." *(33)*

"The artist paints first of all for himself, but the very next person he paints for is the aesthetic consumer, the person who is equipped to enjoy and appreciate." *(23)*

"You can be a giant among artists without ever attaining any great skill. Facility is a dangerous thing. When there is too much technical ease the brain stops criticizing. Don't let the hand fall into a smart way of putting the mind to sleep. If you were so clever that you could paint a perfect eye, I would know that you would always be too clever. Some things are too well done and not done well enough." *(38)*

"Paint what you know and what you think. Keep your mind on such homely things, such deep-seated truths of reality, that there is no room for the superficial. Put over the selected viewpoint of the mind about the subject. Don't be afraid to be human. Draw with human kindness, with appreciation for the marvel of existence. Humanism can be applied to drawing chairs and cobblestones. Look at the work of Daumier." *(41)*

"Study and work and paint pictures. You cannot paint pictures by merely wanting to paint them. All the inspired work of the masters is backed up by a lifetime of hard study. Find your own way of working. You may work three hours a day, or fifteen.

You may work steadily or only when you feel like it, but it is best to get in the habit of working regularly." (*50*)

"An artist who just wishes to paint with nothing in him to paint from, remains an art student all his life. He depends on schools and teachers, and learns methods and manners. The real artist needs no teacher. He will find a way to draw or paint if he has the urge." (*51*)

"Painting is drawing, with the additional means of color. Painting without drawing is just 'coloriness,' color excitement. To think of color for color's sake is like thinking of sound for sound's sake. Who ever heard of a musician who was passionately fond of B-flat? Color is like music. The palette is an instrument that can be orchestrated to build form." (*109*)

"The effort to do the impossible leads to creative work. It is impossible to paint every leaf on a tree. Trying earnestly to do so results in a creative symbol, as in Rousseau." (*52*)

"You don't have to understand pictures. I really feel that an artist can make a good one without understanding it. Most people think that they understand a picture when they have recognized the subject. That isn't understanding. I like the slang expression 'to get' the picture. You can say that about any kind of work, representational or abstract, if you pay enough attention to it. You can't expect to know a picure at a casual glance. It may be that when you really know them, you will learn to like the ones you disliked at first." (*24*)

ON DRAWING

"Drawing is one of the three means of communication between spirits, like speech and music. You wouldn't say nowadays, with pride, 'I can't understand a book. I never learned how to read.' Everyone should be able to draw a little the way we write a little or whistle." (*18*)

"There is no one way of drawing that is right. Nor is it good to be dependent on any one way of doing things. The greatest masters were always searching and groping toward more powerful, significant form, forcing the technique to suit their desires. Delacroix's *Notebooks* are full of observations about the problem of finding a better way to say what he was after." (*50*)

"It is good consciously to study the devices of drawing, to practise methods of painting. This knowledge must become part of your subconscious equipment or it will bother you when you are trying to create. Make laborious studies to find out how things are made in nature and to increase your technical ability. But do not be afraid to loosen up and have a good time making a picture. When you .make a drawing for fun it is apt to be good because you are not hampered by the idea of making Art. In a good drawing you make use of all the information and ability you have been storing up while studying." (*51*)

"Drawing is the cornerstone of the graphic, plastic arts. Drawing is the coördination of line, tone, and color symbols into formations that express the artist's thought. Drawing and composition are the same thing. They can't exist separately. The artist sees order in life, that is one of the important things he has to say about it. To formulate his visual images he must have order in his thinking and order in his expression. A sense of the structure of things, of their geometrical composition, the ability to see order in nature—and then the technical ability to compose these plastic ideas, is essential to the artist. But if you go out and see nature through a formula of composition you won't go very far." (*53*)

"Line is the most powerful device of drawing." (*58*)

"The important thing to bear in mind while drawing the figure is that the model is a human being, that it is alive, that it exists there on the stand. Look on the model with respect, appreciate his or her humanity. Be very humble before that human being. Be filled with wonder at its reality and life. There is a human creature that lives and breathes and feels, a thing with a mind and character of its own—not a patchwork of light and shadow, color shapes." (*87*)

"Find your own technique. Form your own color concept of things in nature. I have no rules for fine color to give you. There are some facts about the craft of painting and the use of the palette which may prove helpful to you. The important thing is to keep on drawing when you start to paint. *Never graduate from drawing."* (*110*)

ON ETCHING AND LITHOGRAPHY

"Etching is a way of drawing—purely a drawing technique. The line is a symbol which expresses without equivocation the thought of the artist. The beauty of an etched print is in its significant linework used to define and describe things. A quality of etching, which gives it a special character shared with line engraving, lies in the fact that the ink lines are raised in relief when the bitten plate is run through the press and printed. The raised surface of those lines gives them more textural significance in a very subtle way." (*178*)

"The classical linework of the masters was used to make things and texture and light and shade. An etching without drawing and composition is nothing, just a technical *tour de force*. Look at the etchings of Rembrandt and the line drawings in *Punch* by John Leech. Any kind of linework you don't find in their work is hardly worth having." (*178*)

"The beauty of lithography is in those rare, tender tones that you get only by drawing on the stone itself. A drawing that is made on paper and transferred to stone is not properly a lithograph, it has none of the qualities of a fine print. The stone has a finer surface than the finest paper in the world. It is like some wonderful crisp silk. When it is surfaced with a fine grain you can get very delicate tones and exquisite lines on it." (*186*)

ON TEACHING

"If I am useful as a teacher it is because I have dug into my own work. Teaching lashes me into a state of consciousness; I find myself trying to prove in my work some of the things I dig out of my sub-conscious to pass on to others. Many an instructor passes on only what he learned as a student. But an artist today, if he has assimilated the meaning of the ultra-modern movement, may have advanced to a greater understanding of the meaning of art than he had thirty years ago. In the last hundred years art has been so diseased by the influence of the camera that any creative artist who is conscious of the technique of tradition should endeavor to pass on what he can about the language of art." (*6*)

"Again and again, I have said: I don't want to interfere with your way of seeing, if you are seeing Things. I have no tricks to teach you. I don't want to teach you any one way to draw. I don't want to teach you my opinions, but if you can get hold of my point of view I don't think it will hurt you. I am here to help you. I want to help you find a purpose, a reason for painting. I can tell you some things about the 'how' to paint. Not any one 'how.' Then you must find your way through your own experience and hard work." (*7*)

"Teaching has taken years of my life. But I feel that I must do it, that I must reach as many students as I can to arouse in them the creative spirit, and to teach them as best I can, some of the technique of the great tradition of art." (*7*)

A FINAL COMMENT

"Though a living cannot be made at art, art makes living worth while. It makes living, living. It makes starving, living. It makes worry, it makes trouble, it makes a life that would be barren of everything—living. It brings life to life." (*35*)

CHRONOLOGY

1871 Born August 2, Lock Haven, Pennsylvania.

1876 Moves to Philadelphia, where he later attends Central High School with William Glackens and Albert C. Barnes.

1887 Begins work at Porter and Coates, booksellers and fine print dealers.

1888 Teaches himself to etch with *The Etcher's Handbook* by Philip Gilbert Hamerton.

1890 Goes to work for A. Edward Newton designing novelties, calendars, lettering. Joins evening freehand drawing class at Spring Garden Institute.

1891 Becomes a free-lance designer of novelties, advertisements, certificates, and diplomas.

1892 Begins work in the art department of the *Philadelphia Inquirer*. Shares studio at 705 Walnut Street with Joe Laub. Enters a class in cast-drawing at the Pennsylvania Academy of the Fine Arts under Thomas Anshutz. Meets Robert Henri through Charles Grafly.

1893 Helps found Charcoal Club, a brief breakaway from the Academy. Rents Henri's studio at 806 Walnut Street with Laub.

1894 First public recognition of illustrations and poster style in the *Inland Printer* and the *Chicago Chap Book*.

1895 Starts work for the *Philadelphia Press* on the Sunday Supplement staff.

1897 Begins to paint seriously (mainly portraits), inspired by Henri.

1898 Begins to paint Philadelphia city scenes. Spends a brief trial period in New York but returns to work on the *Press*. Meets Anna M. (Dolly) Wall.

1900 Included for the first time in the Pennsylvania Academy's Annual Exhibition. Also exhibits at the Carnegie Institute and the Art Institute of Chicago.

1901 Marries Anna M. Wall on August 5.

1902 Begins first major work in etching: 53 plates as illustrations for a deluxe edition of the novels of Charles Paul de Kock.

1903 Leaves *Philadelphia Press* art department but continues making word-charade puzzles for it until 1910.

1904 Moves to New York in April.

1905 Begins series of ten city-life etchings.

1907 Instructor at the Pittsburgh Art Students League from October to December.

1908 Exhibition of The Eight opens February 3 at the Macbeth Gallery. Begins to make lithographs in May.

1909 Meets John Butler Yeats, father of the poet William Butler Yeats. Introduced to the Maratta color system by Henri.

1910 Exhibition of Independent Artists opens on April 1. Joins Socialist Party.

1911 Beginning of MacDowell Club exhibitions.

1912 Becomes acting art editor of *The Masses*.

1913 Represented by seven works in the Armory Show. First sale of painting *Nude in the Green Scarf* to Dr. Albert C. Barnes.

1914 Resigns from the Socialist Party and stops contributing to *The Masses*. First summer at Gloucester, Massachusetts.

1915 Receives bronze medal for an etching at the San Francisco Pan-Pacific International Exposition. Meets Gertrude Vanderbilt Whitney.

1916 First one-man exhibition at Mrs. H. P. Whitney's studio, January 26–February 6. Begins long-time association with the Kraushaar Galleries. One-man exhibition at Hudson Guild. Teaches privately at Gloucester during the summer and then at the Art Students League.

1917 Hangs the first exhibition of the Society of Independent Artists at the Grand Central Palace. First one-man show at Kraushaar's, March 19–April 7.

1918 Made President of the Society of Independent Artists.

1919 First trip to Santa Fe with Randall Davey.

1920 Buys house in Santa Fe, where he spends four months a year.

1921 First sale of a painting to a major museum: *Dust Storm, Fifth Avenue,* to the Metropolitan Museum of Art.

1928 Begins new technique of underpainting and glazing. Subject matter now includes more single figure pieces.

1929 Elected to the National Institute of Arts and Letters. Substitutes tempera for oil underpainting and begins using linework superimposed over glazes. Death of Robert Henri.

1931 Receives Carroll H. Beck Gold Medal for *Vagis the Sculptor* at the Pennsylvania Academy. Made honorary member and elected President of the Art Students League. President of the Exposition of Indian Tribal Arts.

1932 Joins staff of Archipenko's art school, where he teaches drawing and painting until February, 1933. Resigns as President of the Art Students League.

1933 Refuses an invitation from Moscow to show with the American Section of the International Bureau of Revolutionary Artists.

1934 Elected head of the George Luks School and teaches there until May, 1935.

1935 Returns to Art Students League and continues to teach there until 1938.

1937 Etches 16 plates for W. Somerset Maugham's *Of Human Bondage.*

1938 Retrospective exhibition at the Addison Gallery of American Art, Andover, Mass.

1939 *Gist of Art* published.

1941 Testimonial dinner at Petitpas' by the directors of the Society of Independent Artists in celebration of its twenty-fifth anniversary and Sloan's twenty-fourth as President.

1942 Receives first prize for the etching *Fifth Avenue 1909* in the Artists for Victory exhibition. Elected to the Academy of Arts and Letters.

1943 Death of Dolly Sloan on May 4.

1944 Marries Helen Farr, a pupil and long-time friend of the Sloans, on February 5.

1945 Twenty-two paintings, some etchings, and lithographs in the Artists of the *Philadelphia Press* exhibition at the Philadelphia Museum of Art.

1946 Seventy-fifth anniversary exhibition at Dartmouth College.

1948 Retrospective exhibition at the Kraushaar Galleries.

1950 Awarded gold medal for painting by the American Academy of Arts and Letters. Elected to the American Academy of Arts and Sciences.

1951 Death on September 7 of post-operative complications at Hanover, New Hampshire.

1952 January 10–March 2, retrospective exhibition at the Whitney Museum of American Art.

NOTES

1. Unpublished notes of John and Helen Farr Sloan, Sloan Collection, Delaware Art Center, Wilmington. Sloan's memory was faulty at times about dates. He was actually sixteen years old and did some of the work during the blizzard of 1888.

2. *Ibid.*

3. *Ibid.*

4. The members of the Charcoal Club were Vernon Howe Bailey, Edward Wyatt Davis (father of Stuart Davis), William Glackens, W. Gosewisch, Fred Gruger, Robert Henri, Joe E. Laub, Carl Lundstrom, Harry Ritter, J. Horace Rudy, John Sloan, and W. E. Worden.

5. John Sloan, *Gist of Art: Principles and Practise expounded in the Classroom and Studio, recorded with the assistance of Helen Farr* (New York: American Artists Group, Inc., 1939), p. 1.

6. Bruce St. John, ed., *John Sloan's New York Scene 1906–1913* (New York: Harper & Row, 1965), Introduction, pp. xv–xvi.

7. *Ibid.,* p. 33.

8. *Ibid.,* p. 118.

9. *Ibid.,* p. 191.

10. *Ibid.,* p. 318, and (in italics) Unpublished notes.

11. *Ibid.,* p. 391.

12. *Ibid.,* pp. 395–96.

13. *Ibid.,* p. 379.

14. *Ibid.,* pp. 305–6.

15. *Ibid.,* p. 310.

16. Zigrosser is the former curator of prints at the Philadelphia Museum of Art. In 1956, when the museum acquired the master set of Sloan's etchings, which included various states—tissues, sketches, lithographs, and posters—Zigrosser prepared the initial catalog.

17. Peter Morse, *John Sloan's Prints* (New Haven: Yale University Press, 1969), p. 386.

18. *John Sloan's Paintings and Prints,* catalog for the 75th Anniversary Retrospec-

tive, Carpenter Galleries, Dartmouth College, Hanover, New Hampshire, June 1–
September 1, 1946.

19. *Gist of Art,* p. 259.

20. *Ibid.,* p. 265.

21. Sloan's Indian paintings are quite different from those done by George Catlin
or Alfred Jacob Miller. Both of the latter artists actually lived among the Plains
Indians, and their paintings were portraits or scenes of the everyday life of the
Indian. They were not, as was Sloan, primarily interested in recording tribal rites
or ceremonials. The Indians depicted in their works were then autonomous and
powerful, those of Sloan's time were reservation Indians struggling to survive and
keep alive their religious rites and customs.

22. *Gist of Art,* p. 281.

23. *Ibid.,* p. 140.

24. *Ibid.,* p. 300.

25. *Ibid.,* p. 325.

26. *Ibid.,* p. 44.

27. *Ibid.,* p. 45.

28. *Ibid.,* p. 56.

29. *Ibid.,* p. 1.

30. *Ibid.,* p. 110.

31. *Ibid.,* p. 100.

32. *Ibid.,* p. 125.

SELECTED BIBLIOGRAPHY

WRITINGS BY SLOAN

"Art Is, Was, and Ever Will Be." In *Revolt in the Arts,* ed. by Oliver M. Sayler. New York: Brentano's, 1930, pp. 318–21.

"Artist, Dealer, and Buyer." *Creative Art* 2 (February, 1928): 19–25.

"Fragments from the Teachings of John Sloan." *Art Instruction,* October, 1938.

Gist of Art: Principles and Practise expounded in the Classroom and Studio, recorded with the assistance of Helen Farr. New York: American Artists Group, 1939.

"The Independent: An Open Door." *Arts* 2 (April, 1927): 187–88.

"Indian Art." *Rotarian,* March, 1941, pp. 18–21.

"The Indian as Artist." *Survey* 67 (December 1, 1931): 243–46.

Introduction to American Indian Art. With Oliver La Farge. New York: The Exposition of Indian Tribal Arts, Inc., 1931.

John Sloan's New York Scene 1906–1913, edited by Bruce St. John. New York: Harper & Row, 1965.

"Looking for a Lord." *New Freeman* 1 (March 15, 1930): 15–16.

"My Recent Encounter." *Creative Art* 2 (May, 1928): supplement 44–45.

Introduction to *Patterns and Ceremonials of the Indians of the Southwest,* by Ira Moskowitz and John Collier. New York: E. P. Dutton, 1949.

"Presidential Points." *The League* (Art Students League publication), Winter, 1931–32, p. 6.

"Presidential Points." *The League,* Spring, 1932, p. 4.

"The Process of Etching." *Touchstone* 8 (December, 1920): 227, 238–40.

"Randall Davey." *New Mexico Quarterly Review* 21 (Spring, 1951): 19–25.

"Souls of Our Cities Seen in Colors." *The New York Times Magazine,* February 22, 1925, pp. 4, 23.

"What Is Good About the League." *The League,* Spring, 1931, pp. 3, 8.

CONTRIBUTIONS TO EXHIBITION CATALOGS

For one-man shows: Hudson Guild, 1916; Addison Gallery of American Art, 1938; Renaissance Society, University of Chicago, 1942; Dartmouth College, 1946.

For other exhibitions: Society of Independent Artists, *14th Annual Exhibition,* 1930;
Metropolitan Museum of Art, *Robert Henri,* 1931, pp. 11–12; Whitney Museum of
American Art, *Glenn O. Coleman,* 1932, p. 8; Newark Museum, *George Luks,* 1934,
p. 12; Society of Independent Artists, *26th Annual Exhibition,* 1942; Philadelphia
Museum of Art, *Artists of the Philadelphia Press,* 1945, pp. 7–8; American Artists
Group, Inc., *John Sloan,* 1945; Art Students League of New York, *A. F. Levinson,*
1947; Whitney Museum of American Art, *Juliana Force and American Art,* 1949,
pp. 34–42; Art Students League of New York, *75th Anniversary Exhibition,* 1951;
University of Minnesota, *40 American Painters,* 1951.

BOOKS ABOUT SLOAN

BROOKS, VAN WYCK. *John Sloan: A Painter's Life.* New York: E. P. Dutton, 1955.

GALLATIN, A. E. *John Sloan.* New York: E. P. Dutton, 1925.

GLACKENS, IRA. *William Glackens and the Ashcan Group.* New York: Grosset & Dunlap,
1957.

HENRI, ROBERT. *The Art Spirit.* Philadelphia: J. P. Lippincott, 1923.

HOMER, WILLIAM INNESS. *Robert Henri and His Circle.* Ithaca and London: Cornell
University Press, 1969.

LARKIN, OLIVER W. *Art and Life in America.* Rev. ed. New York: Holt, Rinehart &
Winston, 1960.

MATHER, FRANK JEWETT, JR. *John Sloan.* New York: American Art Portfolios, Series I,
1936.

PACH, WALTER. *Modern Art in America.* New York: C. W. Kraushaar Galleries, 1928.

PÈNE DU BOIS, GUY, *John Sloan.* New York: Whitney Museum, American Series, 1931.

PERLMAN, BERNARD E. *The Immortal Eight: American Painting from Eakins to the
Armory Show.* New York: Exposition Press, 1962.

REID, B. L. *The Man from New York: John Quinn and His Friends.* London and
New York: Oxford University Press, 1969.

ST. JOHN, BRUCE, ed. *John Sloan's New York Scene 1906–1913.* New York: Harper &
Row, 1965.

EXHIBITION CATALOGS

Addison Gallery of American Art, Andover, Massachussetts: *John Sloan Retrospective
Exhibition,* 1938.

Art Students League, New York: *Fifty Years on Fifty-Seventh Street,* 1953, p. 102.

Brooklyn Museum, New York: *The Eight,* 1943–44.

Carnegie Institute, Pittsburgh: *An Exhibition of Etchings by John Sloan,* 1937.

Dartmouth College, Hanover, New Hampshire: *John Sloan, Painting and Prints,* 1946.

Kraushaar Galleries, New York: *John Sloan Retrospective Exhibition,* 1948.

Lehigh University, Bethlehem, Pennsylvania: *The Muriel and Philip Berman Collection,*
December, 1966, to January 30, 1967.

Macbeth Galleries, New York: *Exhibition of Paintings (The Eight),* 1908.

Metropolitan Museum of Art, New York: *Life in America,* 1939, p. 27.

Museum of Modern Art, New York: *Paintings by Nineteen Living Americans,* 1929–30.

Philadelphia Museum of Art: *Artists of the Philadelphia Press,* 1945.

University of Missouri, Columbia, Missouri: *A Selection of Etchings by John Sloan,* 1967.

Walker Art Museum, Bowdoin College, Brunswick, Maine: *The Art of John Sloan, 1871–1951,* 1962.

Whitney Museum of American Art, New York: *New York Realists, 1900–1914,* 1937.

Whitney Museum of American Art, New York: *John Sloan 1871–1951,* 1952.

Wilmington Society of the Fine Arts, Delaware Art Museum: *The Life and Times of John Sloan,* 1961.

Wilmington Society of the Fine Arts, Delaware Art Museum (special exhibition for the Traveling Exhibition Service, Smithsonian Institution): *John Sloan,* 1963–64.

INDEX